5

RENEWALS
RENOUVELLEMENTS
This Passport is hereby renewed
Valid until ...

Chief Passport Officer

CANCELLED

6

VISAS

BERGEN
17 JUL 1935

7

VISAS

26

VISAS

HOLTET
INNR 19 SEP 1937

Indrejst den
30 DEC. 1937

12

VISAS

Paskontrol
17 JUNI 1936
BERGEN

JAVORINA
23 VIII 1936

13

VISAS

WIZA PRZEJAZDOWA Nr. 1064

Za Konsula Generalnego:

14

VISAS

UTREST
AUG. 1936
DALS-HÖGEN

PASSKONTROLL
INNR -2 AUG. 1936
KORNSJÖ

20

VISAS

ENTRADA

VISADO Y AUTORIZADO PARA PERMANECER EN
ESPAÑA DURANTE TRES MESES
STA. CRUZ DE TENERIFE
23 MAR. 1937
EL COMISARIO-JEFE

21

SALIDA
VAPOR Bruñas
SANTA CRUZ DE TENERIFE
-7 ABR. 1937

24

VISAS

Bremer Bank Filiale der Dresdner Bank
Wechselkasse Lloydreisebüro

PASSKONTROLL
INNR 17 AUG. 1937
HOLTET

25

VISAS

PASSKONTROLL
INNR 27 JUN
SVINESUND

Utrest Nr
Svinesund

PASSPORT.
PASSEPORT.

UNITED KINGDOM OF GREAT BRITAIN AND NORTHERN IRELAND.
ROYAUME-UNI DE GRANDE-BRETAGNE ET D'IRLANDE DU NORD.

No. of Passport
No. du PASSEPORT — 48109

NAME OF BEARER — Mr JOHN BELAN
NOM DU TITULAIRE

ACCOMPANIED BY HIS WIFE
(Maiden name)
ACCOMPAGNÉ DE SA FEMME
(Nom)

children
enfants

CANCELLED

John Simon

This Passport contains
32 pages.
Ce passeport contient
32 pages.

My Family and Other Spies

My Family and
Other Spies

ALISTAIR WOOD

MICHAEL  JOSEPH

PENGUIN MICHAEL JOSEPH

UK | USA | Canada | Ireland | Australia
India | New Zealand | South Africa

Penguin Michael Joseph is part of the Penguin Random House group of companies
whose addresses can be found at global.penguinrandomhouse.com

Penguin Random House UK
One Embassy Gardens, 8 Viaduct Gardens, London SW11 7BW

penguin.co.uk

Penguin
Random House
UK

First published 2025

001

Set in 13.5/16pt Garamond MT Std
Typeset by Jouve (UK), Milton Keynes
Printed and bound in Great Britain by Clays Ltd, Elcograf S.p.A.

The authorized representative in the EEA is Penguin Random House Ireland,
Morrison Chambers, 32 Nassau Street, Dublin D02 YH68

A CIP catalogue record for this book is available from the British Library

HARDBACK ISBN: 978-0-241-72635-8
TRADE PAPERBACK ISBN: 978-0-241-72637-2

Penguin Random House is committed to a sustainable future
for our business, our readers and our planet. This book is made from
Forest Stewardship Council® certified paper.

Blether. A Scottish word, meaning foolish talk,
nonsense, exaggeration.

But in our family it meant quite the opposite.

It covered anything that was true but
to outsiders would *sound* like foolish talk,
nonsense or exaggeration.

This included any mention of where my
mother worked, what she did for a living, even
where we lived. And, heaven forbid,
any mention whatsoever of my father.

Rest assured, what follows is pure,
unadulterated blether.

Contents

Introduction

'I don't suppose we'll ever really know
the truth about J. B. Wood, will we?'

Harold Shergold, SIS Soviet Bloc
controller 1954–71, to author

As far back as I can remember, once or twice a year my mother would drive us up to London to spend the day with 'Shergy' and his wife, Bevis, at their Richmond Park home. I have photographs of my brother and I feeding the deer, boating on the Pen Ponds, up to our knees among the reed beds. But of course I have no photographs of Shergold himself, long since weeded out, more likely never taken in the first place.

Close friends of my mother ever since she stepped off the train into the deep end of the so-called '*Agentsumpf*' or 'agent-swamp' that was Berlin in 1949, they remained so throughout her life – Shergy gave the eulogy at her funeral. In the years since, he kept in occasional touch, and every now and then I'd be press-ganged into dog-walking duties round Richmond Park, he and Bevis having spent their retirement years training guide dogs for the blind. So I was met with much excited tail-wagging by his latest recruits, Westley and Larry, when I arrived at his home, the ground-floor apartment of a flat-roofed, modernist house backing directly onto the park itself.

Shergy was by now well into his late eighties, and his health had begun to fail. His breathing was not good and he had a rota of (mostly Kiwi) carers 'who keep an eye on me', one of whom had prepared lunch for us, laid out ready on the dining-room sideboard. First things first, he insisted we head across the road to the Star & Garter Home, a residential care home for ex-servicemen and -women where Bevis had spent the last months of her life. He was keen to show me a glass-topped display case of her athletics medals (she competed in the shot put at the 1948 Olympics) installed on the first-floor landing in her memory. Our slow progress up the main staircase was not helped by a constant stream of people stopping to wish him well: anyone and everyone knew Shergy, it seemed. Later though, as he got his breath back and we peered down at Bevis's various certificates and medals, he twinkled, 'Of course, no one here knows who I am.'

During lunch he kept the conversation to everyday matters: his health, dogs past and present, family, what I was up to, after which he shuffled me through to the sitting room, motioning to two fraying armchairs. The room was much as I remembered: the heavy desk with the familiar black upright typewriter in one corner, the same two paintings of Venice and, behind me, the low bookcase with its well-worn school textbooks. My mother had once teasingly asked what job I thought Shergy did, and I can remember guessing that he might be a (rather genial) schoolmaster. As he had been once, only for the Second World War to map out an altogether different path for him.

Just two books referenced his second career. *Battleground Berlin*, jointly written by an ex-KGB officer and two of Shergold's former CIA colleagues, told the story of Cold War

Berlin from both sides, but it contained little if anything that my mother and her Berlin friends used to 'natter' about. On the other hand, Tom Bower's *The Perfect English Spy* did, and even included a distant, slightly blurred photograph of Shergold walking one of his dogs down to the ponds, a rare time he'd been caught on camera.

Normally anything to do with 'the office' – as Shergy and everyone in our family referred to the Secret Intelligence Service (SIS) – would be held back until I had my coat on ready to leave, and even then it would be for perhaps a minute or two at most. Nor do I recall there ever being much mention of my father, a subject best avoided. But then not having been brought up by J. B. Wood, I had no great personal interest in the subject, as I was quick to point out. 'No, of course not. Why would you? No. Why ever would you?' Shergy agreed.

Perhaps this visit would have been no different had not fate intervened. One moment he was sat upright in his armchair, the next he was doubled over, struggling for breath. No expert, I hesitated (correctly, it turned out) to slap a frail eighty-something man on the back. It was touch and go – desperate stuff – before he finally managed to crane his neck into a position where he could gulp some air. A few moments to collect himself, then a wry smile: 'Wouldn't have looked good, would it?' No need to decode: finding the son of an ex-employee of frankly 'questionable loyalties' standing over the still-warm body of the former head of SIS's Soviet Bloc operations might have raised a few eyebrows in certain quarters.

On the unspoken understanding that this might well be our last such meeting, with a series of nods, frowns, prompts, anecdotes and the occasional name, Shergy proceeded to run me through the facts about J. B. Wood as he knew them and steered me towards the truth as he understood it: their time together in Berlin, operations they'd worked on, the frustrations of working with him and, not least, the reasons for his summary dismissal from SIS. Only now I was hearing the true version of what exactly had led to this, rather than the 'official' version.

Driving home that evening I was aware that my visit had been less a spilling of beans, more a briefing. 'I very much enjoyed your visit and the opportunity it gave me to reminisce and think of past events and former colleagues,' Shergy wrote afterwards. 'The older one gets, the more one tends to live in the past. I suppose that this particularly applies to those of us who live alone.'

For Shergy, it seemed, J. B. Wood remained unfinished business, and I was being asked to fill in the gaps – though quite how he expected me to succeed where the finer minds of SIS had come up short he gave no clue, other than to suggest that 'these days I suppose you could always try the Russians'. More to the point, it had long been inculcated into me, not least by Shergy himself, that no good could ever come of having anything to do with my father.

Given the unlikely prospect of any relevant SIS files ever being released – if any still exist – in attempting to piece together something of my father's story, I've had to resort to an additional, unexpected source: my own upbringing, the majority of which was spent 'above the shop', within the four (very high) walls of the SIS training camp. But for this most unusual, not to say impossibly unique head start, very little of what follows could have come to light. Nor, of course, would I have had 'by a long way the most important and influential officer of the post-war period' to set me on my way.

A few months after our get-together Shergy sent a short note to say that Larry had died, leaving just Westley, the last of his dogs, and that 'since I last saw you, I have had a further relapse health-wise and my breathing is very much worse than it was when you were here'. And then one evening, driving out of Richmond Park, I glanced back only to see a 'For Sale' sign across the road from the old Star & Garter Home.

There had been no notice in any newspaper, not a single obituary, not even – at his insistence, legend has it – a funeral.

PART ONE

Staick House, Eardisland. Despite online posts lamenting its
abandoned state, JBW's cousin was still living there, August 2000.

Brother, mother and author reunited following
brother's kidnapping, April 1959.

1.

Southampton Docks car park

'We're just going out for a loaf of bread.
We might be a while.'

J. B. Wood, 23 July 1958

Given that one of the few things I – or anyone else for that matter – could say for certain about my father was his place of birth, this seemed as good a place as any to start.

The village of Eardisland, a picture-book cluster of half-timbered, 'black and white' medieval houses, features regularly in competitions such as Herefordshire in Bloom and Best Presented Village; presumably the judges of such competitions would be gently dissuaded from venturing over the small bridge at one end of the village, beyond which stands the fourteenth-century Staick House, until recently all but uninhabitable following several decades of neglect. It was here that my father spent the first four years of his life, and where his cousin Francis – known to everyone locally as Mush – was still living.

Despite various online posts lamenting the house's abandoned state, the village shop were quick to reassure that despite appearances it was still very much inhabited. My first mistake was to approach the house by the front door, marking me out as a passing tourist at best. Only after

3

several attempts – I should keep trying, Mush keeps odd hours, they encouraged – did I detect signs of life, only to be told in no uncertain terms that no, he had no relatives, not even distant ones. Explaining who I was, or rather who my father was, seemed to register, though the door remained shut – permanently, as it turned out – and I was directed round to the back of the house.

If the front door was seldom if ever opened, the back kitchen door was rarely if ever closed, even in the depths of winter. Though Mush lived entirely alone (his mother, a noted beauty and fashion model in her time, had died in childbirth, leaving him to rattle around the house on his own for the best part of ninety years), he was no hermit, with a large blackened kettle kept permanently on the go for anyone who cared to drop by, and a hundred or so (unwashed) mugs crowded onto the kitchen table, amongst, around and through which a resident mouse happily went about its way – to which Mush paid no attention either then or on any of my subsequent visits. Washing up involved a flick of the wrist to dispatch any dregs through the open doorway, followed by a cursory wipe with a page of old newspaper – only for me, a privilege not extended to his own mug or anyone else's.

The last time my father had been to the house would have been when he was at Cambridge, Mush seemed to think. Though just a boy at the time, he remembered how everything and anything electrical or mechanical had been got out ready for his cousin's visit – 'he could tell what was wrong just by looking at it' – pointing to a primitive wooden wireless cabinet, presumably still left out in the hope that he might drop by again some day. Certainly his Eardisland relatives had always assumed that he would end up doing something technical, become an engineer of some sort per-haps, given that he'd always been tinkering with wireless sets and suchlike from an early age. They thought that was what he was doing at Cambridge, so if anything they were dis-appointed to hear later that he'd ended up in 'the Foreign Service'.

But he never did drop by again, leaving everything and anything electrical or mechanical to remain where it was gathering dust, and that was pretty much the last that his Herefordshire family heard of him. Worried that my trip had been a wasted one, Mush suggested I might want to see my father's old bedroom before I left – though he doubted whether there was anything of his still in there, not that he'd been inside it for a while (Mush-speak for several years).

In the short time I'd been at the house I'd seen enough to suspect that the room was unlikely to be preserved Brontë-like exactly as was, but even so . . . Just finding my way to the staircase required negotiating decades of debris, all left lying where it fell. With no electricity, what little light there was came courtesy of mice having chewed through the curtains and the garden having long since broken and entered through the house's mullioned windows: what in the half-light looked like ivy-patterned wallpaper turned out to be ivy-covered wallpaper. Additional random hazards included missing floor-boards, a grandfather clock lying flat on its back with its innards spread out mid-autopsy, and a huge, menacing wooden propel-ler overhead (Mush had an aeronaut uncle famous for having been the first man in England to fly upside down). Only the full-size billiard table in the next room held out the possibil-ity of ever being brought back to life, should anyone think to clear the ceiling from its surface.

Feeling my way up the windowless staircase – which wound its way around the pipes of, eccentrically, a church organ – I passed by Mush's bedroom (not for the squeamish), then angled my way along a sloping corridor. Since doors had a habit of jamming, sometimes for years on end, he'd armed me with a hammer, though in the end a shoulder was all that was needed, opening up a small, square room unexpectedly filled with sunlight. But sunlight was all that it was filled with. No carpet, no furniture, not even wallpaper (mice again) – just a mound of yellowed newspapers and magazines gathered up bonfire-like in the centre of the room, out of which poked a few faded blue struts of a child's cot.

And so I came away from Eardisland none the wiser. Back to where, for my part, this story really began: my own early childhood. Not that I had much to go on here either. Just a snip of blue ribbon and a tuft of downy hair, a dozen or so greetings cards (mostly storks carrying baby-bundles) and a *My First Year* album – in which my father noted that I looked like his own father – though *My First Two Months* would have been more apt, since the remaining months are all crossed out by a diagonal biro line. I also have several boxes of family photos, yet somehow just a single one of me as a baby.

Home was a rhododendron-lined street near Woking where we'd moved shortly before I was born, bringing with us the latest in a long line of duffle-coated au pairs, hired in the hope that they might spoon-feed my brother (and the soon-to-be me) a little of their German or, more recently, Finnish, depending on which country our father was being posted to. But his Helsinki posting had come to an abrupt end, followed by an equally abrupt departure from the Foreign Office, or more exactly the Secret Intelligence Service (SIS). He'd taken a job in Belfast to tide him over, returning in time for my birth, but then one sunny July morning, as I lay on a blanket in the back garden, my mother stretched out on the grass beside me, he'd leant out of an upstairs window and called down to say that he was just going out for a loaf of bread and might be a while.

It would have been quicker to take the path through the woods at the back of the house, but since he'd various other bits and pieces to see to, in the end he decided to take the car. And my brother. And discreetly tucked two passports into the glove box. His route probably took him past the local bakery, but he didn't stop, heading for, well, who knew where. The other passport was my mother's, taken so she couldn't follow.

The police advised that he had likely returned to Belfast, but as the days ticked by and with still no clue as to their whereabouts, she approached her former employers for help, taking the train up to Waterloo every few days to update them. But – officially at least – SIS was not in the business of tracking down ex-employees, still less interfering in their domestic affairs. Only when our pale-blue Vauxhall Wyvern turned up in Southampton Docks car park did anyone think to check through the various ships' manifests, which duly revealed husband and son as having embarked on the SS *Homeric*, which had set sail for Montreal that same evening.

As it turned out, her desperate commutes up to town were not entirely wasted. On one such journey she'd found herself sitting next to the local conveyancing solicitor who'd overseen the purchase of her house, who agreed to

7

act on her behalf – and who eventually managed to track down her missing son. And with that off she set, replacement passport in hand.

A few months later and there I am, on that same blanket, on that same patch of grass, looking quizzically over at my new-found brother as he looks quizzically down at me. As well he might.

I, of course, knew nothing of all this. Nor would I, certainly for a good few years yet, and even then only the bare facts: it would take half a lifetime to fully unravel the events of that July morning. But then I had more than just family secrets to navigate.

'Next week we are going sailing
with the Shergolds.' June 1964.

Mother's (modest) SIS salary meant we could
finally afford a new car. Which is to say,
a very old car, August 1966.

Aunt A (Agnes Miller), c.1955,
also ex-SIS.

2.

Woking

'I may be going back to "the office". Don't faint.'

Mother, letter to Aunt A (also ex-SIS), March 1966

As luck would have it, our mother was not the only party to have taken an interest in the whereabouts of her errant husband. Unlike their fictional counterparts, the Russians went about their business with a refreshing lack of cloak or dagger, occasionally dialling the heavy black Bakelite phone in our front room, Woking 4786, and asking where he was. Apparently they had 'an agreement', which, true to form, he had not adhered to. Undaunted, my mother batted back their enquiries. She had no idea where he was, but should they have more success than she was having, perhaps they would be so kind as to pass on the relevant details?

Her own motives for tracking down her husband were rather more straightforward. Despite having been one of the Foreign Office's ablest linguists, fluent in several languages, he had a curious blind spot, seemingly unable to master the word for 'alimony' in any tongue – leaving her to bring up two small boys single-handed, which along with the expense of retrieving my brother and endless legal fees (we were being made Wards of Court) had long since exhausted any

11

savings she may have had. A retired army brigadier and his wife across the road helped out with a little typing work here and there, but for us the make-do-and-mend years were set to last a while yet: 'He has James's vest and pants, J's trousers and shirts, Timmy's sweater, J's coat and football boots, and a cap (too big) belonging to an old boy' – supplemented by the occasional woollen jumper knitted by her aunt on the No. 14 bus up from Putney.

As soon as I was old enough for school she took a part-time job with a local engineering firm, the money welcome, the routine less so: 'The work goes into the "In" bin, you bash it through and then fling it in the "Out" bin. Only four of us (out of fifteen) admit to shorthand, the others have more sense.' But if her Woking existence was a far cry from her Berlin days, no one was any the wiser. 'I made few friends, as it was all too difficult to explain.'

If anything, it was the house itself that shed a little light on her former life, and piece by piece, find by find, introduced us to our father, John Bryan Wood. Or JBW, as he was called by one and all, family included. The endless Russian, Finnish, Swedish, Norwegian, Spanish and German language books; the camera equipment stashed away under the eaves; stacks of coins on a high shelf which, much like a 'Penny Falls' arcade machine, would trickle down if nudged hard enough (though the bank wouldn't change foreign coins, certainly not East German coins). Most obviously it was our garage, with his workbench still much as he'd left it, covered in mounds of sawdust caked to a hard crust. In icy weather we'd sprinkle some of the sawdust across the driveway, but as we dug deeper we came across shards of brown glass, the remains of dozens of lozenge-shaped radio valves, some still with their original filament wires – hardly ideal gritting material – along with several biscuit-tin lids onto which clusters of metal components had been soldered: cup-shaped objects resembling the top half of a bicycle bell, with various wires and hollow cylinders, all coated white by corroded batteries. Above the garage was a small attic space which, as we grew taller, eventually came into reach: balancing on my brother's shoulders, as he in turn stood on a chair, I'd hauled myself up into the darkness where, spreading myself flat to avoid falling through the joists, I uncovered two shotguns hidden under the thick strips of orange-yellow lagging. Our enthusiasm for such finds, a steady stream of which continued to turn up throughout our time in the house, was not shared by our mother – they were all promptly confiscated never to be seen again. Much like their original owner.

Though out of sight he was not entirely out of contact, even managing the odd birthday present down the years, if nowhere near our actual birthdays: a five-dollar bill; a model Phantom jet airplane; a miniature chess set; even a gold Omega watch, housed in a smart pale-blue box – which I would need to take good care of, his handwritten note cautioned, as it had been handed down from his own father. All these would arrive in envelopes and parcels plastered with blocks of improbably exotic stamps from the likes of Hong Kong, Iraq, Indonesia, Canada, the US and Vietnam. Clearly, wherever our father was, and whatever he was doing, he was leading a rather more colourful existence than that of a part-time secretary in a local engineering firm. But that was about to change.

Ironically, the Russians had unwittingly done our mother a favour, their phone calls elevating her troubles above the merely domestic and gradually ushering her back into the fold. As well as occasional lunches and sailing trips with Shergy and Bevis, every so often (thankfully not too often) her fellow 'ex-Berliners' would descend en masse to dispense gin and sympathy, their raucous laughter penetrating up through the floorboards. Summoned (a shrill whistle up the stairs) to put in an appearance – best to get it over with – I'd sidle in to where they were all sitting, my mother as usual slumped horizontally in her armchair, feet flat against the wall, skirt hitched up, holding forth as they took it in turns to ruffle my hair, after which I was free to escape back up to my room.

Eventually, word reached her that 'Registry' – where SIS stored all its files – were looking for people to help lighten the load. Given the nature of the material, the position was only open to ex-employees, on the basis that they had already proved themselves entirely trustworthy. Unfortunately her application suffered from her husband having been dismissed from SIS for being entirely untrustworthy. As a result, after the usual security checks 'yet more security checks' were needed, before eventually Tru in Personnel was able to confirm her return (a word or two from former boss Shergy likely seeing her over the line).

The job title would be Junior Executive, Tru cautioned, which my mother took to mean 'another word for clerical no doubt, but anything will be a relief from engineering' – and with that she was back with 'the office', which was now 'a very different kettle of fish, new, hardly recognizable,' she wrote to her aunt. SIS had moved from its rambling Broadway headquarters near St James's Park to the suitably nondescript concrete and glass of Century House, a ten-minute walk from Waterloo Station. 'Not a patch on the old rabbit warren, but nice to have a window.' Her husband need never know. Nor, in all probability, did the then head of SIS, who a decade earlier had ordered her husband's dismissal.

Registry had by this time become little more than a dumping ground, choked with an ever-mounting back catalogue of records, leads, reports and personnel files – which in those far-off, pre-digital days all had to be sorted, indexed and filed away by (entirely female) hand. 'Twenty-odd – and I mean odd – women to check the work off. Vapours and moods on all sides,' with a backlog of 'hundreds of files, cupboards overflowing with work, and with just one doddery seventy-year-old to do it.' Though likely as humdrum as it was hush-hush, the job was not without its perks – 'I collect the scraps from the canteen for the cat. I think folk imagine I carry them home for the boys' – while the salary, though modest, meant that she could finally afford a new car, which is to say a very old car, even the occasional luxury: 'Went berserk – bought myself a new dress.' On the last Friday of the month, payday, she'd head across Waterloo Bridge for dinner at the Savoy Grill with her 'office' chums, supplemented by the occasional outing a little higher up the SIS food chain: 'The chief and his sidekick are going to be there so I hope to make an impact – if I can't do it in tomato trousers I shall never do it.'

For the next five and a half years she took the 7.57 up to Waterloo, then walked down to Century House ('office tel. 01 928 5600, x 498'). 'I can relax and put my feet up in warmth and comfort, drink at the bar with civilized human beings, Communist or not, and eat meals which don't have to be prepared or washed-up after. Bliss,' she wrote to her aunt, before arranging to meet 'for a proper natter over a sticky bun behind Waterloo Station' to update her with chest and arm measurements for my brother and me in time for our Christmas jumpers.

Theirs was a shared history: her aunt had introduced her into SIS the first time round. It was standard practice for the vast majority of secretarial staff (with rare exception, the only position open to women at the time) to be recruited via family, though unlike most, my mother and her aunt were not from the well-to-do home counties set or a senior armed forces family – far from it.

My mother was born in Glasgow, the daughter of a local insurance manager, and though they soon moved south she retained a little of the language, if not the accent: about was 'aboot', trousers were 'breeks', while in those more innocent, early days 'blether' simply referred to the tall tales and exaggerated stories that all young girls and boys like to tell. Home from the age of twelve was in the seaside town of Whitley Bay, a suburb of New-castle, where she attended the local Monkseaton High. Like many girls of her background, her horizons didn't extend much beyond the local secretarial college (opting against Durham University), somewhere along the way acquiring a young submariner boyfriend. But the safe if rather predictable path she was starting to tread came under intense pressure every summer with the visit of her Aunt Agnes. It was never quite clear exactly what her aunt did, still less how she had come to be doing what-ever it was she did. All the family knew was that she had spent most of the war in Cairo, spoke a little Arabic, had learnt to ride (camels) and, when not knitting jumpers for the offspring of Embassy staffers stuck in draughty English boarding schools back home, busied herself arranging travel permits for the likes of Freya Stark and, less enjoyably, dealing with the explorer St John Philby. Philby was renowned as the first European to have crossed the forbidding Empty Quarter; he was a Muslim convert, trusted adviser to Ibn Saud (the future ruler of Saudi Arabia) and by all accounts – including her own – a difficult man. No doubt she gave as good as she got. Aunt Agnes was an acquired taste, with the unfortunate combination of an independent mind lacking independent means, and had long since decided against sacrificing a life of adventure on any marriage altar, which would have meant giving up her job with the Foreign Office. Or, more accurately, with Middle Eastern Intelligence.

Auntie's rescue mission saw my mother exchange Whitley Bay for a hostel on South Kensington's Cromwell Road, the move made easier by the unexpected demise of her submariner boyfriend (someone having forgotten to close off a valve while his submarine was in dock). Despite the hostel being 'supervised by an old dragon of an SIS matron who was supposed to keep them out of mischief', it didn't stop her enjoying the full merry-go-round of dinners and dances, likely a step up from Whitley Bay's Rex Club. With the possibility of a foreign posting for the lucky few, she honed her Pitman shorthand and signed up for evening classes at the nearby Institut Français. Having been the only girl in the hostel who had never been to London, she now found she was one of the few who had never been to Paris. Nor would she. A few weeks later she was sitting up on deck crossing over to Hamburg, then heading down to the small spa town of Bad Salzuflen where, in the immediate aftermath of the Second World War, SIS had set up its German headquarters.

After an all-too-brief induction course, the not-yet-twenty-one-year-old Margaret Miller, very much the young ingénue, boarded the overnight train to Berlin with its blacked-out windows, arriving – after endless checkpoints – at the epicentre of the Cold War.

Quite how her aunt, Agnes Miller, had been recruited was always something of a mystery, but it was all the more surprising given her unpromising start in life, having been orphaned at a young age and packed off from her native Glasgow to live with a distant relative in South Africa. The Agnes that I knew as a boy (always referred to simply as Aunt A) was already well into her sixties and had long since left SIS, emerging unscathed but for a frozen (palsied) right hand, most likely from having had an ice-cold gin and tonic clamped to it for several decades. Her (meagre) pension meant that she was still putting in the hours as a part-time secretary in the BBC newsroom, invariably volunteering for the less popular slots – night shifts, bank holidays, Christmas Day – time-and-a-half money, which she would splurge on our annual outing to Leicester Square cinemas or the Bertram Mills Circus. 'When the boys write their memoirs, I am sure Auntie's treats will have a chapter to themselves . . .'

With her pleated skirts and heavy woollens, she must have cut an incongruous figure among the denim-clad, long-haired backroom staff of the 1970s BBC, but then she must have cut an equally incongruous figure in the Foreign Office of the 1930s, her accent more Clyde than Tweed, a thorn – or thistle – among debs. But a little night-school Arabic had been her passport to a wider world, even if it meant having to share a cabin with 'Elizabeth C-B, a rather silly girl I travelled to Cairo with'.

'Cairo at that time was truly a Paris of the East, and to me it was paradise. Perfect hot climate, a comfortable way of life, breathtaking women,' wrote one of her (male) SIS contemporaries. It was paradise for Aunt A too, if for rather more aesthetic reasons, meeting the likes of Wilfred Thesiger, Freya Stark, Lawrence Durrell – and an inebriated Winston Churchill. As the war turned in the Allies' favour, she moved up from Alexandria to Baghdad (paying to have Gertrude Bell's gravestone cleaned) and then across to Tehran, enjoying – or enduring – an overnight bus trip sat alongside one Hossein Alā, future Prime Minister of Iran: 'I knew more about day-to-day living, he knew more about the quirks of the English language. The night and day we spent together was one long horrid pun. He loved them.' She ended up in Damascus at the end of the war, only to volunteer for the next conflict: 'I was in Jerusalem in 1946–7 [. . .] the walls were lined with Palestinian Police with walkie-talkie sets and tommy-guns. I suppose it was the ugliest-looking precautions I saw in all my riots. I don't like these tommy-gun things.'

Given the choice, she would have opted to stay in the Middle East, but soon enough she was criss-crossing the Iron Curtain, from Istanbul to Belgrade, running into Durrell again: 'When we were in Belgrade he didn't write much that I know of'; to Budapest, where the Embassy bar opened 'promptly at 5.30 so that the staff could get together and bring a little brightness into their enclosed Iron Curtain lives'; to Vienna, 'in a flat owned by a Countess who had done three years hard labour in Switzerland for spying for the British, but it hadn't soured her apparently as she was always keen to let her flat to Embassy people. But cold, my God, how I suffered'; to Trieste, arriving in time for the 1953 Coronation celebrations held in the Duino Castle overlooking the Adriatic, only to find herself being mistaken for an Italian, despite her platinum-blonde hair: 'Kept being shepherded into the Italian groups at the party and had great difficulty in getting back to my buddies . . .'

And then there was Warsaw.

I have a letter posted to her from a 'Room 9', confirming that 'some of your overseas service ranked as unhealthy service'. Nowhere more so than Warsaw. She'd been helping distribute food and clothing parcels via local Catholic churches – possibly hoping to pick up a little word-on-the-street low-level intelligence in the process – only for her contacts to be taken away one by one for questioning. Even in a country boasting 36,000 government agents, who in one (busy) night shift had arrested some 5,000 'suspects', this seemed more than coincidental. Only when she stopped putting her expenses through the books, opting instead to use her own money, did the situation improve, prompting her to think the unthinkable: that someone within the Embassy might be a 'fellow traveller' (as she termed it). A slippery slope that, rightly or wrongly, began to imbue her with a distrust of the service itself. Rightly, as her diaries would later record, when not one but two of her former colleagues were unmasked as double agents. 'I was in Beirut with [George] Blake and Warsaw with [Harry] Houghton and so help me I don't remember either of them. I do know that a damn good clean-up is long overdue and the ones they don't sack for fellow travelling they can sling out for inefficiency.'

'The office' posted her back to the Middle East, 'lent as a gulf expert', where she ran into Thesiger again as he headed into Oman, 'though he didn't get permission', and dealt with the eccentric – 'E, the British representative in Bahrain, twice married. The first time during the war, a Belgian. This lasted nine days as he came home one night and found her in bed with a RAF type. Now spends most of his time and all his holidays with his second ex-wife and her new husband. Odd, but then E was odd' – and the undesirable – 'Sarraj was head of Syrian Intelligence in my time in Beirut and a very bad man he was too. Today we are calling his enemies rebels, but if they win they will become our dear, dear friends – and so it goes. Hope the rebels win.'

By way of a thank you her farewell posting was to her favourite watering hole, Beirut, a city she knew well – well enough to head up into the hills in high summer to estivate. Estivate? 'To live in the hills above Beirut is to estivate. Had quite forgotten about estivation allowances until it caught my eye again.' Of an evening they'd head down to the port, more often than not calling in at The Normandy or the St George's Hotel, where she could always count on meeting familiar faces, few more familiar than St John Philby's son Kim, then employed as Middle East correspondent for the *Observer*, having left 'the office' under a cloud. Perhaps she had more licence than most, having known him since he was a schoolboy, but after one too many (no doubt ferocious) gin and tonics, she'd sounded off, loudly accusing him of being one of her 'damned fellow travellers'. Not the done thing. But all was soon forgiven and forgotten, a later diary entry noting that 'Kim's father has died. The *Sunday Times* obituary seems a little off the beam and the *Observer* I think is the better one as it was written by Kim. What will happen to his natural wife and children now? I suppose they'll go back to S. Arabia to the old black tents. Poor Kim, he is alone now, wife having died. The old boy was fond of his grandchildren, and, of course, cricket. Does his real wife go into mourning or does she just ignore the affair? No mention of the family is made in the obituary. No mention of Kim.'

Of course in the end even Kim let her down, though by then she was largely beyond caring. Her diary entry for 6 March 1963 notes: 'What a week. Aunt Betty committed suicide and Kim Philby disappeared, the whole thing in the papers on the 4th; too soon to say if Kim has taken a slow train to Moscow, he may have been murdered. That would be better than another scandal. Odd that I don't seem to care any more, but there it is I don't. Only glad I got out in time. "EH" was right when she said to me one day: "What would you do if you suddenly found you had been working for Stalin all the time?" She spoke truer than she knew. Well "I ken noo." Still, I wish it had been anybody but Kim.'

But by this time Cairo, Alexandria, Baghdad, even Philby himself were already 'like something from a different life'. Certainly as far as anyone in Room 3051 of Broadcasting House knew she was simply ex-Foreign Office – and the nearest her diaries come to any mention of the Cold War is a walk up to the Soviet Embassy to catch a glimpse of Yuri Gagarin, the first man in space: 'Much more handsome than his photographs. Just a shame he is Russian.' There was still room for the occasional pasted-in obituaries of Foreign Office mandarins and Arabists she'd known, but even these tended to be sandwiched in among waspish observations on the drinking habits of the newsroom's male presenters ('John as drunk as a coot on the last night of the shift') or the unsuitable marital choices of its female presenters ('Pretty girl, small, smart and elegant, throwing herself away'). Where once she had splashed out on front stalls seats in the opera houses of Vienna and Trieste, now she was reduced to traipsing down to Covent Garden at the end of a night shift to queue for rehearsal tickets, her salary just about enough to 'keep a roof over my head, however leaky'. And though she remained in touch with one or two former 'office' colleagues, she avoided get-togethers and reunions, tarnished by her Warsaw experience, seemingly seeing her so-called fellow travellers everywhere she looked.

Not least within her own family.

Mother 'getting spiked again', April 1972.

Aerial view of the Fort.

View from our upstairs
window, indoor firing
range (white-domed
building) in foreground.

3.

The Fort

'There is some possibility of my being offered
the job down on the south coast.'

Mother, letter to Aunt A, July 1971

Unsurprisingly perhaps for someone who'd served her SIS apprenticeship in Berlin at the height of the Cold War, the joys of Registry (and Woking) began to wear thin for our mother. '5 ½ years in one job doing the same thing ad infinitum gets a bit wearisome. I should also like to re-enter the world of men again.' The need for a new chimney proved the final straw – a rusting aerial wire clamped round its base had caused first the plaster to crumble and then the brickwork itself, for which our absent father was apparently to blame. And so she'd put her hand up for an opening at the SIS training camp on the south coast.

The job came with a small terraced house, No. 2 MSQ (Married Staff Quarters – technically, at least, she was still married), which meant she could rent out our Woking home and save on her ticket up to Waterloo ('one pound a day now!'). Solvency, or near enough. Our new home was one of a row of six built to house some of the construction workers on the training camp, a Napoleonic coastal fort. On one side of us lived George, the camp's lead driver, on the other one of the 'General Duty' (GD) staff. During school holidays she shared a bedroom with our grandmother Maisie, drafted in to keep an eye on us (her daytime TV commitments notwithstanding); my brother had the other bedroom, while I had a downstairs room fronting on to the pavement. Being a Ministry of Defence property the house was decorated in the traditional MOD manner, which is to say not at all, nor had it anything by way of a garden, to our mother's relief.

When she started at the training camp, she'd written to Aunt A that 'there are about eighteen men & me here. Personnel thought me sufficiently matronly for the situation.' A few months on she was writing to say that, matronly or not, she had 'found a tame ex-Royal Marine' among the eighteen, followed soon after by the news that she was 'getting spiked again' – reassuring her that 'no, he is not another Broadway beagle', Aunt A clearly of the opinion that 'the office' was still riddled with 'Broadway beagles', whatever they might be.

JBW had unexpectedly cleared the way a few weeks beforehand by asking for a divorce which, given that he was 'not the star I would want to hitch my wagon to without legal backing', she took to mean that there was a third (by her reckoning, fourth) 'Mrs W in the offing'. Her own (re) marriage was a quiet affair, with our grandmother and the camp's Commanding Officer (CO) as the sole attendees, the idea being to keep everything 'very dark as I knew I wouldn't stand an earthly chance of keeping the Woking house if JBW knew I was getting married again – and news does travel.'

Her new husband was the Administration Officer (AO) of the training camp, responsible for its day-to-day running, which required him – and therefore now us – to live on the premises. And so once again we were on the move, if only half a mile or so down the road.

From the very first, despite MTE being painted in large letters above its entrance, I pretty much knew that our new home wasn't really a Military Training Establishment, not least because I never saw anyone in uniform there. But being thirteen years old I barely gave it a thought. Of far greater concern was the news that friends and classmates wouldn't be allowed inside. I was to make my own way there from No. 2 MSQ, a simple enough route that passed directly in front of the first tee of the local golf club, whose members had possibly never seen anyone approach the camp on foot, let alone a boy wheeling a metal trunk. Play temporarily suspended, I passed under their silent gaze, then followed the single-track road across a bridge. The road straightened out, then dipped down into a huge dry moat some sixty feet across, surrounded by an outer fence topped with razor wire, before coming to a halt in front of two huge pale-blue wooden doors at the foot of a sheer block-stone wall some 80 feet high. Instead of surveillance cameras, laser beams, motion detectors, pressure mats and suchlike, there was just a large, rusting doorbell which gave off a metallic rasp, following which heavy boots echoed along the flagstone entrance tunnel and an expressionless eye peered down through a small wired-glass hatch for possibly longer than was necessary, before a smaller entrance cut into one of the massive wooden doors opened and in I stepped.

There shouldn't be any problems, my mother had reassured, they knew to expect me. Certainly the guard – Head Guard as it turned out – had been expecting someone of my name, but clearly not someone of my age. Equally clearly, he did not approve – with some justification, given the true nature of the establishment. His name was Fleming, an irony that had likely never occurred to him or anyone else inside the camp, so far removed was the reality of day-to-day life there from the world of James Bond.

Fleming escorted me through the entrance tunnel to where a single pole barred the way to the camp's vast, gravel-covered quadrangle. I was to wait outside the glass-roofed lean-to structure to one side of the barrier – more green-house than guard room – where a sorry-looking Alsatian lay prone on the lino and took no notice of me either then or in all the years I lived there. Eventually Fleming returned, having made whatever calls he needed to make, the pole juddered upwards and I was pointed towards a small road leading up to the original earthwork ramparts, onto which had been built (plonked) a modern, sprawling two-storey brick affair – the Main Mess – at the far end of which I would find my new home, No. 1 MTE. (There was no No. 2 MTE, ours being the only house in the entire camp.)

Since there was no lock on the door (no need), I could go straight in. The house was arranged upside down, with the bedrooms downstairs and living rooms upstairs, to take advantage of the view along the coastline. On one side we overlooked a stretch of moat complete with assault course – climbing walls, stepping logs, monkey bars and so on; on the other we looked across the quadrangle itself, with a cluster of storage huts, an indoor firing range and a small ammuni-tions bunker directly below our house. My allotted bedroom looked out onto a small garden surrounded by a high wall, giving respite from the biting winds that swept round the headland. There'd be plenty to do, our mother had promised, and certainly there was, if only at weekends when no one was about. Soon enough our mother was reporting back to Aunt A that all was well: '[They are] taken out to sea in the launch, being given target practice in the range, they fish on the private beach, there's a tennis court & a golf course on the doorstep – not to mention fresh sea breezes.'

On weekdays, with training courses in progress, I was encouraged to keep a low profile. Unfortunately, my idea of keeping a low profile was not the same as my mother's. Crouched forward, chin resting on handlebars, I discovered that by freewheeling down the hill from the Main Mess I could silently glide beneath the single pole, past the guardhouse and the comatose Alsatian and along the entrance tunnel with no one any the wiser. If the outer doors had been left open, as they often were in summer, I was out and away – if not, no matter, the smaller inner door had just a simple mortise lock. 'It's good fun playing with the guards,' I wrote to Aunt A. 'I zip down on my speedy new bike, turn the corner and wiz [sic] through the main entrance. Of course they don't know what to put in the registra [sic] book, they obviously find it a bit trying.'

The problem of what to do with a (trying) young boy on the loose inside the SIS training camp was partially solved by the camp's CO. A keen sailor, but with nothing like the salary to fund it, to save on mooring fees he would overwinter his yacht in the quadrangle, and wondered whether my brother and I might want to earn 'some loose change' by scraping down the hull, a task largely devised to keep us – especially me – out of harm's way, but which inevitably resulted in the camp's workforce – training instructors, GD men, mechanics and 'tech boys' – gradually growing used to seeing a young boy around the place. And vice versa. The 'tech boys' dealt, of course, with all things technical (domestic TV repairs included, if asked nicely), the 'mech boys' with all things mechanical – trucks, cars and outboard engines (bicycles included, if asked nicely); anything and everything else was dumped on the GD men, mostly ageing ex-servicemen who helped out in the kitchens or with more mundane tasks such as cleaning windows – outside tradespeople being unlikely to be granted security clearance.

The yacht was laid up to the side of the long, brick building which faced directly onto the seafront, originally the Fort's gun battery. The entire upper floor had been converted into offices, each with a direct view looking out to sea – provided one stood on a chair, the windows being just below ceiling level. The ground floor comprised a row of casement workshops, a large garage complete with hydraulic lifts and inspection pits at one end, a photography studio and adjoining darkroom at the other. The remaining casements were mostly given over to the 'tech' boys, while those nearest the central access tunnel leading to the camp's shingle beach housed a jumble of diving equipment, oxygen tanks and inflatable dinghies. The building was bookended by two rather basic and, during winter months, very damp, barely habitable accommodation blocks (known simply as the East and West Wings), beyond which lay the remains of the original outer wall defences: two red-brick double-height former gun batteries, largely roofless, whose floors had long since rotted away, home only to nesting seagulls.

Come Friday afternoons, when most courses finished, we pretty much had the run of the place – with the exception of the indoor firing range which, needless to say, required the presence of one of the camp's weapons instructors. Inside this windowless, white-domed building was an obstacle course of plasterboard partitions and random doors, which had to be navigated in total darkness. Automatic pulleys and levers released cutout figures which randomly sprang out from all angles, each with a phosphorescent target, so that the instructors could assess would-be officers' suitability for 'work in the field'. (Kim Philby had once been put through his paces there.) However, our initial enthusiasm for all this, or certainly our mother's, rather waned when a stray bullet ricocheted off an exposed nail head, taking out an instructor's eye. Following which I was gently steered towards the training camp's abandoned and heavily pot-holed tennis court, no less hazardous in its own way. The court was situated on the strip of land between the camp walls and the outer perimeter wire. Aside from a helicopter landing spot, marked with a large 'H', this was largely disused, which meant we occasionally stumbled over random pieces of hardware such as the short stretch of railway line used for explosives and sabotage training, left over from the camp's Second World War heyday when it was home to the Special Operations Executive (SOE), otherwise known as the Ministry for Ungentlemanly Warfare, tasked with creating havoc behind enemy lines by whatever means necessary.

Since we were the lone residents of the camp – lone boy for the most part after my brother got into Oxford – the tennis court was destined to remain abandoned (tennis, I soon discovered, being rather better for having someone on the other side of the net). Instead I spent the best part of a summer holiday measuring out a croquet course in front of our house, croquet being just about the only sport I could practise on my own. But if my solitary existence occasionally had me wondering quite what our mother's marriage had got us into, her new husband could be forgiven for having much the same thought. No sooner had word reached Century House that he was seeing our mother than he found himself being invited up to London, ostensibly to discuss potential ways to improve operational efficiency or some such, in reality a pretext – as Shergy later cheerfully admitted – for her former Berlin boss to give him the once-over, just to be sure she wasn't repeating the mistake she'd made first time around. But any similarity ended at a shared first name – her second husband inevitably becoming 'John II' – while any concerns about his predecessor's offspring going to live within the very bowels of the organization that had dismissed him were discounted on the basis that it was standard practice never to use surnames in the training camp – a practice all but undermined by the curiously high number of staff called John: a John F ran the photographic studio, a John E skippered the training camp's launch, a John M was the chief training officer, a John W the incoming camp CO, and, of course, John II. As for my brother and myself, this was further reduced to a simple letter – I was no longer Alistair, simply A, my brother no longer Jonathan but J, just as our Aunt Agnes was only ever Aunt A and our mother (Margaret) simply M. True to her training, a Pitman-esque shorthanding of everything and everyone.

Despite its location, the training camp turned out to be anything but the quiet backwater our mother had feared. As the camp's sole female employee, she was on call both day and more especially night, exhaustingly so, with a seemingly never-ending round of welcoming drinks and end-of-course dinners (long dress required): 'I meet some quite interesting folk at the "special" dinners – even the occasional drop of royalty no less.' And with SIS finally starting to recruit female graduates, her arrival at the camp was all the more timely – aside from the lack of female staff within the camp itself, there was not a single female instructor or lecturer, indeed there was barely a female officer in the entire service. Not that she was complaining too loudly. 'The ratio of men to women is about 40:1. Life begins at 43!'

Nor, for my own part, was life within the four (very high) walls of the camp quite as solitary as it had first appeared. Given the sheer expanse of quadrangle and accompanying 'fresh sea breezes' that whipped round the headland, a boy with a bicycle was never going to be bereft of company for long. Soon enough the tech boys, GD men and staffers had me transporting random pieces of equipment from one corner of the camp to another. My errand-boy duties did not go unrewarded: the GD men would leave an extra lunch from the canteen on our doorstep, John F took me up to Southampton to watch the football and John E smuggled my brother and me aboard the camp launch boat for fishing forays along the coast.

That said, not all the camp instructors were quite so thrilled at the sight of a young boy freewheeling across the quadrangle – or to be more exact, the sight of JBW's offspring turning up in SIS's own backyard.

Work outing aboard FPB (fast patrol boat), my mother nearest camera.

John Wyke (& family),
'in his heyday regarded
as SIS's leading
technical expert.'

'I rode (drove? flew?) a helicopter up to Wales, did a trip in a hovercraft,
so it is not all routine.' Mother, June 1972.

4.

No. 1 MTE

'Don't mention this in front of the boys any
time as I really don't feel strong enough to
explain their father to them yet.'

Mother, letter to Aunt A, 11 June 1967

I first met Peter Lunn in the stern of the camp's FPB (fast patrol boat) known simply as the Fort Launch. Powered by twin Rolls-Royce engines, the boat had originally been commissioned for situations where speed might be called for, such as depositing or extricating employees on or from unfriendly Baltic shores. However, with the 1970s oil crisis making running costs prohibitive and with the lack of enthusiasm for such adventuring within the current SIS, the launch was now all but mothballed in the nearby naval dock-yard, with just the occasional outing along the coast to keep its engines ticking over.

Quietly spoken, with a slight lisp and being (just about) medium height (by the age of fourteen I was already taller than him), Lunn would not have been most people's idea of a British Secret Service agent. Indeed, from a distance – I'd often see him entering and exiting the Main Mess from our kitchen window – in his suit and tie he could have passed for middle management in an insurance office. However, this belied a wiry athleticism of someone half his age, honed by a lifetime's devotion to the ski slopes. Now, stripped to the waist, he was checking the oxygen tanks and various pieces of diving gear, and wondered if I might want to explore the murky depths with him, though he couldn't guarantee I'd be able to see much beyond the end of my arm. Given the tidal currents along our stretch of coastline and the fast-running waters that swept at right angles to the camp's shingle beach, I thought better of it. Even so, I made a point of umming and ahing for a moment or two before declining, in case he might think less of me. I needn't have worried. He undoubtedly did think less of me, being cut from an altogether different cloth.

Lunn had worked alongside JBW in Vienna, and was no admirer. Back on dry land, I learnt I had made the correct call. 'Who knows what might have happened down there?' my mother wondered out loud, to Lunn's amusement.

Prior to our move to No. 1 MTE our father was seldom if ever mentioned – still less explained – his cause not helped by the irregular trickle of envelopes and parcels, plastered with those blocks of improbably exotic stamps, having long since dried up. Only now, here we were, surrounded by the very people who had worked alongside him and who – for better or, in Lunn's case, for worse – knew him only too well.

Though Lunn had officially retired from SIS, he was still a regular lecturer at the Fort. When not otherwise engaged on SIS business (and often when he was), Lunn would head for the slopes at every opportunity (even interrupting his questioning of Kim Philby in Beirut to go skiing). He had introduced most of SIS's Vienna and Berlin stations, including my mother, to the slopes of Garmisch-Partenkirchen, where he was a familiar figure having captained the 1936 British Winter Olympics team (deliberately avoiding the opening ceremony, loath to give the stiff-arm salute to the watching Hitler). Despite his reputation as 'a complex man, for whom physical exertion and danger possessed an almost spiritual dimension', he would happily stand in as impromptu barman behind the cubbyhole bar in the Main Mess, where he kept a personalized tankard. Most weekends he liked to head home – or to the ski slopes of Mürren, where the Lunn family owned a chalet – at the earliest opportunity, and though he may have been less than impressed by my enthusiasm for underwater adventure, it didn't stop him enlisting me come Friday lunchtime to help wash up behind the bar or to straighten up the chairs in the small theatre room where he lectured. Clearly the sins of the father – whatever they might have been – would not be foisted on the son.

The theatre room was little more than a converted office, with a blue velvet curtain strung round a slightly raised platform and disagreeable plastic seating. A row of black and white photographs along one wall showed every SIS chief from Mansfield Cumming (1909–23) through Dick White (1956–68) to the newly appointed Maurice Oldfield (1973–). Of necessity, Lunn's case histories were largely confined to operations that had been 'blown', which meant that recruits were subjected to a steady diet of past failure, the best known of which was a 450-metre tunnel dug under the Russian-occupied sector of Berlin to tap the KGB's communication cables. Lunn had run the British side of the operation.

I knew nothing about the so-called 'Operation Gold', still less of my own parents' involvement, though this was hardly surprising: to judge by my mother's old Kodak prints, life in Berlin was a constant merry-go-round of boating on Lake Wannsee and the Havel, tennis and swimming at the Blau-Weiss (Blue-White) Club, cantering through the Grunewald and hot glühwein served high up in the Austrian Tyrol. Even when she did talk about her time there, which wasn't often, it was still mostly all ski runs and tennis parties, the only exception to her self-censorship – now that we were living in the training camp – being a very occasional reference to the tunnel operation, which to her bemusement (annoyance) 'everyone seems to claim credit for – except for the people who actually worked on it'. As for her own involvement, this she dismissed as nothing more than 'a walk-on part', though what exactly a walk-on part entailed she never did say.

But others did.

Unable to bring outside catering staff into the training camp, she'd occasionally cajole me into ironing a shirt and helping out at one of her dos, which mostly involved nothing more demanding than serving White Russians (the cocktail), Snowballs and suchlike and handing round bowls of Twiglets (it being the 1970s). Despite the supposedly parlous state of the post-war SIS, judging by the noise levels at her get-togethers the current 'office' was in rather better shape. This was largely down to former chief Dick White, who, some twenty years earlier, had been drafted across from MI5 to oversee a radical overhaul of the service, but more recently owed something to SIS finally being headed up by one of its own, Maurice Oldfield.

Once or twice a year Oldfield would pay a visit to the training camp, the cue for the various instructors and senior officers to crowd into our upstairs sitting room as he wandered over from the Main Mess. Back then the identity of 'the chief' was by and large kept out of the public eye, and but for my mother pointing him out I would have struggled to imagine the 'rumpled, homespun figure with owlish glasses' being head of Britain's Secret Intelligence Service. But even a part-time wine waiter could see that he was very much among friends, whereas my only memory of Dick White was of a rather patrician figure standing alone in the stern of the Fort Launch while everyone else huddled round a thermos flask in the cabin, chatting away. (Oldfield's immediate predecessor was rarely mentioned, other than my mother's occasional reminder that he had had to resign when his son was arrested on drugs charges, should I be tempted to dabble.)

But for a later scandal concerning his own private life, Old-field would have been looked back on as one of SIS's abler chiefs, appreciated for being both 'an excellent companion and classless in outlook' – not least within our own household: one of his last acts before retiring into academia was to sign off John II's promotion from AO to CO of the camp, no small achievement for a relative outsider, let alone someone brought up in rural Norfolk with little formal education. Under Oldfield, SIS would open its doors ever wider – and more especially the camp's vast wooden doors – to include all the various branches of the intelligence and security services, along with one or two (dubious) foreign agencies, a rapid expansion that was not without its teething problems: '30,000 main meals last year – it's like running four or five large hotels, dos nearly every night & mostly long dress. The head of training is in hospital after a nervous breakdown.'

Oldfield was a career officer who had spent much of his thirty-something years of service overseas, largely in the Far East, and so understood what the job involved at ground level. One of the ways his hands-on experience played out – which certainly endeared him to the likes of my mother – was that he knew better than to judge SIS's rank and file solely on the basis of the Foreign Office's rigid grading structure, especially those who applied themselves to tasks slightly above their pay grade as and when circumstances demanded. And in few places was this truer than in the Berlin of the Cold War. No coincidence then that the only press article my mother ever cut out and kept was a 1979 *New Statesman* appreciation of Oldfield on his retirement, highlighting in orange marker pen his contempt for 'those who snatch credit and copyright for the work of hundreds who dwelt in necessary obscurity'.

However, within the four walls of the training camp such obscurity wasn't deemed quite so necessary, and over the course of various such dos – at which there were invariably one or two ex-Berliners present – anecdote by anecdote I would learn something of what she'd been doing away from the ski slopes and the Blau-Weiss Club, even a little of what her 'walk-on' part in the Berlin tunnel operation had involved. And no one was more keen to relive past glories – and failures – than John Wyke, who in early 1973 arrived as the new CO of the camp.

Because it was, superficially at least, a Military Training Establishment, Wyke had to reacquaint himself with his former army rank of lieutenant colonel, despite having spent most of his career with SIS. In his heyday he was regarded as SIS's leading frontline technical expert, not least by MI5's Peter Wright, who granted him rare praise in his 1987 book *Spycatcher*, be it for shinning up telegraph poles at night under the noses of EOKA terrorists in Cyprus, tapping Russian communication lines in Vienna or spending hours flat on his back in total darkness connecting the crucial 'taps' at the business end of the Berlin tunnel. But for his reputation – many of SIS's operations would never have got off the ground, or under it, without him – Wyke might well have been pensioned off in Dick White's overhaul of the service, but instead he had remained with 'the office', wings clipped, his appointment as the camp's CO a final hurrah before retirement.

Wyke would have liked nothing better than to return the camp to its Second World War SOE roots, but even a teenage boy could see that those days had long gone. The assault course in the moat beneath our house remained entirely unassaulted, the railway track laid for explosives training was long weeded over, the Fort Launch was all but decommissioned and the muffled gunfire from the indoor range was at best sporadic. Cycling across the quadrangle one midwinter morning, I stopped next to where the veteran instructor John ('Jimmy') Munn, submariner sweater over a plain office shirt, stood waiting for that week's recruits to arrive. Munn had run SOE's North African training camp during the Second World War and been an instructor at the famous Camp X in Ottawa, so he was a last reminder of when the ground beneath our feet had been home turf for SOE. I followed Munn's silent gaze as one of the camp's blue transit vans drove through the entrance tunnel, George behind the wheel as usual, flashing his headlights and giving Munn a wry smile before swinging up to the Main Mess and dropping off his smart-suited Oxbridge passengers, overnight cases in hand, bright green Marks & Spencer bags flapping in the sea breeze, hunched against the cold.

Wyke was a man of many and varied talents. An unlikely if highly accomplished ballroom dancer, no sooner had he arrived than he set about livening up the end-of-course dinners by clearing away the furniture and taking to the floor,

41

requiring my mother to take a pair of flat pumps to every dinner. He was a skilled if not entirely practical carpenter, carving a large piece of exotic timber he'd picked up on his travels, which he then installed as a mantelpiece in the Main Mess. (And which in due course fell onto the foot of the visiting head of MI5, no less, leaving him on crutches for several weeks.) As a keen amateur historian (penning historical dramas for BBC Radio in retirement), he believed that no self-respecting naval fortification should be without a cannon and arranged for a surplus 32-pounder to be sent down from the Tower of London, overseeing the construction of a carriage to house it, then press-ganging several of the GD staff into positioning it here, there and everywhere in the quadrangle, before deciding it would look best up in front of the Main Mess – initially facing down the slope, then to one side, then the other. Wyke himself was something of a loose cannon. He'd arrived with wife number three (number two an old 'office' friend of my mother, awkwardly) along with – to Head Guard Fleming's further dismay – twin infant girls they'd recently adopted. Unfortunately the only accommodation available was the set of dreary, dark, damp rooms directly over the entrance tunnel, sparking off a volley of complaints from Wyke to Century House for the duration of his two-year stint as CO, eventually resolved by the purchase of a pleasant detached house – after he had retired.

Alongside an at times exhausting ebullience – he could barely manage a straight face for his passport photograph – Wyke had a rather unfortunate trait given his line of work (or a marvellous habit, depending on one's point of view), being a brilliant raconteur ('consummate bletherer', as my mother put it). To make matters worse he was a very fast eater, often finishing courses before his fellow diners had barely started, with the result that he often had the stage all to himself. Entertaining as this might be, his loose tongue had caused him problems down the years: aside from being a little too free with his opinions about his former SIS boss Dick White, he still blamed himself for having matter-of-factly updated a certain George Blake on what he was working on during one of their fishing trips together on Grunewald's lakes during his time in Berlin.

Finding to his surprise – and delight – that JBW's ex-wife and offspring were his new (and only) neighbours presented him with the perfect opportunity to relive past glories. Squeezed round the circular table in our small upstairs dining room, we would be treated to the full Wyke repertoire, including his work on the preparatory stages of the Berlin tunnel operation with my father, whose subsequent dismissal from the service he saw not just as a miscarriage of justice but as a wholly unnecessary result of the paranoia that had gripped SIS following the defection of Guy Burgess and Donald Maclean, and Kim Philby's subsequent exit.

Wyke's championing excepted, JBW was something of a pariah figure, even within his own family, a state of affairs that John II felt the need to rectify, especially when he learnt that my brother and I had yet to meet JBW's mother – our grandmother – despite her living just an hour's drive away. And so a few weekends later off we set.

Her house was at the end of a single-track lane, a surprisingly remote spot given its Surrey address, overlooking a series of ancient carp ponds banked by a thick covering of beech trees. Strictly speaking, this was not the first time I had visited. Many years earlier, driving back to Woking from a birthday trip to the seaside, my mother had stopped the car at the top of the lane and, engine running, pointed down to where our 'other grandmother' lived. Up until then I wasn't aware that I had another grandmother – we didn't even know her name (Gladys). But barely had the news sunk in than we were on our way again, and that was that.

This time we would be venturing down the lane. Unbeknown to my brother and me, John II had taken the precaution of having a fellow SIS officer exercise his dogs near the house beforehand, on the off-chance that JBW might be putting in one of his trademark unscheduled appearances. This was not entirely without precedent. A few years before, at her wits' end financially, our mother had arrived at the house, cap in hand, only to find JBW halfway up a tree, chainsaw in hand. 'I went down to see Ma Wood. He was staying with her at the time but was up a tree and refused to come down so didn't speak to him [. . .] & shortly afterwards the bank wrote to say the money was paid, so presumably she brought some influence to bear.'

The coast duly confirmed clear, we entered via a dilapidated conservatory, windows broken, to be met by a colossal bronze eagle perched at a precipitous angle, so large that the floorboards had given way – along with two small, rain-sodden dogs who, as quickly became all too clear, were free to do what dogs will do whenever and wherever they pleased. The ground floor was bedecked with vases, pots and pans collecting a steady stream of water which descended directly through the ceiling above, the noise of which, along with the yapping dogs and the accompanying chimes of no less than four grandfather clocks – each with its own idea of the time – explained why JBW's mother had not heard us arrive. And why she always wore a heavy black coat indoors whenever it

44

rained. Getting up from her armchair she shooed away her dogs, poked the fire with her walking stick and apologized for the (indoor) weather. Like the house itself, she had what might reasonably be described as an unkempt look, her black coat doubling as a dog blanket as soon as she sat back down, though the eye – or certainly this teenage boy's eye – was mostly drawn to the large mushroom-like cysts protruding from her scalp, which she made no attempt to hide, or possibly had never noticed. ('How nice to be so uninhibited,' our mother noted.) Doing away with any formalities she launched into an uninterrupted stream of questions, comments and observations, interspersed with something of her own history, reminiscences about people she had known (Kipling, for instance) and places she had been (pretty much everywhere), all the while somehow managing to keep off the subject of her son, other than a brief mention of a road trip she'd taken with him a few years back – all the way to Istanbul, at the age of seventy-three. Clearly she was of a rather different order to our other grandmother, with whom I'd spent the previous Saturday afternoon – and countless other Saturday afternoons – watching the wrestling on ITV through a fug of Embassy Regals.

Tea arrived in unwashed cups with, by way of disinfectant, the option of an accompanying whisky, following which she suggested my brother and I help ourselves to whatever we wanted from the bedroom at the top of the stairs. There was no electricity in the top half of the house but just enough natural light to make out various dismantled radio parts scattered across the floor, a tattered white Cambridge rowing blazer, some trout rods and, in amongst a bundle of foreign-language books, a dusty stamp album – the opening page headed 'Only six known sets in the world.' Which our mother, correctly suspecting they might be valuable, made us put back. Mistake.

As we were leaving, John II tactfully enquired as to his predecessor's current whereabouts, but she had no idea where he was, still less when he might return, only that he was prone to descending on her without warning every few years. And so we came away two trout rods to the good but little further on with regard to our father other than the impression – given the Cambridge blazer and his sharp-as-a-tack English mother – that he might be English. How wrong can you be.

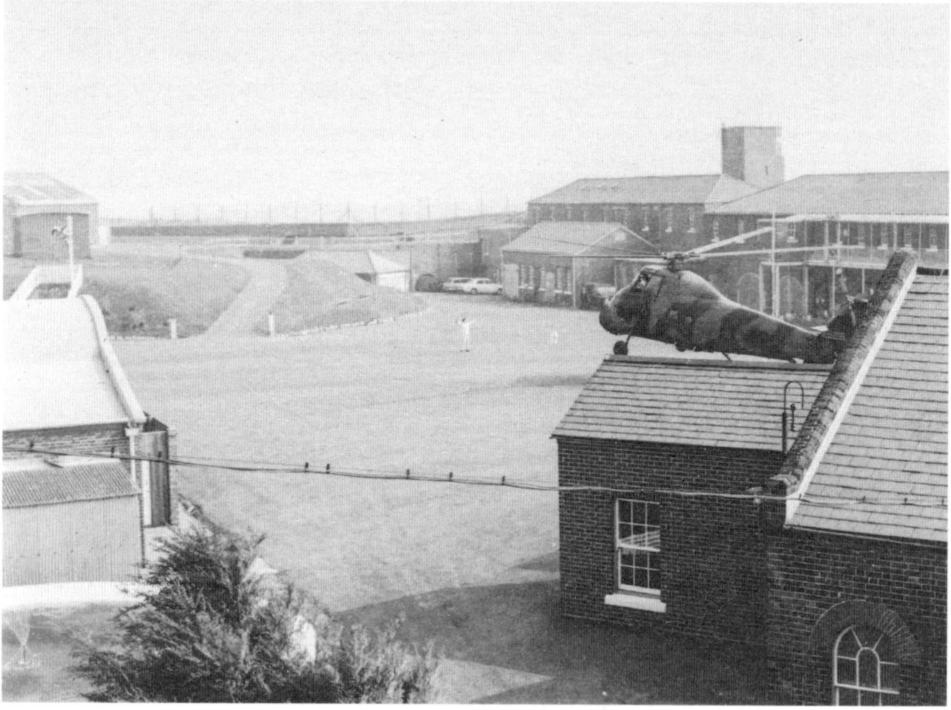

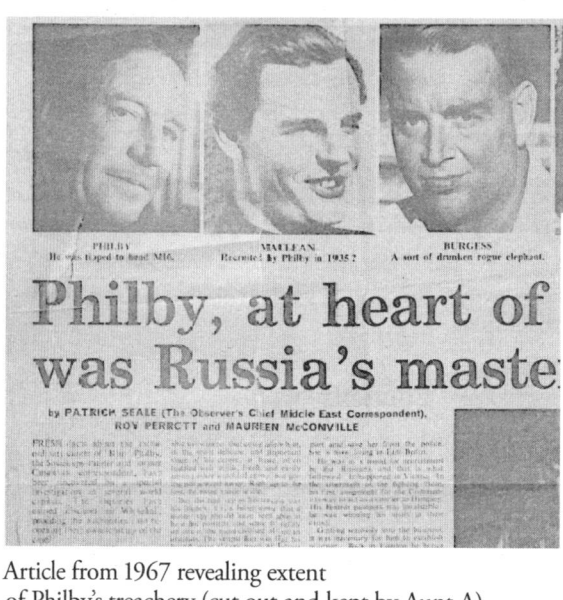

Foreign heads of state would land inside the camp, away from prying eyes.

PHILBY
He was tipped to head MI6.

MACLEAN
Recruited by Philby in 1935?

BURGESS
A sort of drunken rogue elephant.

Philby, at heart of was Russia's maste

by PATRICK SEALE (The Observer's Chief Middle East Correspondent), ROY PERROTT and MAUREEN McCONVILLE

Article from 1967 revealing extent of Philby's treachery (cut out and kept by Aunt A).

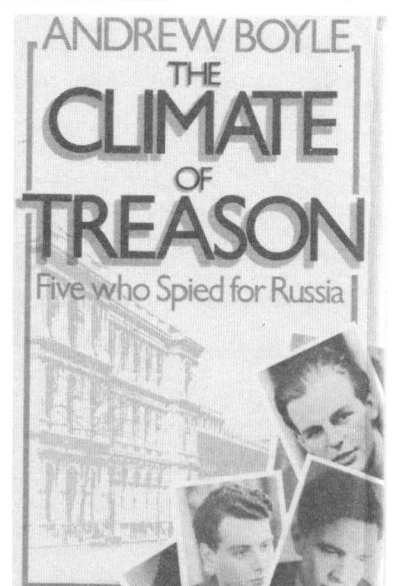

With up to twenty-five others suspected of having spied for the Soviets, even I had my doubts about my father, November 1979.

5.

Lynchmere

'News of [JBW's] return to these shores was soon
doing the rounds up at head office, a bit of a stir.'

Mother to Aunt A, Christmas card note, 1979

In the years since Kim Philby turned up in Moscow in
1963 there had been endless newspaper articles and books
speculating on who else might have been involved. Most of
which my mother took little notice of, other than the occasional Chapman Pincher article in the *Daily Express*, not least
because she had barely heard of most of the names being
bandied around – aside from Philby himself. 'I see Kim
Philby has vanished now. One only needs to read the daily
rag to keep abreast of one's old friends and acquaintances,'
she wrote to Aunt A at the time, though in truth he was little
more than a passing acquaintance and the last time she'd run
into him had been July 1961, on a post-JBW recuperative
visit to Beirut. So when she heard via 'the office' grapevine
that the so-called 'Fourth Man' had turned out to be the Surveyor of the Queen's Pictures (Sir Anthony Blunt), this only
confirmed her belief that it was all a world away from the
circles she moved in and far removed from the quiet backwater that we inhabited, our address sufficiently anonymous
for it to be matter-of-factly listed in my school handbook,

with just that rusty entrance barrier and equally rusty Alsatian to suggest otherwise.

Security was only ramped up for rare visits by foreign heads of state – the Shah of Iran, King Hussein of Jordan – the camp's gravel quadrangle having been tarmacked over so that their helicopters could land safely out of sight from prying eyes. On such occasions the chief weapons instructor would spreadeagle himself across the flat roof of our house ready to pick off any intruder, though even this was eventually discontinued for fear of taking out a hapless golfer retrieving a wayward ball. Otherwise, there were occasional security warnings courtesy of the Irish Republic Army (IRA), at the time engaged in an extensive bombing campaign on the UK mainland, with government buildings marked out as a prime target. Warnings were graded Bikini Black, Amber or Red according to the level of threat, but given our relative anonymity these never rose above Black, during which the only visible precaution was that the camp's entrance doors would remain shut. A more pressing concern – certainly for John II, as the camp's Admin Officer – was the annual visit from the local council's buildings inspectors: despite the historic importance of the fortifications, back in the early 1960s permission had (somehow) been granted for the construction of the Main Mess and adjoining accommodation blocks – including our own house – seemingly with the proviso that the foundations would not be dug too deep. As a result walls had a tendency to fall down whenever the wind got up, including one in our own garden, taking out a flowerbed and two deckchairs.

However, 'Bikini Blacks' and tumbling walls would soon be the least of our problems. The journalist Andrew Boyle, having effectively outed Anthony Blunt, was now claiming that 'at least another twenty-five unnamed spies' had been working for the Russians. Whether my father had made the cut or how high up in the pecking order he might be was unclear, but given his abrupt dismissal from SIS, the omens were not good. Even I had my doubts, remembering the steady stream of discarded radio valves, half-bicycle bells and corroded batteries that had turned up throughout our time in Woking, further fuelled by some local schoolboys' discovery of a Russian dead-letter drop halfway up a silver birch tree in nearby Martyr's Lane, a mere five-minute cycle ride from our old house. For years to come I would await the revelations from sources such as the Mitrokhin Archive and the Venona transcripts with much the same degree of trepidation as I used to await school exam results.

The fear was that, should worst come to worst, Fleet Street might not take kindly to his offspring being housed within the very bowels of the organization that had dismissed him – however mundane the reason for our ending up there.

Against this backdrop, with impeccable timing, in October 1979 JBW's mother – Gladys, our 'other grandmother' – died, raising the prospect of him returning for the funeral. Given that no one knew where in the world he might be, still less how to get hold of him, it seemed a distant prospect. And even if he did, our mother reassured (herself), he would likely sidle in once the service was underway and slip out before the end, as was his way. Nevertheless, on the off-chance that he might turn up, I made a point of wearing the gold Omega he'd sent me from Saigon all those years ago, if only to show willing. It had of course turned out to be a fake – admittedly a good one – made in one of the small workshops that had sprung up in the Mekong Delta, most likely from the village of My Tho. Unsurprisingly, it had long since stopped working.

The funeral was held in our grandmother's local church, in the village of Lynchmere. We were the first to arrive, the vicar assured us, only to find a lone figure occupying the front pew. Having never seen JBW from the front let alone the back, I couldn't be sure, unlike his ex-wife – who calmly marched up the aisle, tapped him on the shoulder and greeted him with, despite everything, a surprising degree of warmth. With his high forehead and thinning, back-swept hair, my first impression was that he looked not unlike the American comedian Bob Hope, albeit a rather war-torn, haggard version ('seedy, yellowing, ageing and toothless' according to our mother), complete with transatlantic – if barely audible – mumble. He was wearing a crumpled, slightly inappropriate chocolate-brown suit, lapels noticeably fraying and rather too short in the sleeve – short enough to see that he was wearing not one but two watches on the same wrist. Watches obviously his thing, I remember thinking.

After introducing him to John II (to bemusement of vicar), then to his sons (to further bemusement of vicar), our mother set about the lengthy process, to be continued after the service and beyond, of attempting to wheedle out of him where exactly he had flown in from (Zambia) and, less successfully, what exactly he was up to and who the current Mrs Wood might be. Setting the pattern for the next few days, during which even the most straightforward question would be met with a marvel of muttered obfuscation. But as she pointed out to him, goodness knows, he'd been through tougher interrogations.

There was a smattering of elderly attendees, oblivious to the domestic complications of the front rows, a few of whom braved the driving rain and joined us at the burial ground, where – slightly alarmingly – JBW calmly leant over the empty grave as his mother's coffin was lowered in, camera in hand. Afterwards he agreed to join us for, under the circumstances, a surprisingly relaxed late pub lunch (dried-up shepherd's pie), laughter included. Given the unexpected air of détente, our mother made the impromptu suggestion he might like to join us for the weekend – and further questioning. To which, equally unexpectedly, he agreed.

The plan was that he follow behind in his hire car as we headed down the A3 (only this time without our mother's passport tucked away in the glove box). As we wandered out to the pub car park, my mother, worried that we might get separated somewhere along the way, suggested it might be better if I rode with JBW to help navigate. A daunting prospect, certainly more daunting than Peter Lunn's offer of a first dive into the murky depths of the Solent. And whereas back then I'd made a point of umming and ahing for a moment or two before declining, here there was no such hesitation – I opted for the safety of the back seat of John II's car. It wasn't so much the prospect of being left alone with the father I hadn't met for twenty years – scary though this might be (what to say? where to begin?) – but more especially it was JBW himself, who was a world away from all the SIS officers I'd grown up with in the training camp, with their sensible jackets and ties and regulation short back and sides. Whereas JBW looked – and, frankly, smelt – like he'd just stepped, if not straight off the battlefield, then certainly straight out of the bush. Which turned out to be not so wide of the mark.

For all that, his welcome had been warm enough, and whenever I checked back to see that he was still following on behind, he'd give a cheery smile; on one occasion, stuck in traffic, an expansive wave of the hand – duly reciprocated. Or so I would like to think. But try as I might, somehow I couldn't quite raise my outstretched arm more than an inch or two, the ten yards between our cars not so much the problem as the twenty-year gap since our last meeting. And so the moment passed; the arm slumped back down, as did his; opportunity lost.

Thankfully the possibility – or impossibility – of JBW staying in the training camp itself was avoided. John II had been promoted from AO to CO a few months earlier and, courtesy of John Wyke's badgering, the post now came with a four-bedroom house a mile or so down the road. Entering through the side kitchen door, my mother offered to take JBW's coat, declined on the basis that she would simply go through all his pockets. No matter, she'd already sneaked a look back in the pub, she said, questioning how exactly he had come by a Canadian passport.

The weekend did not get off to the best of starts, our dried-up shepherd's pie coming back to haunt. Then again, there's nothing quite like an orderly queue for the toilet in the small hours for getting to know one's far-flung relatives. Forewarned of JBW's intelligence, not least by Harold Shergold, the plan was that we should stick to subjects that we might know more about than him. Unfortunately, there were no subjects that we knew more about than him – even my brother's specialist hobby, conchology, failed the test, JBW having supplied various museums with examples of exotic-sounding seashells he'd picked up on his travels, most recently from the beaches of Mozambique. Instead he spent the best part of the long rainy weekend talking us through (judiciously edited highlights of) his life, from his early years in Mexico through to Vietnam, including some of the scrapes he'd survived and a few of the more interesting people he'd come across along the way, Leon Trotsky included – somehow managing to entirely omit any mention of his years with SIS.

With the rain easing – and John II having lent (donated) JBW a fresh shirt – we headed off to a local book fair, our mother accompanied by her two husbands (to the bemusement of her bridge club friends), followed by a windswept walk along the seafront. Of course it's not entirely beyond the bounds of possibility that JBW had yet to realize that his former wife (in the absence of alimony) had returned to the fold and was back with 'the office'. However, this was not something she was prepared to leave to chance: the slightly circuitous route she chose skirted the entire perimeter fence of the training camp.

Unlike our pub lunch, clearly a dish best served cold.

In amongst a huge pile of rubbish ready to be thrown out I spotted a blackened, cross-shaped object. His OBE.

JBW's papers: a rare window into the life – correction, lives – of a frontline agent, Mexican lottery tickets & passports (genuine) included.

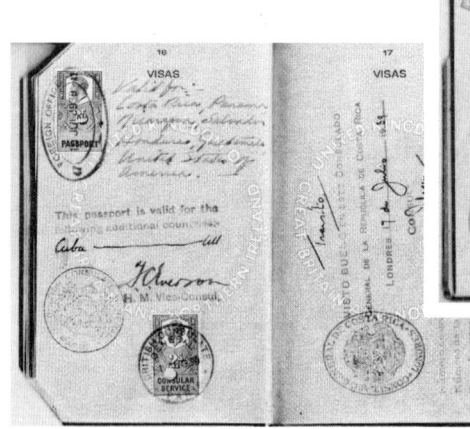

6.

Happy Eater car park

'I don't suppose his present spouse knows
anything about the boys, so this will pose
problems for him. My heart bleeds.'

Mother, letter to Aunt A, 1979

To add extra frisson to the weekend, should extra frisson
be needed, we learnt that JBW's mother had made her will
out to my brother and me, cutting him out entirely. The lawyers couldn't say how he reacted to the news, only that it was
met with silence, as was their attempt to soften the blow by
pointing out the relatively small size of the estate, the more
valuable items amongst the house's vast jumble having all
been stolen – stamp album included.

The robbery had been dramatic enough to have made the
papers. 'Mr Wood returned to find the men, wearing stock-
ing masks, lying in wait and was knocked unconscious with
either a large stick or an iron bar as he entered the kitchen.
When he came round a few minutes later, he was blindfolded
and being tied to a chair in the sitting room. His mother, who
was not hurt, was also tied to a chair with flex, rope and the
leads from two small dogs [. . .] He later received medical
treatment for injuries to his head and left forearm.'

Iron bars, blindfold and injured forearm notwithstanding,

JBW's former SIS colleagues were not convinced. They questioned the timing of the robbery, taking place as it did a few months after his mother made out her will and on one of the rare occasions he had been in the country since the mid-1950s. A coincidence too far for those who by trade didn't set much store by coincidence. Though one of the robbers was later remanded in custody, with 'police expecting other arrests', it made little difference: such was JBW's reputation within 'the office' that many years later, finding myself sat next to a former SIS officer at dinner, I was told that the feeling was still that, given his track record, he'd probably had a hand in it somewhere along the line. Which in turn told me that JBW was unlikely to ever be granted a fair hearing.

In the aftermath of the robbery his mother's furniture and remaining effects had been stored away in a warehouse depository, all of which now needed to be sorted through, preferably before he left the country. Given that the warehouse was just along the coast in Chichester, it would have made sense for him to stay on an extra day or two, if only for convenience's sake.

Unfortunately this was far from convenient. On Monday nights the BBC were showing John le Carré's *Tinker Tailor Soldier Spy* saga, possibly the only time the fictional world overlapped with that of the camp's instructors, who would crowd into our small television room to watch it, every seat taken – I had to lie on the floor and peer up at the screen – during which they kept up an intermittent commentary, trying to remember le Carré's real name and whether they might have come across him in Germany or Austria (maybe, perhaps; no, probably not, in my mother's case), or else trying

58

to match up the cast with real-life counterparts, one or two of whom might have been in the room for all I knew.

The following morning we headed across to Chichester, while JBW, having had to make himself scarce for a day, rejoined us from, well, he never did say where. The lawyer was on hand to see fair play, a local auction house for probate purposes. There were three large containers to be unloaded, unwrapped, then loaded back again – promising a long day ahead. Sensitive to the fact that our father had grown up with most of the contents, we agreed that he should keep anything of sentimental value. There turned out to be quite a few items of sentimental value – a whole container's worth – but no matter. Otherwise, he spent most of the day sorting through several tea chests of papers and newspaper cuttings he'd amassed over the years, more than a few of which, I couldn't help but notice, were related to his former occupation. It was late evening before we were anywhere near finished, and as we waited for a taxi to take us to the station I picked out a box of dried-up shoe polishes from the huge pile of discarded packing paper and rubbish, from which I retrieved a blackened, cross-shaped object. 'I think that's probably mine,' JBW volunteered, ambling over and giving it a shine on his sleeve. It was his OBE.

In the rush to catch the last train back to London we never did get to say a proper goodbye. Instead, JBW simply got out his camera, fired off a snapshot of the two of us as we climbed into the taxi and gave us a knowing smile, just as we gave him a knowing smile back. 'Knowing' smile? Though we'd only spent a few days with him, we already knew better than to ask when we might be seeing him again, still less ask for an address, a phone number, or even which country he might be going to. Even the most mundane enquiry would, of course, be met with his trademark evasion and deflection. Not that we thought badly of him for it, quite the opposite. It simply went with the territory, was part of his make-up, who he was; if anything it only added to his mystique.

And with that we went our separate ways, our father, still wearing one of John II's shirts, heading off to, well, who knew.

A few days later the lawyer rang to say that various items from our container had gone missing. No need to trouble the police, we reassured, much easier to simply head back to Chichester and jemmy open our father's container, where, sure enough, we found the missing items. Soon the lawyer was in touch again, saying that the local Barclays bank were holding a few additional boxes, which we would also need to collect. Though they belonged to JBW, he had deposited them in his mother's name – with the result that she had (unknowingly) been paying for their storage over several decades. The bank had made several attempts to track him down, but without success – like anybody else who had ever attempted to track him down. And so the lawyer, possibly no longer of the belief that an OBE was quite the guarantor of probity he had previously supposed, suggested that strictly speaking they now belonged to us.

Since the boxes were stored off site, the bank arranged for them to be handed over – for reasons known only to themselves – in the car park of a Happy Eater on the A3, where a bemused storage clerk arrived to find not one Mr Wood, but two. However, as we appeared to be in possession of the necessary paperwork, and it being a Saturday, in the end he decided it wasn't his problem, and began unloading large boxes. There were perhaps a dozen in all, mostly crammed with the sort of pastel-coloured files found in pretty much any office drawer, though possibly not the contents. JBW had presumably filed all this away with the intention of sorting through it at a later date, which of course he had never quite got around to.

But we would.

The majority of the files turned out to contain endless reams of philosophical and spiritual teachings, all typed out on wafer-thin sheets of paper, interspersed with various photographs of a bearded, berobed mystic. Only one file related directly to his former profession (helpfully stamped 'Top Secret') – mostly background traces on suspect characters. Others were crammed full of tiny photographs all no bigger than a thumbprint – there were maps of South America; a Russian notebook; a left-luggage receipt from Estonia; dozens of blank postcards of landmarks from Mexico to Budapest and everywhere in between; two passports (genuine); a bundle of old love letters – from various women in various languages; several UN personnel reports; a crumpled $1 Mexican lottery ticket (¡*Premio Mayor $100,000!*); a framed formal photograph of King Haakon VII of Norway in full uniform; and, though I didn't think anything of it at the time, a slightly blurred photograph of my brother and me playing outside the garage of our old Woking house.

Our unexpected windfall resulted in a terse note from JBW to the lawyer, postmarked Rome, complaining that our jemmying open of his container had been 'underhand', and presuming that our Happy Eater cache was doubtless 'destined for our mother'. Not so. Having only just fallen in with our father, we were reluctant to fall out with him so soon; besides, we knew full well that if we were to hand the various files over to our mother there was little hope of them ever being returned, just as everything we had unearthed in our old Woking home – random radio parts and the occasional gun included – had all been confiscated, never to be seen again.

The correct decision. Having wound down her job at the training camp, our mother had taken on a part-time welfare role for 'the office', which amongst other duties involved checking up on former employees across south-east England, hoovering up any work-related papers or documents they might have in their possession and steering them away from any thoughts of supplementing their pensions by spilling the beans on past activities. Intelligence officers were expressly forbidden from discussing their work, less still who they had been working for, with even the very existence of SIS yet to be officially acknowledged. However, not all its officers followed the rules to the letter, not least its former chief Dick White, who had discreetly confirmed the identity of the so-called 'Fourth Man' to Andrew Boyle, effectively giving him licence to publish *A Climate of Treason*. Much to Margaret Thatcher's annoyance. And my mother's.

'I sometimes wonder if one isn't doing all this [vetting of ex-employees] simply to leave the field free for one's superiors,' she'd remarked huffily one morning when about to set off on yet another of her 'welfare' visits. She would go on to enjoy a revenge of sorts. In her semi-retirement she joined a writer's course, occasionally sending off her efforts to local papers and magazine competitions – but glossy romances and romps in the heather had rather had their day. Write about what you know, her tutor urged, and so she did. Out went the heather-covered glens and flame-haired heroines, to be replaced by a rather more familiar backdrop: 'Berlin in the late 1940s was a dangerous city. It was the meeting place of East and West, a divided city, and one in which completely opposed ideologies played sinister games of espionage and intrigue as they strove to exploit the instability of those early post-war years . . .'

The change of style did not go unnoticed and soon enough she, or rather her various aliases – Felicity Gray or Susan Leigh or Maggie Ferguson or Meg Mackay – were winning 'second prize for a competition in *Woman & Home*'s Diamond Jubilee Short Story Competition', followed up, she wrote to Aunt A, 'by a thing called "The Livinia Hammond Cup" – came joint-second – we had our photos in the evening paper – such is fame'. The judges noted how 'the writer knows the setting – or seems to, which is just as good' with the next instalment, *The Decoy* by one Maggie Ferguson, praised for its authenticity. 'It feels like a true story!'

Unfortunately it was, and this too did not go unnoticed. A series of thinly disguised reminiscences for her local hospital radio proved her undoing: a bedridden former SIS officer called her out, and Felicity Gray, Maggie Ferguson et al. were obliged to put down their pens – or rather, to put the cover back on the 'Smith Corona C400 typewriter – worth £200!' that she had won in *Writers Monthly*'s 'Perfect Murder' competition.

Thwarted in her literary ambitions, she took up bridge, attended whist drives and art classes with her Alverstoke neighbours (the 'Alverstocracy'), visited her old Berlin chums for tea and cake (rather than gin and sympathy) – and helped out here and there with a little 'office' work.

Though the days when female staff had to resign on marrying were long gone, there was still a dearth of female instructors, so from time to time she found herself seconded to act the part of the fearsome ambassador's wife, the self-styled Lady d'Arcy. Hapless young recruits would have to make their way over from the training camp to our house and explain why they would be unable to attend an official function that she – as Lady d'Arcy – had specifically invited them to. A test not so much of how inventive they were but of how well they stood up to cross-examination under pressure. They had my sympathy. The simple answer would have been to bypass the problem entirely and calmly accept the invitation, Rule One being to always buy time wherever possible, and yet in all her career as Lady d'Arcy none of the recruits thought to do this. And so they were faced with the same reddening of the neck, gradual raising of the voice and scraping at the carpet (not unlike a bull ready to charge) that I knew only too well.

Never more so than in late 1987, when I managed to get hold of a copy of former MI5 staffer Peter Wright's *Spy-catcher*, at the time still banned in Britain. In the book, Wright detailed how the service went about the more nefarious side of its business, in the process confirming both the whereabouts of the training camp itself and the identities of some of its senior instructors and visiting lecturers (Wyke, Lunn and Shergold included). A few pages in, she'd paused a moment or two, the warning signs (reddening of neck, etc.) the cue for me to retreat out of harm's way – but after a page or two more at most she was done, the book closed shut, never to be seen again. And with that Lady d'Arcy returned to her bridge classes and her whist drives and her art classes, while I returned to London and my Happy Eater cache of pastel-coloured files, destined to remain on top of various bedsit wardrobes for a few years yet.

From time to time I'd take down a dusty file, hoping to decipher the endless reams of philosophical teachings and spiritual tracts – and largely failing, despite enlisting the likes of Rumi, Gurdjieff and the Bhagavad Gita in my search for enlightenment. Just as my attempts to decode the various letters, manuscripts and missives were invariably hamstrung by my knowledge of Finnish, Albanian, Russian, Viet, Tibetan and the more obscure Nāgarī scripts not being up to scratch.

Nevertheless, I was aware that the files offered a rare insight into the life – correction, lives – of a frontline agent, and whenever I found myself working in a part of the world where my father had been, I would try to tack on a day or two by way of research. And he had, at one time or another and in one guise or another, been in most parts of the world.

For a good few years I was able to dine out on my findings; I can only hope that what follows is half as enjoyable, or else I will have failed to have done my subject justice. As marvellously shady a character as my father was and – in an admittedly crowded field – as duplicitous as he was, it made for an anything but a dull life.

PART TWO

Canada, 1923. JBW's peripatetic childhood: the perfect grounding for an (im)perfect spy.

I.

Eardisland. And beyond

'I was under the impression he didn't attend
any school. I thought the Woods just
circumnavigated the world.'

Dorothy Maclean, letter to the author,
September 1999

My initial attempts to try and unravel the proverbial riddle
wrapped in a mystery inside an enigma that was JBW had
not got off to the best of starts. Even the one thing I thought
I knew for certain – his place of birth – had turned out to
be slightly wide of the mark: he was born in a neighbouring
cottage rather than in Staick House itself. I had come away
from Eardisland empty-handed.

Unlike JBW all those years ago.

Having repaired whatever wireless sets, electrical goods
and machinery had been left out for him by his Eardisland
relatives, he'd helped himself to a little of their family history, in an early indication of his ingrained tendency to
dissemble. Mush's mother had been half-Norwegian – from
Hasvig in the far north; the young JBW had visited Norway
many times and, by the time he got to university, spoke the
language more or less fluently – certainly fluently enough to
have exchanged the red, white and blue of his own country

(nothing to be proud of in the Cambridge of the 1930s) for the red, white and blue of Norway. But this newly acquired nationality was little more than a finishing touch. Long before his visit to Eardisland, long before he went up to Cambridge, the die had been cast, with JBW having already acquired much of the skillset of an imperfect spy, courtesy of a childhood like no other.

Over time I've learnt something of his family history, though there was little to signpost what lay ahead; rather, a familiar story of solid Victorian achievement: Derbyshire lead-mining stock on the maternal side, rags-to-riches Lancashire cotton merchants on the paternal side. Nor was there anything much by way of academia – his grandfather exiting Balliol with 'a gentleman's 4th', his father, John Atkinson Wood, leaving Charterhouse School at the age of sixteen to start work with the (aptly named) Duff Development Company in Kelantan, north-east Malaysia. Occupation: apprentice rubber planter. Salary: $50 per month plus accommodation, passage not included.

However, unlike most apprentice rubber planters, within a year his father was exchanging Latin and Greek for near-fluent Malay, even tackling the Kelantan dialect (said to be impenetrable to most Malays). And in the absence of any local Christian places of worship, he would head into the state capital, Khota Baru, to attend the local mosque, one of the country's oldest, or else the Buddhist temple, with the result that the only souvenirs of his time in Kelantan – various tiger claws aside – were a well-thumbed copy of the Koran, a Buddhist bible and a statue of the Buddha. By no means a classical education perhaps, but certainly an eclectic one, which in time he would pass on to his own son.

In the summer of 1914 he returned to England to marry

the nineteen-year-old Gladys Eleanor Greenhough of Staick House, Eardisland. But the prospect of war and the resulting demand for rubber made for a short honeymoon, with the *Birmingham News* reporting that the newlyweds would be heading back to Kelantan. They returned when general conscription was introduced, but after the birth of what would be their only child, John Bryan Wood on 12 August 1916, his father left for the Belgian front.

As a highly skilled, self-taught mechanic, he was drafted into the RNAS (Royal Naval Air Service), forerunner of the RAF, tasked with keeping its fleet of Nieuports airborne, being finally demobbed in 1919 and returning to Staick House. But it would be a short stay: before long they would leave both Eardisland and England behind, heading off into the proverbial sunset for who knew where, or for how long.

And so it began.

Father, mother and the four-year-old JBW headed first to New York, then up to Toronto. Canadian immigration recorded their intention to settle permanently, a document that JBW would one day make good use of (or certainly attempt to). But instead they simply kept going. And going. To Vancouver, Alaska, San Francisco, across the Pacific to New Zealand via Hawaii (and a typhoon – JBW's first brush with mortality), then back across the Pacific, through the Panama Canal and up to New York, a second, longer stay in Canada then down to Buenos Aires, up to Rio de Janeiro, back across the Atlantic to Portugal, then Barcelona, home to England – for all of three weeks – back to the US and Canada and to New Zealand (once again with a view to settling permanently) – until eventually, having circumnavigated the world not once but twice, the now eleven-year-old JBW settled down to life in Antibes, in the south of France.

Having spent significant chunks of his early years at sea, by the time JBW arrived back on dry land he had acquired an unusual hobby, one that would do his future career prospects no harm. The loss of the *Titanic* and the First World War had resulted in high-frequency radio being installed as standard equipment at sea, enabling ships to communicate over vast distances; whereas most young boys grew up with Meccano and *Boy's Own* adventure stories, JBW had shortwave radio and his trusty *Phonetic Alphabet Morse Code* guide. Judging by his collection of 'Radio Transmission Acknowledgments', he must have been a familiar figure in the ships' communications rooms, with a steady stream of certificates winging their way across the globe from the likes of Bandoeng, Batavia, Macao . . . and far-off Tynemouth, all later pasted in scrapbooks or pinned up onto bedroom walls, along with rough diagrams of the primitive wireless sets he constructed, using whatever he could find on board: discarded biscuit tin lids, copper wiring, spare plyboard, old battery units.

Equally key to his future career, given his lack of formal education (a term or two at most in various countries, useful provenance in later life), his parents encouraged him to learn the language of whatever country they happened to be in or – better still – whatever languages the various ships' crews spoke: by the time they settled down to life in Antibes his schoolboy *cahiers* were filled with spidery column after spidery column of French, Spanish, Portuguese, Greek and Norwegian.

But a life on the ocean wave, no matter how formative, was scant preparation for life in a traditional English public school. With its dreary focus on the classics rather than modern languages, its boaters and blazers and emphasis on team games, Winchester College must have seemed a daunting prospect for someone whose idea of sport was an occasional game of deck quoits and who had likely never worn so much as a school cap. And so it proved. 'His mother said they put him down for Winchester but he refused to go.' In desperation, they managed to get him into the newly founded and rather more progressive Bryanston School, but this too was not for him (or vice versa), and after a year he headed back to Antibes. They spent the summer there, only to then resume their endless circling of the globe, in many ways mapping out (literally) the life that their son would go on to lead and explaining the young JBW's gift for languages.

But more exactly demonstrating his talent for reinvention.

The reality turned out to have been rather more mundane, not that future wives or employers or his own offspring need ever know it. Far from continuing on with life on the ocean wave, he instead spent his teenage years attending Courtenay Lodge, an idyllic-sounding school by the Thames, where 'conversational French is a special feature of the curriculum' and 'thorough individual attention is given, and every care taken to understand the individual needs of each pupil, especially of those who are unfitted for public school life'.

'So glad John is enjoying his new school. Do come south,' their Antibes neighbours encouraged, but he wouldn't be heading south any time soon, staying put at Courtenay Lodge for the next four years, fine-tuning his ear for languages (few of his classmates had English as a first language). And if scholastic achievement for the most part took a back seat to messing about in boats on the Thames, there was always Messrs Davies, Laing & Dick of

Gloucester Road, SW7, last refuge of the 'must try harder' public school boy cramming for Oxbridge. Following which JBW duly headed up to St Catharine's College, Cambridge, to read Medieval and Modern Languages, by now more or less fluent in French, Spanish and Portuguese. And, of course, Norwegian.

No surprise then that many – indeed most – of his Cambridge contemporaries would have no idea that he was even English. But then John was no longer John. He was now Jøn.

JBW (far right) and 'fellow' Norwegians, 1934.

JBW's Norwegian driving licence, sporting
what looks uncannily like a five-pointed
communist star on his lapel, 1938.

His shiny new Hudson 8 Tourer put something of a dent
in his socialist credentials, 1937.

2.

Norway

'Kjære elskede Jøn!'

Cil Egeberg, letters to JBW,
1936–41

One of the joys of being Wards of Court – a restriction
put in place following my brother's kidnapping – was that
up until the age of eighteen neither of us would be allowed
to leave the country without the Court's permission. Which
meant that the Great British Package Holiday, which
boomed in the 1960s and early '70s, was sadly destined to
pass us by. Good thing too, our mother would remind us
(every summer), having read how the Cambridge spy Donald
Maclean's offspring had ended up in the industrial grey of
Kuybyshev, a closed city several hundred miles from Moscow.
A prospect which, however unlikely or irrational, she could
never entirely rule out, what with our father 'being so completely unpredictable': 'I don't fancy a chase to the Far East
after my dash to the Far West.'

Kindly Woking neighbours would invite us to accompany
them and their children to the impossibly-exotic-sounding
Costa Brava or Costa del Sol, only to be told that 'the lawyers
wouldn't agree to them leaving the country'. And so Bourne-
mouth it was. Leaving us to spend endless summer holidays

77

squabbling over who got the top bunk in our (maternal) grandmother's modest first-floor flat – which was within walking distance of the bucket-and-spade delights of Boscombe beach, surely preferable to the hammer and sickle drear of the collective farm. If rather less glamorous than the summers that our father had enjoyed back in the early 1930s.

From the age of fourteen, at the end of every summer term JBW and a Courtenay Lodge friend, scion of Bergen's Westfal-Larson shipping family, would take the ferry over from Newcastle to stay in the coastal hamlet of Fana, a few miles to the south of Bergen. His devotion to all things Norwegian likely originated with his Herefordshire family's connection to the country, furthered by his parents hiring a retired Oslo tutor, 'The Professor', who was wintering in Antibes, to teach the young JBW something of the language.

Though I knew nothing of my father's childhood travels when I was growing up – possibly just as well, all things considered – grainy black and white prints of sails being hoisted, fish gutted and fjords sculled would frequently turn up in drawers and boxes throughout our time in Woking; for a few years his faded Norwegian sailing pennant adorned the top of our Christmas tree (in lieu of anything from him under the tree) until replaced by a plastic Angel Gabriel. Judging by the postcards of red-timbered fishermen's huts in and around Bergen's islands and inlets (Northeimsund, Rosendal, Eidfjord) the majority of his endless summer daylight hours were spent on the water, and by the time he went up to Cambridge he'd already put down roots of a sort, a single-masted wooden 'Oselvar' boat, which he kept moored at the local sailing club. Within a few weeks of arriving at St Catharine's he'd acquired a Norwegian girlfriend, Cecilia Egeberg, 'Cil', who was studying English at one of the town's language schools, their letters, penned after lingering farewell teas at the Lyons' Corner House before one or other caught the boat train, written Rosetta Stone-like, duplicated word for word in Norwegian and underneath in English.

Unsurprisingly, he opted for Norwegian as his additional tripos language, which along with his (recently acquired) Hasvig ancestry and framed photograph of King Haakon VII in full naval uniform led many of his fellow undergraduates to assume that he *was* Norwegian, with any traces of Englishness dismissed as little more than an accident of birth, having left at the age of four. But his more immediate Cambridge circle were not so easily taken in: his German friend Erica, who had always known him by his middle name, recalled how 'one afternoon there were about ten visitors from different countries. I got the idea that each one of them should sing their National anthem. Bryan, an Englishman, always wanted to be a Norwegian, so he sang the Norwegian anthem, surprising everybody.'

Though JBW – or Jøn, as he now preferred to be known – was far from the only Cambridge undergraduate in the 1930s looking to distance himself from the land of their birth, feeling 'repugnance for its dreary, unjust and uncultured society, with its impotent ruling class and its dull and puritanical middle classes', few took it to such extremes: despite the sparsity of foreign students, not a single one of his Cambridge friends was English. Erica's visitors belting out their national anthems round the piano that day had included Jan Willemstein (Dutch), Pelle Mortensen (Swedish), Vatsaraja ('Raja') Bhanot (from Uttar Pradesh, India), the Hungarian 'Ali' and Martin Allwood (who despite his surname was also Swedish), together with his closest friend at the time, Bill Hathaway, an American.

79

Hathaway had enjoyed a similarly peripatetic early child-hood, before ending up in Munich, where his father was the United States Consul General. With the Bavarian capital increasingly at the centre of world events, for any politically aware Cambridge student this was too good an opportunity to pass up – soon enough JBW's regular ferry ride across to Bergen gave way to a dog-leg drive via Munich in his patched-up, bald-tyred Alvis, running repairs made along the way (like his father, he was a more-than-competent mechanic): 'Tram to Yselhaven 10 ct. Rotterdam dock unloading fee 2f 50ct. Antwerp 5L Esso @ 2.75 frcs. Tip for bloke pushing car in Delft 10ct.'

Hathaway Snr's State Department career had mostly been spent out of harm's way, with stints in Dominica, Dublin, Bombay, Puerto Rico . . . and Hull, and back in 1927 he had likely expected his next posting to be more of the same, with the added bonus of his Ledererstrasse office being directly above one of the better restaurants in Munich's Old Town. But it was also just a twenty-minute walk from the König-splatz's Braunes Haus, home to Hitler's nascent National Socialist party, where he would be a frequent visitor over the following decade and, as such, an invaluable source of firsthand information to Washington – to the extent that by 1936 his reports were being submitted directly to President Roosevelt in the White House.

On Sundays he would invite Reuters and visiting foreign correspondents to join him on a gentle ramble around the countryside close to his Pullach home, a few miles outside Munich. The walks were to all intents and purposes off-the-record briefing sessions, to which Bill and his new Cambridge friend were also invited, JBW doubtless tagging along at the back of the group, quietly taking it all in. And so began my father's *Realpolitik* education, not in the drinking clubs, debating societies and ivory towers of Cambridge but at the sharp end of world events, firsthand witness to the various parades, rallies and patriotic fervour sweeping all before it, with Erica, Bill's German girlfriend, on hand to give her own guided tour of the city, her running commentaries rather more candid than anything to be found in JBW's dog-eared copy of Baedeker's *München und Südbayern*. In many ways she and Bill were an unlikely couple, Erica speaking barely a word of English, the hopelessly gangly Bill – close to six and a half feet tall – towering over her. They'd met at an English-language night school, which Erica had joined for no better reason than she enjoyed watching American movies, whereas Bill had turned up to meet a former school friend who was learning English for rather less frivolous reasons, being one of several Jewish residents for whom Hathaway Snr was urgently trying to arrange US entry visas, likely prompted by a visit to the newly built Dachau concentration camp on the outskirts of Munich.

Erica had grown up in the Berlin of the Weimar Republic, experiencing severe rationing, street violence and hyperinflation before moving to the Bavarian capital, arriving in time to cast her vote in the '*Ja oder Nein*' ('For or Against Hitler') election. Braving the attendant Brownshirts and ignoring their requests to swear loyalty to Hitler, she was surprised – or not – to find that hers was one of only three '*Nein*' votes cast in the district, despite almost everyone she knew, family included, being opposed to Hitler.

In the years leading up to the election Hitler was a familiar enough sight around town, he and his entourage sometimes taking the corner table in the same Osteria Bavaria restaurant that her parents ate in. So when one morning Erica ran into an old flame from her Berlin days – to her disgust now wearing the uniform of Ernst Rohm's Sturmabteilung militia – boasting that he had a pass to the Braunes Haus, if only out of curiosity she took him up on his offer. After stubbornly replying to the Braunes Haus guards' '*Heil Hitler!*' with the traditional Bavarian greeting of '*Gruess Gott!*', she'd gone inside, but with most of the building off limits, all she saw was endless red-carpeted corridors flanked by closed doors, after which her chaperone ushered her down to the basement restaurant. But no sooner had she sat down than one of the guards rushed down the stairs, shouting: '*Der Führer ist ange-kommen!*' Hustled upstairs, she found herself being corralled into a welcoming party. 'I knew the dreaded moment would come when Hitler would be across from me. His hand shot out. I couldn't possibly shake hands with the "scourge", as my family referred to him [. . .] a frown appeared on Hitler's forehead, his hand wavered [. . .] I looked around, met only hostile eyes, but not for long. All eyes were on Hitler, who was now walking away towards the side entrance of the house. I was conscious of all the angry uniformed men around me, yet inwardly I was suddenly completely at peace.' Unsurprisingly, Erica heard no more from her Sturmabteilung admirer, and within a few weeks had (wisely) decided to flee Munich and join Bill in Cambridge.

Having witnessed the gathering storm firsthand, JBW was soon to be seen standing out in the rain opposite the Cambridge Corn Exchange of a Saturday morning, alongside his Swedish friend Martin Allwood, 'a fanatical pacifist. Often, I saw him standing on some street corner handing out pamphlets.' As has been well documented, many of their fellow undergraduates were choosing a slightly different path: over 200 in JBW's year alone threw in their lot with the cause and joined the Communist Party of Great Britain, a statistic which certainly did not escape the notice of the Soviets' new Cambridge recruiter, Theodore Maly. 'Go search for those hurt by fate or nature,' Maly's Moscow controllers are said to have urged, but it seems unlikely that the nineteen-year-old owner of the gleaming new 2880cc Hudson sedan parked opposite the St Catharine's quad would have struck passers-by, still less Maly, as having been overly troubled by either fate or by nature.

At the end of his first year at Cambridge, JBW learnt that he was the sole beneficiary of various family trust funds set up by his Lancashire mill-owning antecedents. Being an only child of an only child, he received a sizeable sum, far more than they had likely intended and certainly more than his mother considered healthy or felt comfortable with: contrary to outward appearances (Staick House) she had grown up without 'so much as two pennies to rub together'. Her one concession to her son's sudden wealth was the purchase of the shiny new – and solidly robust – Hudson 8 Touring Sedan, replacement for the barely roadworthy Alvis, which he had managed to write off in the Munich snow, ending upside down in a roadside ditch, somehow emerging with only a small scar at the corner of one eye to show for it.

The trust funds paid out some £900 a year, rising to £1,300 when he was twenty-five (about £115,000 in today's money), putting something of a dent in his socialist credentials. The funds would continue to flow into his Cambridge bank account up until the day he died – not that anyone in the years to come would ever know it to look at him, still less to marry him, but explaining in no small part how he managed to go on to lead the life he did, a high-wire act of vertigo-inducing duplicity, albeit never without a financial safety net.

On 10 June 1936 JBW and the Hudson 8 arrived in Munich for his now regular stopover, before heading up through Germany and Denmark and on to Cil's Fredrikstad home a few miles south of Oslo, with a red, blue and white ensign fluttering atop the Hudson's hood, true Norwegian patriot that he was, or certainly believed himself to be. But instead of the endless summer days of his youth spent messing around in boats in and around Bergen, he was now teaching English in the small Swedish town of Mullsjö, courtesy of his fellow Cambridge pamphleteer, Martin Allwood.

Allwood was a man of no little energy, going on to write more than fifty books, and no little charm, persuading no fewer than seven women to marry him. He'd grown up in a small town a hundred miles east of Gothenburg, where his father hosted a hugely successful English-language course on Swedish radio, which at its height attracted close to 400,000 listeners a week. On the strength of this he had founded – and built – a summer language school in the rural hamlet of Mullsjö. The school was noted for its highly innovative 'immersive' teaching method, where students talked, read and listened *only* to the language they were learning. Looking to introduce open conversation forums along the lines of Cambridge's debating societies, Martin's father employed his son and two of his Cambridge friends, JBW and Raja Bhanot, as tutors. A photograph in a book chronicling the history of the school shows them outside one of the chalets, JBW incongruously dressed – given the woodland setting – in a white double-breasted jacket. For Bhanot, it was the start of a long association with both Mullsjö and Swedish literature, which he would later translate into Gujarati and Hindi, while Allwood, aside from taking over the school itself, would go on to professorships in Europe and America and to found the Swedish Authors' Society. But of the three, it was arguably JBW who would benefit most from the school's *direkt metod*, his three summers at Mullsjö likely as instructive as his modern languages course at Cambridge. Headphones on, ears clamped to language tapes or his trusty Marconi tuned to far-off radio stations sometimes for days on end, aerial slung round the chimney of his Grantchester Road digs, he would immerse himself to the exclusion of all else. In an age when few English people bothered with languages, he would go on to master Dutch, Russian, German, Finnish and Danish, along with '*quelques connaissances d'arabe et du portugais*', a smattering of Romansh, Albanian and Tibetan (the lower slopes of) – in addition to the Norwegian, Swedish, French and Spanish he already had, or certainly was well on the way to having. Mullsjö would also do his future career prospects no harm.

Thankfully Cambridge's extended summer break still allowed time for a (by his standards) short motoring holiday, possibly more glamorous than any driving I was doing at much the same age. Which is not to say that life in the SIS training camp was without its perks: being off-grid it was as good a place as any to learn and with as good – albeit as unorthodox – an instructor as one could wish for in George, the camp's lead driver. Lesson 1: Mirror, signal, clutch. Lesson 2: Gears. Lesson 3: How to shake off a pursuing vehicle. But whereas I was endlessly criss-crossing a tarmac quadrangle in my battered Triumph Herald, JBW was happily exploring the mountains and valleys of mainland Europe in his brand-new Hudson 8.

Leaving Norway, he and Cil drove down through Denmark, Germany and Austria to Hungary, then 'from Budapest we went east to Debrecen into Romania then out to Kosice. From there we went over the Carpathians to Krakow. Warsaw was our next stop, where we stayed a couple of days with a friend from Cambridge. We have come up through East Prussia and the Baltic States and have now got back to the more northern regions of Europe.' At the end of August they reached Estonia, before finally arriving back in Bergen, only to head 300 miles up the coast to 'his' ancestral home, Hasvig, then hurrying back to Cambridge in time for the new academic year. A Cambridge that was now consumed by Spain and its long-predicted Civil War, which had finally broken out earlier that summer.

Like many, quite likely all, of his Cambridge contemporaries, JBW was soon rallying to the cause, donating a chunk of his new-found wealth to the Dependents and Wounded Aid Committee and putting his Spanish to good use translating pro-Republican pamphlets, handed out from his usual stump outside the Corn Exchange. He joined the International Society, and even managed to squeeze in a short spring 'holiday' in (Nationalist-held) Tenerife, at the time just about the only part of Spain for which one could still obtain a visa.

As his interest in the febrile international situation continued to grow, correspondingly his devotion to his Modern Languages tripos began to wane, not helped by its focus on the traditional rather than the modern, with as much emphasis on the literature and history of its subject countries as on the language itself. Unlike Mullsjö. Or, come to that, his Grantchester Road digs, Marconi receiver dial at the ready. By now all but fluent in Norwegian – to the extent that even 'fellow' Norwegians took him for one of their own – he began to devote his energies and intellect to all things electrical and mechanical (as his Herefordshire relatives could vouch), developing a full-blown interest in the sciences, evidenced by a prescient mini thesis on the effects of bovine methane gas emission along with an award from the Engineering faculty's tutors – explaining how someone with his linguistic abilities ended up with a 2.2 (albeit a 1st in Norwegian), to the disappointment of his parents and others, who harboured hopes of a career in the diplomatic service for their gifted if, as was likely becoming all too clear by now, increasingly wayward son.

In June 1938 he received his Bachelor of Arts degree, posed for his graduation portrait, attended the St John's College ball, then headed over to Rotterdam to begin his customary touring of the Continent, including (unbeknown to his parents) a detour to spend a week in Republican-held Barcelona before escaping up through the Pyrenees to Andorra. Normal service resumed, he then headed up to Oslo to celebrate his twenty-second birthday with Cil, as ever taking the scenic route, each country visited (Austria, Belgium, Czechoslovakia, Denmark, Danzig, Estonia, Finland, Germany, France, Holland, Hungary, Italy, Latvia, Lichenstein, Lithuania, Luxemburg, Monaco, Norway, Romania, Spain, Sweden, Switzerland and Yugoslavia) dutifully ticked off on his new Norwegian driving licence, the front cover of which shows an understandably jaded-looking JBW, bags under his eyes, sporting what looks uncannily like a five-pointed communist star insignia on his lapel.

With no pressing need to find gainful employment – or certainly employment that would pay anything approaching the quarterly stipend from his trust fund – after much discussion with his parents he opted for a course in economics at the Sorbonne – if only to perfect his French. Economics, as my mother could attest, was never a subject for which he showed much aptitude (proverbial economy with truth excepted).

After finishing off at Mullsjö, he set off for Paris, his circuitous route more scenic by the mile perhaps, but through a political landscape that by the summer of 1938 was growing uglier by the day. From Denmark (8 August) he headed across to Danzig, driving down through Poland into Germany – stopping off with the Hathaways – before crossing into the newly annexed, post-Anschluss Austria (11 August), spending four nights in Vienna then going east to Hungary (16 August) – detouring to Budapest (17 August) to pick up new passport (Nationality: British. Occupation: Government Employee, curiously) – then on through Romania and Croatia (18–20 August), up to Slovenia (22 August), back into Austria (23 August), across to Liechtenstein (24 August) back to Munich, followed by a nineteen-day tour through the heartlands of Nazi Germany (25 August–12 September) before exiting into Switzerland (15 September) and heading across to Paris and the Place du Panthéon to begin his two-year MA.

Or not, as the case may be.

VOWS.

1. I will keep silence during each meal.

1a. I will keep silence three hours during the day.

1b. I will keep silence from sunrise to sunset.

1c. I will always keep silence.

2. I will omit saying the word "my" in conversation.

2a. I will omit saying the word "I" in conversation.

3. I will wake before sunrise and practise.

4. I will exercise my mind with the given instructions for the prescribed period of time.

5. I will totally abstain from meat, living on a purely vegetable diet.

5a. I will not smoke or drink.

5b. I will live on milk, give up tea and coffee.

6. I will speak no evil, I will hear no evil, and I will see no evil.

7. I will say to no one a harsh word.

8. I will not tell a lie, even in jest.

9. I will keep myself free from emotions and passions.

10. I will take life ungrudgingly, without complaining about any one or about anything.

———————————————

JBW's daily vows – dutifully observed (with varying degrees of success).

3.

Suresnes

'Vow No. 8. I will not tell a lie, even in jest.'

JBW's daily vows

If JBW's parents and his Cambridge friends believed that he had gone to Paris simply to study economics or perfect his French, they were of course mistaken.

Certainly all those pastel-coloured Sorbonne files (erroneously) handed over to my brother and me in the Happy Eater car park contained precious little in the way of economics – none at all, to be exact. In place of Keynes and Adam Smith read Vyasa, Gurdjieff and the 'selected' thoughts of Hazrat Inayat Khan (all thirty volumes), with page after page, file after file of spiritual tracts, devotional poetry and endless lists of 'selfless actions'.

For example: Series One, File One: 'CONCENTRA-TION'. 'Concentrating uses abstinence against the constant and uncontrollable activity of the mind,' it headlines, before, over several hundred ('opening') pages, exploring the difference between 'Gathas', 'Gathekas' and 'Gathers', explaining thermodynamic principles, electromagnetic behaviourism, the various properties of crystals ('It is natural that resistances along different faces or axes of the crystal are different, the same as lines of fracture, and other mechanical qualities differ'), liquids ('Viscous substances tend to the vitreous state and the others to crystalline or crystalloid states'), gases ('The Zero group are vehicles for ether and if they were not present in the atmosphere the etheric or akashic element could not touch this sphere'), energy ('Fire and electricity are definitely Jelalic while phenomena such as fluorescence and phosphorescence are Jemalic') and the significance of numbers: '32 is a perfect number: the 32 paths of Moses, the 32 qualities of Buddha; 32 are the number of bones in the back . . .' And so on. And on. All meticulously transcribed onto thin, double-sided sheets to be learnt by rote – not to mention all 700 typed-out verses of the Bhagavad Vita.

The key to JBW's alternative and exhaustive curriculum – which must have left little if any time for economics – lay in a few black and white photographs randomly salted away here and there of a bearded man dressed in simple white cotton with a winged-heart pendant, sitting cross-legged playing a sitar-like instrument (a veena), staring intensely into and through the camera, every last inch and topaz bead the Indian mystic.

Hazrat Inayat Khan is credited with having first introduced the Islamic creed of Sufism to the West. Originally a musician, he'd been taken up by Ruth St Denis, a pioneer of modern American dance, whose tours of the United States gave him the chance to showcase Indian and Sufi music and the perfect platform to promote his creed of 'universal worship', which embraced the philosophies behind each religion rather than one particular doctrine or deity: 'a pure light which becomes diversely coloured as it is filtered through the different religions'. His message went down especially well with liberal-minded West Coast devotees, known as 'mureeds'. Hoping to repeat this success in mainland Europe, Inayat Khan took his music and accompanying Sufism on the road, lecturing in European capitals and relying, as was the Sufi way, for board and lodging from fellow Sufis and mureeds, one of whom, a wealthy Dutch follower, funded the purchase of a family home in the leafy suburb of Suresnes, a few kilometres west of the centre of Paris – and the Sorbonne.

One of the last stops on Inayat Khan's endless travels had been a 1924 visit to Oslo, where he was greeted on the dockside by the city's small Sufi community, among them Halvor Egeberg and his then seven-year-old daughter Cecilie, affectionately known as 'Cil'.

Egeberg it was who, many years later, would first introduce his daughter's Cambridge boyfriend to the teachings of Hazrat Inayat Khan and Sufism. Cil aside, quite what drew the young JBW to Sufism isn't clear, though his father's abiding interest in Buddhism and Islamism since Kelantan likely played a part. His fellow Cambridge undergraduates would remain largely unaware of the double life he had begun to lead, with his spiritualist beliefs confined to (unsuccessful) attempts at dowsing or occasional group outings to Glastonbury Tor and Stonehenge in the Hudson 8; any interest in Sufism was simply put down to an interest in Norway, and more especially Cil.

But convert he did, as various photographs from his time in Norway show: JBW, chin cupped in hand, paying earnest attention to one of Egeberg's talks; attending a Christmas get-together with other mureeds at the newly built (and modestly named) Egeberg Castle; he and Cil dwarfed beneath the Egeberg Christmas tree, the fairy long since displaced by the Sufi winged emblem.

Every morning JBW would set off from his fifth-arrondissement lodgings on the twenty-minute stroll to the

Panthéon-Sorbonne's Faculty of Economics. Or, just as often, the twenty-minute train ride out to Suresnes. Despite Inayat Khan having passed away ten years earlier on a visit to India, the house was still the de facto centre of the movement and home to his wife and children, including daughter Noor and her brother Vilayat. The centre hosted an annual summer school, attended by young Sufis from across Europe – or in JBW's case, from just across the Seine, near enough for him to fully immerse himself in Sufism and to start living the life of a true mureed, helped along the path of true enlightenment by study, practice and prayer under the guidance of a murshid or shaykh, and attending the occasional talk by fellow Paris resident Gurdjieff. Not that it was all 'Gathas', 'Gathekas' and 'Gathers' and no play. The centre's gardens hosted a constant round of informal gatherings on summer evenings, one local remembering how before the war 'the house was always full of light and parties'. Partying commitments notwithstanding, the young JBW would rise every morning before dawn to light a candle for each of the six main religions, then prostrate himself for the first of three daily prayer sessions with repeated (if slightly muted) chants of '*Allāhu akbar*' (he was lodging with a local family), followed by his 'wazifas', phrases similarly repeated over and over to purge negative thoughts. On the wall above his bed he'd pinned up a list of daily vows, which he would continue to observe, or attempt to observe, for the rest of his days – with varying degrees of success.

    1). I will keep silence during each meal.
        a. I will keep silence three hours during the day.
        b. I will keep silence from sunrise to sunset.
        c. I will always keep silence.

2). I will omit saying the word 'my' in conversation.

    a. I will omit saying the word 'I' in conversation.

3). I will awake before sunrise and practise.

4). I will exercise my mind with the given instructions for the prescribed period of time.

5). I will totally abstain from meat, living on a purely vegetable diet.

    a. I will not smoke or drink.

    b. I will live on milk, give up tea or coffee.

6). I will speak no evil, I will hear no evil, and I will see no evil.

7). I will say to no one a harsh word.

8). I will not tell a lie, even in jest.

9). I will keep myself free from emotions and passions.

10). I will take life ungrudgingly, without complaining about any one or about anything.

In fairness, he never smoked (Vow 5a).

Having meditated daily ever since his induction back in Norway, the next step was to try and master an intense form of Sufism, '*murāqabah*', said by devotees to be 'the gateway to mystical thought and the enlightened self'. The believer was encouraged to 'open his or her heart to receive divine truths, spiritual enlightenment, spiritual abundance, prosperity and bounteous spiritual gifts', which, if practised often enough and intensively enough, was said to grant the true believer a spiritual sixth sense, affording a clear premonition of what might be about to happen in any given situation, even to intuitively sense possible danger. This was a practice he would continue long after he had (outwardly) abandoned Sufism. Not that future colleagues, my mother and her Berlin friends included, would be any the wiser – other than noticing his eccentric habit of occasionally disappearing beneath the surface of swimming pools. 'Remember how he used to swim down to the bottom of the pool & used to lie on the bottom in a reclining position, sometimes for minutes on end?'

With Suresnes almost a home from home and with Vilayat Khan, son of the founder, now a close friend, the young JBW was being marked out for greater things within the movement, not least on account of his language skills. After attending the Sufi summer school in Suresnes, he called in on his parents at their Surrey home, suggesting that economics and the Sorbonne might not be for him after all – unsurprising, given his attendance record – before attempting to persuade them that having spent a year perfecting his French, he should spend a further year perfecting his Spanish. And given that Spain was no longer an option following General Franco's victory, he would have to try further afield, to which end he had applied for visas to Mexico, Peru, Bolivia, Argentina, Costa Rica, Panama, Nicaragua, El Salvador, Honduras and Guatemala.

Parents somehow persuaded, in early August 1939 he added a United States visa to his collection, before heading back to Paris to arrange for his belongings, voluminous Sufi files included, to be put into a storage depot back in England.

After a last-minute dash to Paris's Cuban Embassy for yet another visa, he took a taxi to the Gare Saint-Lazare in time for the Cherbourg train, with a steerage ticket to New York on the German liner SS *Europa*, leaving Britain behind, certainly for the foreseeable future.

And Cil.

Their Cambridge friends (and his parents) had always assumed he and Cil would end up together, inseparable as they were, but for whatever reason it had never quite happened. Erica remembered driving through the night with JBW and Raja Bhanot from the language school in Mullsjö to be in time for Cil's twenty-first birthday. 'When we arrived, Cil suggested a swim in the fjord. We took her suggestion and almost froze in the water. It was a festive affair, with many toasts. It had been expected that Jøn would declare himself, but he didn't. A very disappointed Cil said goodbye to us quite sadly when we left. "See you in Cambridge, and thanks for having come."'

And so JBW sailed to New York, planning to go from there to Latin America, leaving Cil to head back to Oslo. On 17 August US customs officials noted that the now twenty-three-year-old JBW ('Height: 6ft, Hair: Reddish, Eyes: Grey. Distinguishing marks: Mole on left side of chin, scar left eye corner [Munich car crash]') was intending to stay with his friend Bill Hathaway in California. Instead he headed up to Chicago, then flew down to Brownsville, Texas, before crossing into Mexico, twelve-month residency visa in hand, courtesy of President Cárdenas's decision to grant asylum to the defeated Spanish Republican leaders and their followers. Quite what his contribution to the Republican cause had entailed would remain something of a mystery, with just a passport stamp and a blank postcard of the main square in Santa Cruz to show for his stay in Nationalist-held Tenerife, just as a blank postcard of the Ramblas was the only souvenir of his week in Barcelona the following July, with his subsequent escape up through the Pyrenees (along with some ten thousand refugees fleeing Franco's forces that month alone) commemorated by a picture of an Andorran cattle trough – blank postcards invariably the only record of JBW's more questionable travels. Nevertheless, his devotion to the cause, financial and otherwise, was certainly solid enough for him to have been granted a visa – and to be accepted as a fellow exile by the growing numbers of Republican '*exiliados españoles*' making their way across the Atlantic.

Which is not to entirely rule out the possibility, however slim, that JBW, with his linguistic abilities, had not been talent-spotted at Cambridge, that long-established recruiting ground for intelligence officers. Certainly one could point to the endless wanderings through a central Europe on the cusp of war; the 'Government Employee' descriptor in his passport – issued in, of all places, Budapest; the endless tiny Minox photographs of factories, industrial sites, railway yards and aerodromes; the sheer number of visas issued for Central and South American countries, a region where SIS didn't have so much as a single operative. But as Shergold, Lunn and others might ask: talent-spotted by whom?

On 28 August he arrived in Mexico City. Four days later Germany invaded Poland, followed shortly afterwards by Chamberlain's declaration of war. Not that events several thousand miles away would have caused him undue concern, committed pacifist that he was – and citizen of steadfastly neutral Norway, as he certainly led everyone to believe he was, albeit with nothing more than a Norwegian driving licence to show for it.

Rio de Janeiro, where JBW arrived in his 'usual lordly fashion', 1939.

T. Ifor Rees, Consul General in Mexico 1938–43, who –
for better or worse – recommended JBW to British Intelligence.

4.

Latin America

'I enclose, for your information, a biography.
My previous experience in Latin America was
mostly wartime 1939–Dec 1940 Mexico . . .'

JBW's (skilfully edited) curriculum vitae, 1960s

If JBW's parents and his Cambridge friends believed that he had gone to Latin America simply to perfect his Spanish, once again they were of course mistaken.

He had gone there to become a Farmer.

To his credit, this was something of a promotion, or elevation, given that in Suresnes he had been a humble Ploughman (the ascending hierarchy of the Sufi order being Labourer, Ploughman, Farmer, Experienced Farmer, Most Experienced Farmer and then the Great Farmer, Hazrat Inayat Khan himself).

The ceremony was held in Rio de Janeiro, where JBW arrived from Mexico City in his 'usual lordly fashion', courtesy of his quarterly stipend, flying first to Havana (explaining the last-minute Cuban visa back in Paris), then boarding Pan Am's Latin America flying boat service, touching down at 100mph on Rio's Guanabara Bay. He was staying at the Sufi Lodge, 579 Rua Julia Ottoni, a large hilltop house with spectacular views over both the city itself and across to the statue of Christ the Redeemer.

The following morning he was presented with a plain-covered exercise book dedicated 'To Farmer John Bryan Wood, with greetings & blessings from Sufi Lodge, Rio', with the inscription: 'Life is an opportunity and it is a great pity if man realizes this too late', catalyst perhaps for his move to Latin America, where the Sufi movement had yet to gain more than a handful of followers, unlike its North American neighbour.

The book opened by listing the levels of the Sufi hierarchy. A Labourer was a novice, a 'mureed', as JBW had been back in Cambridge and Norway, before graduating to Ploughman in Suresnes, which came with its own accompanying watchword: 'Toil'. Now that he was to be a Farmer, he would get a new watchword.

His induction ceremony, 'only to be performed during the first phase of the growing moon', was titled simply 'Z', short for 'Ziraat', which was explained as being 'mystical agriculture, or the spiritual culture of man' and deemed '<u>SACRED AND MOST SECRET</u>: If one wishes to discover whether another mureed belongs to Ziraat, the following dialogue takes place: Q: "Are you interested in Agriculture?" A: "Yes, and especially in Farming."'

The ceremony, held in the grounds of the house, was conducted by the resident country head, Shabaz Best (Experienced Farmer, and former London bank clerk), along with the overall leader of the movement throughout the Americas, Murshida Rabia Martin (Most Experienced Farmer). On a plain white tablecloth Shabaz Best placed a harrow – the symbol of the Farmer – along with incense, a fan and two bowls, one filled with earth and the other with water – earth, wind, fire and water. A yellow cord was draped over JBW's left shoulder, then tucked under his right arm as Murshida Martin began by 'invoking the presence of the Owner of the Farm' (all raise hands) and offering 'whole-hearted devotion to the Great Farmer himself'.

Murshida Martin: 'For what purpose have we assembled here?'

JBW: 'For Farming.'

Murshida Martin: 'What fertilizes the soil?'

JBW: 'The Farmer.'

Murshida Martin: 'What does a Farmer do at night?'

JBW: 'He keeps watch.'

Murshida Martin then set out the various roles and duties of the Farmer, before anointing JBW: 'You will be conscious from this moment of your duty towards the Farm, the workers on the Farm, the Farmers, the Experienced Farmers, the Most Experienced Farmers and the Great Owner of the Farm?'

JBW: 'I will be conscious of my duty.'

Murshida Martin: 'Then, Ploughman, I raise you to be a Farmer on behalf of the Great Farmer, Inayat Khan, and in the name of the Owner of the Farm. May your work be approved by the Owner of the Farm. May your watchword be Courage.' A watchword that would come in useful in the years ahead, though not perhaps in the way that Murshida Martin and her fellow Sufis had intended.

Ceremony concluded, Farmer Wood spent a weekend with Shabaz Best and his family, then headed back to Mexico City. To begin with he stayed in one of the smarter, city-centre hotels (10 pesos a night), doubtless only too happy to find himself living in a country which, in stark contrast to the storm clouds gathering over Europe, was 'alive with every conceivable pattern of colour, raw drama and brilliant overtones'. The capital back then was a surprisingly walkable city of just 15 square miles, with wide sweeping boulevards and vast ahuehuete trees; its Central Park twice the size of New York's, with uniformed guides to help newcomers ward off the local police's customary 'mordida' – a form of semi-official bribe. Free speech was encouraged, corruption discouraged and communists were able to freely go about their business. There was a dazzling art scene – Diego Rivera, Tina Modotti, Frida Kahlo et al. – and the city's restaurants, clubs and bars were there to be enjoyed by anyone who had the money.

Unfortunately, within a few weeks of his return JBW found out that he did not have the money.

Among the stringent measures imposed by the British government on 3 September 1939 had been an overnight block on funds being transferred out of the country. In the past he'd managed to bypass similar – if less draconian – restrictions, often with the help of Cil and her father in Norway. In preparation for his stay in Mexico and visit to Rio de Janeiro, he'd wired his quarterly allowance ahead to a Chicago bank and collected it in passing. True, £200 went a long way back in 1939, but then so did JBW.

Finding himself unexpectedly out of pocket, aside from pinning his hopes on a crumpled $1 Mexican lottery ticket (*¡Premio Mayor $100,000!*), he was forced to explore alternative methods of finance in the shape of an ex-pat currency broker, a Mr Irvine, who with the help of Lazard Brothers had ordered 162 pounds, 13 shillings and 3 pence (over £13,000 in today's money) from JBW's Barclays bank account back in Bene't Street, Cambridge, to be transferred into Mexican pesos. This would come back to bite him.

Just to add to his troubles, as per his visa, he was required to register his presence with the local authorities and with the British Consulate. In normal times a routine, twenty-minute visit at most. Less so in time of war, especially now that all able-bodied British citizens between the ages of eighteen and forty-one were eligible for active service, a prospect that JBW, committed pacifist that he was, had managed to circumnavigate by sailing directly from Cherbourg to New York rather than via a British port.

Then again it can't have been every day that someone with the requisite dark-blue passport, speaking fluent Spanish, a Cambridge graduate to boot, who, more importantly, much more importantly, was also a highly skilled and experienced shortwave radio operator happened to walk in off the street. And, as luck would have it, that someone was rapidly and unexpectedly running short on funds. A consulate with the sort of problems that the resident Consul General, T. Ifor Rees, was facing in 1939 could use a man like that.

On 18 March 1938, amidst raucous street celebrations and a six-hour parade through the capital, President Lázaro Cárdenas had announced the nationalization of Mexico's foreign-owned petroleum industry. British interests were hard hit, having controlled much of the country's oil production while getting away with paying just 5 per cent in royalties to the government. Feathers ruffled, Whitehall had broken off diplomatic relations and recalled its ambassador, downgrading Britain's diplomatic presence to consular status.

Finding a consul with anything like the credentials acceptable to the staunchly socialist and anti-British President Cárdenas cannot have been a straightforward matter, but find him they did.

Unlike the standard Oxbridge intake, T. Ifor Rees had graduated from Aberystwyth with a degree in Welsh, the language perhaps seen as sufficiently foreign for Whitehall to grant him fast-track entry into the Foreign Office. Though his early postings had all been to Latin America – Venezuela, Nicaragua, Cuba and Mexico itself – more likely it was the seven years he had spent in the Basque, and largely Republican, city of Bilbao that made him an ideal candidate for the Mexico post, Cárdenas's administration having supported the Republican cause with both aircraft and arms since the start of the war.

Inevitably perhaps, Rees's Welsh-language skills soon proved useful in Mexico. Overhearing at a drinks party that the Minister for Foreign Affairs had translated *The Rubáiyát of Omar Khayyám* into Spanish, he was able to introduce himself as having done the same, albeit into Welsh. By such unlikely turns are diplomatic tensions eased. Tall, good-looking, with a neatly trimmed moustache and, just to round off the image, more often than not sporting an Indiana Jones-style hat, as his various published travel books demonstrate, he was both a gifted photographer and keen mountaineer, for whom Mexico was a perfect posting (asked to describe the country, the Spanish conquistador Cortés had simply crumpled a piece of paper). However, on the morning of 3 September 1939, T. Ifor Rees woke to find that he had a mountain of a very different nature to climb.

Encouraged by Hitler's observation that Mexico was crying out for 'a capable master' and that with access to its vast mineral wealth and oil fields Germany 'could be rich and great', Admiral Canaris, chief of German Military Intelligence, had long foreseen the need to establish a proper intelligence network within the country, and had tasked German industry with developing a transmitter-receiver powerful enough to send messages over vast distances. The resulting *Agentenfunk* transceivers, or 'Afus' as they were known, were small enough and, at just 13 kilos, light enough to be carried inside a suitcase. Canaris's aim was to establish a series of shortwave stations running down the spine of Latin America, from Mexico down as far as Buenos Aires: the 'Bolivar Network'.

The first station – given the unlikely name of 'Glenn' – was rigged up in the grounds of Mexico City's German Legation, whose trees provided sufficient cover for the 70 feet of wire needed for the transmitter's aerial. Since tests showed that the stream of radio impulses flowed much better north to south than east to west across the Atlantic, the plan was to place relatively low-energy stations in the United States, then beam their signals to high-energy stations in South America for relay to the Fatherland, with Mexico the key station. Staffed by some of the Abwehr's most experienced agents, including the former head of the Nazi Party in Spain, by 1939 it was the largest station anywhere outside of Germany, with a huge smuggling operation sending vast quantities of vital oil back to German-occupied Europe on Japanese and Axis-friendly ships. More damaging still, it was able to transmit details of Allied shipping and North Atlantic convoy routes to any of the forty-three receivers on the second floor of Abwehr's telecommunications centre in Hamburg, and thence to the North Atlantic U-boats, leading to the loss of over two hundred ships in the first three months of the war alone, increasing to close on a thousand the following year.

By contrast, British Intelligence was totally ill-equipped for war, 'with a desperate shortage of suitable receivers and DF [direction finding] equipment as well as trained people to work them'. Nowhere was this felt sooner than in Rees's Mexico City outpost, which found itself acting as the communications hub between London, Montevideo and the Royal Navy in the first major naval action of the war, the Battle of the River Plate, when a small force of British and New Zealand cruisers forced the crippled German battleship *Graf Spee* to run for shelter into Montevideo Harbour; the resulting standoff ended with the *Graf Spee* being scuttled.

This early success was somewhat offset by the fact that, unlike in the previous war (in which Germany had offered to 'repatriate' Texas, New Mexico and Arizona to Mexico in return for their support), Rees could expect little help from north of the border, since President Roosevelt's Good Neighbour Policy ruled out any interference in the domestic affairs of his Latin American neighbours. Added to which, alongside its own homegrown pro-Nazi fascists, the *sinarquistas*, Mexico was also home to the Ausland Organization, probably the most extensive Nazi movement in Latin America, who would openly parade in full regalia and uniforms – Mexico City was home to several thousand Germans, with their own sporting and sailing clubs, bars and beer cellars, even a 'Restaurant Swastika'. Home too, on the very week that war was declared, to the twenty-three-year-old JBW.

Some forty years later, on that rather awkward weekend following our grandmother's funeral, JBW described to us his first meeting with T. Ifor Rees, which in many ways was to prove pivotal to his future career. Officially at least, the Embassy, a discreetly impressive building on the corner of Rio Lerma and Rio Sena, had closed following the breakdown in diplomatic relations, but Rees was clearly not someone prepared to let a crisis go to waste or, more accurately, to let the embassy gardens go to waste. He allowed various groups of Spanish Republican *exiliados* and their families to camp out in the grounds while he and his team did their best to help find them work – preferably as chauffeurs, gardeners and handymen to various pro-Axis embassies and their staff 'whose households were suddenly no longer safe for secrets' (or, in Rees's case, personally commissioning the more talented artists among them, easels, brushes and paints provided).

Given the chances of finding a Consul-General sympathetic to the Republican cause, let alone one who had spent several years in the Basque region and who was a gifted linguist – perversely rare in the Diplomatic Service of the 1930s – it was no surprise then that JBW's involvement with both T. Ifor Rees and the Mexico City consulate was destined to last rather longer than twenty minutes.

Indeed, as an early advocate of humanitarian projects and aid agencies, in particular the Red Cross, Rees's career might have served as a useful blueprint for JBW. But it was not to be, not least since it was Rees himself who would bring my father's talents to the attention of Britain's intelligence services – for better or for worse. For now though, he was happy to overlook any patriotic failings JBW might have in return for his wireless skills, and simply asked him to 'help out', as JBW called it.

When not 'helping out', he was free to come and go as he pleased, even to explore a little of the wider country, though for the time being his lack of funds forced him to abandon any thoughts of visiting the various other Latin American countries he had obtained visas for (presumably for a fact-finding mission on behalf of the Sufi movement). A flurry of letters to and from the San Francisco Sufi community ensued, ending with the suggestion that Farmer Wood should head up to California at the end of the year (or when his money ran out), to work on a small farm Murshida Martin had purchased some twenty miles north of San Francisco, intended as a rural Sufi retreat and education centre along the lines of Suresnes.

His straitened circumstances had necessitated a move to the leafy southern Coyoacán district, his evenings now spent huddled over a beer with his fellow *exiliados españoles* in the cafés and bars of the Calle de López rather than in city-centre restaurants, his weekends spent rowing on Lake Xochimilco or occasionally joining T. Ifor Rees for a hike up the nearby Popocatepetl volcano. Or simply taking in the sights and sounds of his new neighbourhood, coincidentally also home to one Lev Bronstein, better known to the local authorities and to history as Leon Trotsky.

It was JBW himself who first revealed his (hopefully tenuous) connection to the former Bolshevik party commissar and head of the Red Army while talking us through his time in Mexico – and in some detail. Having covered the Russian Revolution at school, here at least I was on firmer ground (but not much firmer) than conchology. Just as I would wander past the guardhouse of the SIS training camp with John Reed's *Ten Days That Shook the World* and Trotsky's *History of the Russian Revolution* tucked under my arm (the irony of which never occurred to me, or them), so too JBW would wander past Trotsky's fortress-like house, often enough to be a familiar face to the guards milling around its entrance, though whether he went inside he never said.

Mexico was not the first time their paths had crossed. Prior to his arrival in the country Trotsky had been holed up in a rural farmhouse in Norway not far from Oslo, which must have seemed too good an opportunity to pass up, all the more so given Erica's encounter with Herr Hitler in Munich's Braun Haus and his friend Raja Bhanot having met

Ghandi. Whether JBW actually met Trotsky face-to-face, either in Norway or Mexico, he never let on, but he was certainly able to describe him in minute detail, before relating his August 1940 assassination, voicing doubts as to whether Jacques Mornard (better known as Ramón Mercader) had been acting entirely alone.

Yet somehow omitting to mention that he'd been living on the same street as Trotsky, or that Mornard had been a fellow student at the Sorbonne.

But if, at the age of twenty-three, JBW was already starting to amass quite a collection of future eyebrow-raisers, he was far from done yet.

Samuel L. Lewis, *c*.1940, 'Head Gardener' at Kaaba Allah, and future spiritual leader of the San Francisco hippy movement.

Vera Corda.

Erica Hathaway with JBW at Kaaba Allah.

5.

Kaaba Allah

'In 1969, an elderly man with long grey hair and a
long grey beard, wearing white robes, deplaned at San
Francisco airport, where he was met by a large crowd
of young followers. "Who is that?" asked a passing
porter. "That," replied the elderly man, who had
heard the question, "is the New Age . . . in person."
The elderly man was Samuel L. Lewis, also known
as "Sufi Sam" [. . .] dubbed by the press as "the
spiritual leader of the hippy movement".'

Mark Sedgwick, *Western Sufism:
From the Abbasids to the New Age* (2016)

At the start of 1940, Samuel L. Lewis, who for many years
was spiritual mentor, guide and closest friend of JBW, was
running Murshida Martin's Sufi school and spiritual retreat,
'Kaaba Allah' (or 'House of God'), one of the first alternative communities in North America, situated near the small
town of Fairfax, north of San Francisco, possibly to the dis-
quiet of its well-to-do Marin County neighbours.

Lewis was a leading light of the West Coast spiritualist
community, seen as likely successor to Murshida Martin as
head of the San Francisco Sufi movement. By all accounts
(not least his own) something of a child prodigy, he had

long since turned his back on material wealth or anything that might be mistaken for a proper job – despite his mother being a Rothschild and his father a senior executive with Levi Strauss – initially choosing to live as a 'dunist' among the sand dunes of the California coastline, which was where he had met the Norwegian Sufi Bryn Bjorset.

Bjorset's 'dunite' existence was merely the latest chapter in a nomadic life which had included working as a jackaroo on a sheep station in Australia, being attacked by a Dayak chieftain while employed as an engineer in Borneo, building ports and railroads in Ataturk's Turkey and going to meditate in a cave only to find it already inhabited – by a Himalayan bear. As one of the first Norwegians to convert to Sufism, he had stood alongside Harvor and Cil Egeberg on the Oslo dockside waiting to greet Inayat Khan – and many years later would pave the way for JBW's move to Paris and Suresnes. It was Bjorset who had first suggested to Murshida Martin and Lewis that the Spanish- and Portuguese-speaking JBW would be perfect casting for Latin America.

Lewis's own conversion was the result of a chance meeting in a Sutter Street bookshop with Murshida Martin, who in turn had introduced him to the Great Farmer himself, Hazrat Inayat Khan, in the Beverley Hills Hotel – where his bearded, be-robed presence must have raised eyebrows, even amongst the 1920s Hollywood set. A compulsive letter writer, Lewis kept up a regular correspondence with JBW on anything and every-thing throughout the war and for many years after. Though occasionally sidetracked by (seemingly successful) attempts to convince JBW of the existence of the likes of Atlantis, Lewis mostly stuck to Inayat Khan's teachings: 'The mystic looks at Chemistry – ditto Physics, ditto Botany, ditto Zoology, ditto Human Anatomy and Physiology, ditto Geology, etc. [...] this is exactly what Inayat Khan asked me to do in 1923.' His constant stream (torrent) of letters, seldom fewer than several pages long, contained expositions of the spiritual properties of various minerals, crystals, gases and suchlike, along with reminders on the importance of reciting one's daily 'wazifas' – preferably in Arabic – before signing off with light-reading suggestions: 'I am enclosing the first ten of the Original papers for the Ikhwan-i-safo', even the occasional nod to what might be happening in the real world: 'Present civilization is doomed and we might have to make the whole world over.'

By upbringing a horticulturist, by profession a soil scientist, Lewis devoted his indefatigable energies and most of his time to the problem of global food shortage. As Kaaba Allah's self-styled 'Head Gardener', he was an early advocate of organic planting, seed exchange, desalination, desert reclamation and suchlike, in the process sowing the seeds for the career that JBW would one day follow. And, more fundamentally, the philosophy that JBW embraced both now and in the years to come: 'A Sufi has no home or family or country.'

Kaaba Allah was run as a collective, and 'Farmer' Wood was expected to contribute in a practical way, an irony that somehow escaped Lewis's letters to Mexico. Given that the nearest JBW had come to any form of agriculture had been his father's passion for bee-keeping, he volunteered to set up a series of hives, only for this to be politely rejected by Lewis on the grounds that 'people here would not like it if you were to start hives in these parts, although I believe that we have no right to refuse any gifts, all coming from God'. Instead, Lewis had a rather more straightforward schedule in mind: 'I have taken up the matter of you staying with us a little while, and while we too are short of funds it is possible to arrange for you to spend some time here in exchange for work. Then you would come and be the chauffeur and do two or three jobs; these are chiefly tree topping and trimming, and floor painting. Would this be satisfactory?'

Clearly it was satisfactory and, all but broke, JBW spent his remaining pesos on a bus ticket from Mexico City to San Francisco, a journey of over 2,500 miles and three days. The US customs officials at the Nogales border crossing noted his eventual destination as 133 Hillside Drive, Fairfax, CA – otherwise known as 'Kaaba Allah'.

As in Suresnes, his days would begin with 6 a.m. prayers, followed by chanting and the recital of his ten daily vows, after which JBW would be let loose on the surrounding hillside slopes 'planting crops, painting fences, constructing pergolas', the idea being that Lewis would give him one-to-one tuition as they worked – 'painting and a few other jobs could be done with you in seclusion, but not the tree work, of course'.

A few photographs from my father's time at Kaaba Allah survive: Lewis standing beneath the entrance arch to the retreat; Lewis showing off their newly constructed pergolas; JBW holding his hand up to the sun (or, just as likely, the camera); a distant female figure hacking away at the undergrowth with a machete. This was almost certainly Vera Corda, destined to be something of a muse to JBW. By training a ballet dancer, as a young girl she'd queued up to see Ruth St Denis's pioneer dance company in her local Modesto theatre, only to come away transfixed by the interval performance of Inayat Khan and his fellow musicians, the sight and sound of which had stayed with her ever since.

As a regular attendee at Lewis's weekly lectures at the Sufi Centre on Stockton Street (now a Gucci store), first thing every Saturday morning she would leave her Irving Street apartment, make the twenty-mile bus ride up to Fairfax, then hike up to Kaaba Allah, returning late Sunday nights. Despite their vastly different backgrounds (Vera's family were in the Kansas City lumber trade), she and JBW immediately recognized that they had met before – first in India, where they'd even lived in the same house, then again in China. Unfortunately, both meetings had taken place several centuries back in their previous lives. And despite the longevity of their relationship it had never been consummated: 'both in China and India [. . .] we were very much in love. But because of the class distinction we could only see each other through bars and at night – we could never be physically together.' Nor would they be this time around, Vera being married to a young navy officer, while JBW would be heading back to Norway and Cil just as soon as his Mexican visa expired. Or so Cil had been led to believe.

In spite of such impediments, with Vera's husband away at sea for long periods, she and JBW were soon all but inseparable, granting him an unlikely entrée into the avant-garde San Francisco ballet world, with mixed results: 'He looked like he'd just stepped off of a farmer's wagon, he didn't press his clothes or clean them or do anything like that – we did it for him, because we just couldn't be seen with him the way he looked, we were embarrassed for him.' Given JBW's (apparent) impoverishment, Vera would continue throughout her life to keep back all her (various) husbands' discarded clothing for whenever JBW happened to drop by – blissfully unaware of his Bene't Street riches (much like his various future wives).

Thankfully JBW's deficiencies on the wardrobe front would soon be solved by the reappearance of the Hathaways, recently returned from Munich. Having finally retired from the American diplomatic service, Hathaway Snr was only too happy to look out some of his old suits for his son's friend who, as in Munich, was soon a regular guest at their new home a few miles north of Santa Barbara. Hathaway's generosity largely stemmed from the (misplaced) belief that if anyone could get his son Bill up and running it was JBW. Having been kicked out of Yale (drink and sloth), Bill had managed to scrape through his Cambridge exams with JBW's help and a steady supply of Benzedrine, before landing a German teaching job at Stanford, prompting him and Erica to take the first available passage from Germany (along with several hundred Jewish refugees), arriving in San Francisco for the start of the academic year.

Only now, true to form, Bill was no longer at Stanford (drink and sloth). Though her husband's sacking came as no great surprise to Erica, nevertheless she'd taken to her bed 'burning up with fever', only for JBW to turn up out of the blue with no prior warning, as was his way.

But he was very different from the JBW that Erica remembered from their time together in Cambridge: the earnest language student she had first met in Munich was now a Farmer. And 'What does a Farmer do at night? He keeps watch.' Ordering her back to bed, 'he took out a pendulum and held it over my body. I had to hold out my hands and he circled it over my fingers. When I woke up, I heard voices. "Erica, should you be up?" Bill asked with much concern. "I feel wonderful." Jøn the healer is responsible!'

Like most of their Cambridge circle (Cil aside), Erica had been unaware of the full extent of JBW's spiritualist leanings, knowing nothing of Suresnes or his visit down to Rio de Janeiro. Nor had she heard of Murshida Martin, Samuel Lewis, Kaaba Allah, wazifas or *murāqabah*. But she would soon enough. '"Have you ever meditated?" Seeing my bewilderment, he said, "Let's sit down. Doing is better than

118

explaining." I sat opposite him and closed my eyes so as not to be distracted [. . .] a huge lion walked towards me, then stopped just inches away. Frightened, I opened my eyes. Jøn smiled. "You didn't mind the lion in the end, did you?"'

A few days later Erica and husband Bill found themselves being invited up to the Sufi Centre on Fourth Street, where they were met by a short, bespectacled man 'with thick lenses that didn't stop his eyes from looking searchingly into the very depth of my being'. Samuel Lewis spent the next few hours introducing them to Sufism and the teachings of Inayat Khan, inviting them to attend his Monday lectures, though if for any reason they could not be there in person, JBW would teach them how to tune in via meditation. With his star very much in the ascendant within the Sufi movement, JBW was soon being earmarked by Murshida Martin as a possible future leader in Latin America, with Lewis his most vocal cheerleader: 'Well, Jøn, when I learn that you are human, I praise God and pray for your enlightenment. If you ever become what some others expect of you, God pity you; you won't be fit to associate with anybody or they with you.'

Unfortunately he was all too human, certainly so far as the British government was concerned.

A Mr Mynors of His Majesty's Treasury had begun looking into JBW's dubious financial arrangements with Mr Irvine and Lazard Brothers and the illegal transfer of funds from his Bene't Street bank account. And Mr Mynors was not one to let such matters slip, no matter how elusive or distant the quarry. And because trouble seldom arrived unaccompanied – certainly so far as my father was concerned – it soon emerged that Mr Mynors was not the only government official to be taking an interest in the young British *exiliado*. Having deftly avoided active service, he now had a Mr Allchin of His Majesty's

Foreign & Commonwealth Office on his case, with JBW marked down as a 'Quitter'. Informal though it might sound, the term 'Quitter' was anything but, being instead the official term given to 'Absentees in the United States of America from the United Kingdom' who, for whatever reason – conscientious objector or otherwise – had refused the call to arms. The upshot was that his name and passport details were included in a list of 'Quitters' forwarded to the British Embassy in Washington and posted up in the various British consulates and offices throughout the United States. More awkward still, the 'Quitter' label came with an immediate blocking order on his Cambridge bank account ('re John Bryan Wood, United States: British absentee from National Service: blocked account No: 54652898 in UK'), stymying any hopes of being able to wire funds across to the States, via an illegal broker or otherwise.

In his defence, JBW's pacifism was partly down to his obeying orders – or instructions – from on high: the Sufi movement advocated Gandhi's line of passive resistance rather than the taking up of arms. They had maintained this stance since the start of the war, though it was coming under increasing pressure from within their own ranks, not least from the offspring of the 'Great Farmer' himself. With German troops closing in on Paris, Inayat Khan's daughter Noor and son Vilayat (JBW's close friend) would manage to get out just in time, escaping via Bordeaux to London; Vilayat volunteered for service with the RAF, while Noor famously ended up with the SOE.

JBW's own pacifist stance was set to be tested rather sooner, when on 9 April 1940 Hitler launched a surprise attack on his home country. Norway, that is.

JBW's Mexican visa photograph.

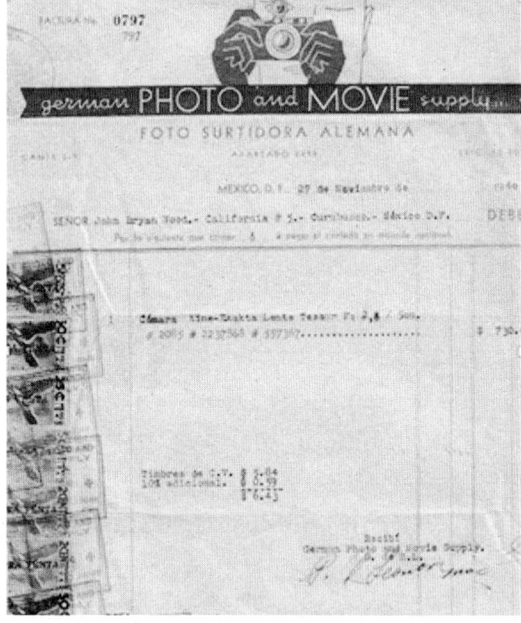

Camera receipt made out to JBW, Av. Río Churubusco – home also to one Lev Bronstein, known to history as Leon Trotsky.

6.

Tenth & Irving, San Francisco

'"What are you going to do now that your
country is at war?" I'd asked Jøn. "I already
have my assignments," he'd replied. I didn't ask
any more questions, neither did Bill.'

Erica Hathaway (Erica Moore),
Eka, volume II (2007)

If my father had any reservations about abandoning his
deeply held pacifist beliefs, he kept them well hidden.

The very next morning, 10 April 1940, dawn prayers and
daily wazifas concluded, he took the bus down from Fairfax to San Francisco, marched into the Norwegian consulate
and volunteered for service as a pilot with the Norwegian
navy (his father had served with the Royal Navy Air Service
during the First World War). Welcome though his application may have been, the consulate quickly pointed out the
slight flaw in his plan: the lack of a Norwegian passport (as
opposed to a Norwegian driving licence). He and his dark-
blue British passport No. C90782 were directed to a more
appropriate consulate in San Francisco, who in turn passed
him on to the Los Angeles consulate while they figured out
how best to use his talents.

At much the same time Churchill, aware post-Dunkirk

that without American help his country's chances of survival were slim at best, was instructing a leading Canadian businessman, William Stephenson, to head to New York and set up an office aimed at persuading neutral America of the merits of joining Britain's cause.

Stephenson made it his immediate priority to give J. Edgar Hoover, the FBI's Director, every assistance possible. With newspapers reporting that Germany's advance on Paris was being helped by the activities of pro-Hitler Fifth Columnists, Hoover's fear was that this might be replicated not only in Latin America, where the German diaspora ran into the millions, but possibly even within the United States itself. That same month, he had set up a Special FBI Intelligence Service to deal with the threat, maintaining that 'the best way to control Nazi espionage within the United States [is] to wipe out the spy nests in Latin America'. Unfortunately, given the restrictions of President Roosevelt's Good Neighbour Policy, to Hoover's frustration the FBI had no authority whatsoever to operate outside of the United States. Unlike Stephenson.

Within days of arriving he was passing on 'all the intelligence from secret sources that he was able to obtain' to the FBI, as a result of which Hoover 'could hardly have been more co-operative' – allowing what was to all intents and purposes a foreign intelligence service to operate on his own patch, reportedly even suggesting British Security Coordination (BSC) as its cover name.

To begin with, Stephenson's efforts were hampered by his new office having just four passport control officers – standard cover occupation for intelligence officers – all four of whom turned out to be bona fide passport control officers, something of a first. Nor could he realistically expect much help from Britain's own Intelligence Service, with just two small SIS stations, Rio de Janeiro (code no. 75200) and Montevideo (code no. 75000), covering the whole of South America, both of which reported directly to London and showed little appetite for answering to a hastily cobbled-together organization – and a largely Canadian organization at that – run by a Winnipeg steel magnate. But the greatest barrier to assembling any sort of realistic intelligence capability in Latin America was the chronic shortage of Spanish-speaking officers throughout the service, resulting in a desperate London 'sending us all sorts of chaps who spoke German, French, Dutch, but not a chap with Spanish or Portuguese'. 'How long will it take you to learn Spanish?' Stephenson demanded of one such new arrival. 'And so I learnt Spanish under great pressure.'

Thankfully, Britain's man in Mexico City, T. Ifor Rees, knew of a young Cambridge graduate who not only had fluent Spanish but also happened to be an expert wireless operator.

'What are you going to do now that your country is at war?' Erica Hathaway had asked when JBW stopped off at their Santa Barbara home on his way back down to Mexico. 'I already have my assignments,' he'd replied. But then, true to form, JBW calmly spent the next few days tackling Tibetan, with the aim of being able to read *The Tibetan Book of the Dead* in the original. Sometime during the course of which he suggested that 'because of the war and Bill's perfect German, there might be a chance of an interesting job down in Mexico'. Knowing her husband only too well, Erica was against the idea but was persuaded by Hathaway Snr's argument that 'it will give us all a breathing space' and that her (unemployed) husband would be in safe hands with JBW. 'He had been a help in Cambridge, so why not again?'

Needless to say, Bill would not be in safe hands.

She'd gone to the bus station to see them off, her husband's parting promise being: 'The Mexican people are as loving as you are, and as soon as I have a job, you'll join me.' In the event, he did not get a job, though for once he was not entirely to blame. Given the presence of Germany's largest Abwehr station on its doorstep, the US Embassy in Mexico City had put together an improvised intelligence-gathering group of volunteers, to which the fluent German-speaking Hathaway was a valuable addition. But no sooner had he started than the group was disbanded on the basis that if word got out it might do more harm than good, as it clearly contravened Roosevelt's Good Neighbour Policy.

On the other hand the Mexican people proved just as loving as Bill had promised, though not in the way Erica would have wanted. Weeks turned into months, which even the worldly-wise Hathaway Snr began to find disconcerting, 'suspecting [knowing] that JBW was collecting information for British Intelligence'. When her husband did finally return, he was pursued by a steady stream of perfumed letters with Mexican postmarks, hidden away under a rug until the pile grew big enough for Erica to trip over. Clearly her husband was not cut out for a career in the dark arts. Unlike JBW.

Half a century later I put to my mother's former Berlin boss Harold Shergold the same question I'd once asked her: how did someone who couldn't bring himself to sing the National Anthem at Cambridge, let alone admit to being English, end up working for the British, albeit unofficially, via the back door? And got much the same answer: 'When there's a war on, it tends to be all hands to the pump.'

War being very much on and hands very much to the pump, on 13 June 1940 JBW duly reported for duty at T. Ifor Rees's Mexico City consulate.

In this, the first real 'radio' war, Stephenson and Hoover's immediate problem was an acute shortage of wireless operators, with the fledgling BSC reduced to trawling civilian amateur radio hams in Canada for possible recruits, none of whom were told how exactly their expertise would be implemented. Fewer still spoke Spanish, nor in all probability had anything like JBW's improvisation skills, able to repair or even build an entire wireless set at a time when spare components, not to mention transmitters and receivers, were now all but unobtainable as a result of the war.

Unlike most boyhood hobbies, JBW's passion for long-range wireless had only increased with age. Given his son's passion for sitting up in all those various ships' radio rooms, scanning far-off receivers or else cannibalizing canteen biscuit tin lids, bicycle bells and the like, on their return to England his father – who had used wireless to direct artillery fire with the Royal Flying Corps – built a radio hut in their back garden, 'a workshop for me when I was about fourteen, where I used to construct radios'. By which time he was already sufficiently adept to be making nightly contact with all four corners of the globe, scrawling in the margin of his school exercise book how he'd 'got Sydney N.S.W. VK2ME on short wave, wonderfully clear'. Even the distractions of Cambridge failed to dim his enthusiasm, aerial slung round the chimney of his Grantchester Road digs, colourful certificates acknowledging his Marconi transmissions from as far afield as Java, Brazil and Colombia pinned up on his bedsit wall. Quite likely JBW had possibly as much – if not more – experience of short-wave radio under his belt as anyone in BSC.

For BSC, the immediate need was for advance warning of potential attacks on the North Atlantic convoys, which were being decimated by Hitler's U-boats, while for the FBI the threat was even closer to home, with Hoover's men aware that the Abwehr already had a spy network up and running within the United States itself. However, their attempts to read German radio traffic were thwarted by a dearth of offshore monitoring stations – other than a relic of the Pro-hibition era, designed to track East Coast bootleggers. (Only in late 1940 would a special Latin American Intelligence division be formed and building work begin on a central monitoring station in Texas.)

The Abwehr's use of Mexico City's 'Glenn' station to 'bounce' a continuous stream of messages from the US to Hamburg placed an even greater importance on BSC's Latin American operation, with Hoover totally reliant on BSC's small band of Wireless Traffic (WT) operators. As a result JBW's days – more commonly, nights – would typically now be spent hunched over his transmission receiver dials, headphones clamped to his ear, patiently looking for traffic, hoping to identify call-names or five-letter groupings, a par-ticular Abwehr operator's radio style or 'fist'. Any encoded transmissions that were picked up were forwarded to BSC in New York and from there to Bletchley Park (which had begun operating before the war had even started), the pro-cess greatly facilitated by Hoover allowing BSC to use the FBI's own communication network in return for their help in Latin America.

By August 1940 US and British decryption experts were beginning to unravel Abwehr codes and starting to listen in on conversations. Such was the success of the intercepts and signal tracking that by the end of the year BSC's efforts were seriously hampering Admiral Canaris's activities both in Mexico City and countrywide (and, eventually, throughout Latin America). Guadalajara was identified as a centre for Abwehr WT operations and a secondary station pinpointed to Veracruz (mysteriously shut down as soon as investigations were launched, collusion with the Mexican police suspected) as JBW's remit – and travel – was widened to cover the whole country. Not that his duties appear to have been confined solely to WT: for someone who the previous year had just a crumpled $1 lottery ticket to his name, he was developing very expensive tastes in high-end photographic equipment, purchasing the latest Kine-Exacta Lente Tessar (a prototype of today's 35 mm cameras) for $730 from, ironically, the German Photo & Movie Supply Company, the receipt made out to John B. Wood, '#5 Calif, Av. Río Churubusco' – the same Avenida as Trotsky.

Whereas at the start of the war the Abwehr all but had the country to itself, its smuggling operations supplying vital aviation fuel to Hamburg and 'Glenn' beaming back a steady stream of economic data and shipping information, twelve months on the intelligence war was being won by BSC – aided and abetted by the same restrictions that had brought JBW's first stay in Mexico to a premature end, with currency transfers from Europe rapidly becoming all but impossible thanks to the tacit support of the US. The sheer size of Canaris's Mexico City station, with its vast network of agents and informants (day rate: $20–30), correspondingly made it the most expensive, and while the local police – on a salary of just 2.75 pesos a day – were often only too happy to turn a blind eye to smuggling operations, forged passports and other clandestine activities, they required sufficient financial inducement to do so. Increasingly short of the pesos, colons, sucres, quetzals, lempiras and cordobas needed to pay its agents either there or in Colombia, Costa Rica, Ecuador, Guatemala, Honduras and Nicaragua, the Abwehr were unable to operate at anything like the same level, so much so that by the time the United States entered the war it was down to just some two dozen agents in Mexico, between them producing 'less valuable information than the shipping schedules from Tampico'.

Not that BSC had the field entirely to themselves, as the 20 August assassination of JBW's Avenida Río Churubusco neighbour demonstrated. A crowd of some 200,000, JBW included, lined the streets to watch Trotsky's open casket go by.

With President Cárdenas obliged to step down at the end of the year – the Mexican constitution prevented him from running for a second term – just to add to Canaris's woes, his successor would not be Germany's favoured (and financed) candidate but 'the steady, cautious, efficient, grey' General Avila Camacho, 'regardless of the vote'. Camacho's main qualification – certainly so far as his northern neighbours saw it – was that he possessed 'the most favourable view of the United States as could be expected' – despite, as one of its journalists noted, being 'about as colourful as a slab of halibut'.

By this time JBW was on his way again, the only souvenirs from his second stay in Mexico as much as he could carry in his overnight bag: a few postcards of Aztec deities and ruins, and a photograph of a nameless bare-shouldered beauty looking up into a cloudless sky, courtesy of his Kine-Exacta Lente Tessar camera. Ongoing investigations into dubious currency transactions notwithstanding, his finances were now healthy enough (courtesy of T. Ifor Rees or more likely British Security Coordination itself) for him to fly via Calexico. After spending Christmas with the Hathaways at their Santa Barbara home, he then headed up to San Francisco to see in the New Year with his fellow Sufis, a 31 December telegram of endorsement from T. Ifor Rees to London no doubt ringing in his ears – or entering his enlightened consciousness:

From: Consul-General Rees, Mexico City.

Volunteer from Mexico.

Has received application from Mr John Bryan Wood, a British subject, to volunteer for service to His Majesty's Government. Gives qualifications and suggests that he would be most suitable for intelligence work.

Registry Number: W1146/19/49. No. 40 (18/82) Dated 31st December 1940

A few days later the *San Anselmo Herald* reported that 'Jøn B. Wood is enjoying his second visit here in Marin County during the past year, and contemplates spending a month at the Sufi School, Fairfax. Wood was formerly connected with the Norwegian Consulate Service, but since the German invasion, he has been working and residing in various parts of Mexico and California.'

Vera Corda questioned why 'Jøn', granted temporary Resident Alien status, hadn't instead simply applied for US residency, on the basis that his homeland was now under German occupation, while Samuel Lewis commiserated with JBW's frustration at not being able to do his bit for king (Haakon VII) and country (Norway). 'Norway: Please be patient. With the understanding of *murāqabah* sooner or later others will pick up your thoughts.'

And with that JBW dusted down his Norwegian driving licence and became once again Farmer Jøn Wood, chauffeur, tree trimmer and floor painter, rising for 6 a.m. prayers, reciting his wazifas and his daily vows, before setting off for a hard day's labour in the fields accompanied by Head Gardener Samuel Lewis, filling in the time while awaiting orders from BSC.

If little had changed at Kaaba Allah since he was last there, the same could not be said of San Francisco. Unbeknown to its citizens, the city was by now 'a logical coordination centre for German and Japanese espionage in the US and a logical headquarters, too, from which to direct Nazi activities in Mexico & South America', headed up by the Abwehr's Captain Fritz Wiedmann. Clearly JBW's daily routine of planting crops, painting fences and constructing pergolas didn't fool Captain Wiedmann and his men. Followed wherever he went, or certainly wary of being followed wherever he went, constantly changing tram or bus, always sitting with his back to the wall, as Vera Corda witnessed: 'When we would be on streetcars, so many times, he would haul me off the streetcar in the middle of the night, took a long time for another one to come – someone was following him.' And just as he had made full use of his *exiliados* connections in Mexico City, in San Francisco it was the turn of his fellow Sufis, who could always be relied upon to provide a roof over his head but who soon discovered that Farmer Wood had begun to plough a very different furrow, as Vera Corda would come uncomfortably close to experiencing firsthand.

Her first-floor apartment on the corner of Tenth Avenue

and Irving Street had always been open house for JBW after Lewis's lectures or Hathaway Snr's social invites, but it was now effectively doubling as a convenient safe house, all the more so for being only accessible via the all-night drugstore on the ground floor. Even so: 'Jøn would always stand against the wall, if there was any sign of shadows or anybody being on the roof-garden, he would just put himself against the wall in the shadow.'

Sufficiently concerned, Vera's husband finally plucked up the courage to demand that JBW's visit should be his last. As it very nearly was. 'I heard the gunshot – but I didn't know that it hit, that it landed in my room, so they were definitely then aiming at him, but because the lights were out and shutters were such that they would definitely protect Jøn [. . .] we didn't see the bullet in the wall till the next day.' A close call, and by no means his last. But then of course, with the benefit of *murāqabah* – said to give the true believer a sixth sense – no doubt he would have seen it coming.

In early April the Foreign Office – not the nimblest of organizations, even in wartime – finally responded to T. Ifor Rees's New Year's Eve telegram:

Volunteer from Mexico.

Refers to Foreign Office letter of 5th April (W1146/19/49) giving particulars of Mr J. B. Wood

States that as applicant seems to be so exceptionally well qualified he should be provided with a passage to this country if he is prepared to accept whatever form of service is considered most appropriate for him when the matter has been discussed with him personally.

Registry Number: W4343/19/49

Only to be promptly overruled by their counterparts in 'Admiralty':

Volunteer from Mexico, Mr J. B. Wood.

Refers to Foreign Office letter of April 5th. (W1146/19/49)

States that there is at present no vacancy for him in Intelligence and Liaison work, nor would his knowledge of science appear to be sufficient for an appointment in technical capacity.

Registry Number: W5504/19/49

With a further telegram confirming that 'the Norwegian Naval authorities are unable to utilize him' and having been rejected by both the British and the Norwegians, JBW returned to Kaaba Allah and his pergola painting, albeit with Captain Wiedmann and his henchmen on his tail and the bowler-hatted brigade (Mr Allchin and Mr Mynors) on his case.

Not that any of this would have worried him unduly: other countries were only too keen to make use of someone with his talents, dubious or otherwise.

The Rockefeller Center, New York, headquarters of BSC (British Security Coordination) during the Second World War.

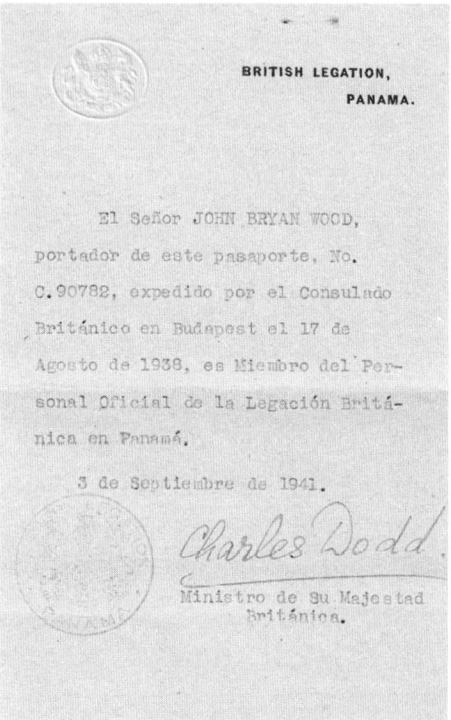

BRITISH LEGATION,
PANAMA.

El Señor JOHN BRYAN WOOD, portador de este pasaporte, No. C.90782, expedido por el Consulado Británico en Budapest el 17 de Agosto de 1938, es Miembro del Personal Oficial de la Legación Británica en Panamá.

3 de Septiembre de 1941.

Charles Dodd

Ministro de Su Majestad
Británica.

Posted to Panama under the guise of 'assistant commissioner'.

7.

Room 3603

'Jøn, I learned, was in "Little Norway", one of
England's secret spy training camps, fulfilling the
assignment he had mentioned to me.'

Erica Hathaway (Erica Moore), *Eka*, volume II

Just as he had done twelve months previously, JBW saw in
the New Year at Murshida Martin's Ashbury Street home.
For most Americans, the war in Europe was a distant threat
at the start of 1941, less so to those present that evening,
their numbers swelled by a group of Jewish refugees Martin
had taken in, whose children would dive under their beds in
terror whenever they heard the wail of a passing police car
or fire engine.

When not otherwise engaged on BSC business in downtown San Francisco, Farmer Wood busied himself with
pergola painting and tree trimming under Head Gardener
Lewis, together with 'Dancing, Music, Diet, Industry,
Handicrafts and Amaliat [sic]', reward for which was Murshida Martin's February announcement that he was 'entitled
to grant First Bayat' – an embossed certificate confirming
that he could now 'initiate applicants prepared to enter the
Sufi order'.

Having long since been earmarked as a future 'sheykh'

or leader in the Sufi movement, likely based in Latin America, as Samuel Lewis saw it, all that was stopping JBW from going on to become 'what some others expect of you' was his habit of speaking in a barely audible mutter. The solution for this, Lewis decided, was for JBW to give an introductory talk before his Monday-night lectures at the downtown Sufi Centre, on the basis that just 'as self-consciousness is the enemy of a speaker, singer, doctor or lawyer, so it is the greatest enemy of the one who concentrates'.

Hathaway Snr put it rather more bluntly. 'I'd love to hear what he has to say. I just wish he'd open his mouth so I could understand him.' Ever since Munich, Hathaway Snr had taken something of an avuncular interest in his son's (quietly spoken) Cambridge friend, suggesting that with his linguistic abilities the young JBW might want to try for some sort of career within the diplomatic service – to which end he'd made a point of inviting him on his Sunday walkabout briefings to foreign journalists, a front-row seat to the gathering storm.

In much the same way, the Hathaways' return to California now gave JBW an entrée into West Coast diplomatic circles. His decade-long stint as Consul General had given Hathaway Snr as clear an insight into what was happening in Germany as anyone in the United States, having met and dealt with the entire leadership of the Nazi party on a regular basis, Hitler included. As a result he found his Santa Barbara retirement plans taking something of a back seat, travelling the coast road up to San Francisco (or else flying across to Washington) more often than he might have wished, to give his thoughts on the current situation or to brief various government departments and news agencies – along with the endless drinks and dinners that would invariably follow, to which JBW was often invited. 'With the Hathaways we were invited to places and parties that were top society in the San Francisco Bay Area,' Vera Corda recalled, 'and if there was anything that was going on politically that he wanted to attend.'

Indifferently dressed and quietly spoken though he may have been, JBW would not have been the first to find the social climate of California refreshingly liberating. And anyone who at the age of twenty-four could speak (or mutter) several languages, had circled the globe, witnessed firsthand the rise of Nazi Germany, visited Austria post-Anschluss and been a near neighbour of the late Leon Trotsky can't have been the worst person to sit next to at dinner or exchange small talk with over drinks. Suffice to say, he was soon a familiar figure within San Francisco's social and political circles, even something of a sought-after figure among its younger members – a connection that would do him no harm in the years to come, given that 'these were not run-of-the-mill people, they would be important people.'

But as Hathaway Snr was no doubt already aware, JBW was not destined for the diplomatic service, or at least not the front-of-house version that he himself and T. Ifor Rees had made a career of. Nor, for all Samuel Lewis's wishful thinking, had JBW returned to San Francisco simply to whitewash pergolas or trim hedges at Kaaba Allah, still less was he destined to end up parading barefoot through the Haight-Ashbury district clad head-to-toe in white robes, chanting and banging on a drum as he performed the Dances of the Universal Peace, as his mentor Lewis would do.

Captain Fritz Wiedmann and his Abwehr associates, on the other hand, clearly knew what JBW was about and why he had returned to San Francisco, just as they knew exactly what he'd been doing in Mexico.

Though, officially at least, JBW spent the first few months of 1941 waiting for the Foreign Office to decide how best to use his talents, BSC were rather quicker off the mark, and enlisted him to help set up their Ships' Observers Scheme.

The aim of the scheme was to cut off the supply of raw materials feeding Hitler's war machine, not least his North Atlantic U-boat fleet, which had been decimating British shipping. The Abwehr had enjoyed something of a head start, having already set up a highly successful clandestine operation that in the opening months of the war had managed to ship vast quantities of oil and cotton back to Germany – in the process chalking up some unlikely successes, including smuggling platinum out in tins of peaches or the drinking cups of canary cages and gold coins melted down into the shape of the brass buckles on trunks.

Merchant fleets tended to be manned by all sorts from all over Latin America and Europe, including large numbers of Germans, who at the start of 1941 began sabotaging ships in American harbours. Fearing that they might attempt to do the same as they were going through the Panama Canal, the US naval authorities were forced to ban German sailors and nationals from boarding any of the boats – as a result of which several thousand found themselves marooned in and around the major ports – San Francisco, Los Angeles, San Diego. Despite this measure, smuggling operations were still rife, exacerbated by the vast numbers of cargo ships and fruit boats plying to and from South America, whose crews were made up of various nationalities, some of whom might not be entirely sympathetic to the Allied cause, certainly if the price was right.

To counter this, the idea was that neutral ships would be joined by an appointed 'observer', whose job was to wire

New York about any suspicious activity, be it pro-German talk amongst the crew, evidence of smuggling, possible Axis agents amongst the passengers, radio messages sent out after a British ship was sighted, along with any sightings of German supply vessels or naval shipping.

Alongside his normal night-time WT eavesdropping duties – trying to determine the nationalities of the various crews on board ships – JBW's day-to-day work was centred on helping the various shipping companies implement the scheme, although he left them to organize the actual recruiting, a Cambridge and Sorbonne education possibly not the best grounding for dealing with Californian dockyard workers. Which left JBW, with his *exiliados* connections, free to concentrate on the Spanish and Portuguese shipping lines, which handled the majority of trade between Europe and the US, in particular the Portuguese Bensaude line, whose manifests listed an ever-increasing number of suspect hands on board.

Given the large number of German nationals still employed in San Francisco's dockyards – though no longer on the boats themselves – his friend Bill Hathaway (still at a loose end post-Mexico) would be a useful recruit, being a fluent German-speaker. Bill was not keen. 'You haven't accepted my suggestion of working in the shipyards yet?' a disappointed if not wholly surprised JBW asked on his return from Los Angeles (where, true to form, he had managed to fit in a visit to one Nyogen Senzaki, a Rinzai Zen monk, trying his hand at 'floating zendo' – a form of Buddhist meditation – in Senzaki's apartment.) He had better luck with Vera Corda, helping her land a job in the Bay Area naval shipyard offices, which came with the added bonus (certainly from JBW's point of view) of a window overlooking the dockyard itself.

By May 1941 the Ships' Observers Scheme (code no. 48907) was fully up and running, with recruits stationed on well over a hundred ships. Despite being one of Stephenson's most successful operations, it was less well received by J. Edgar Hoover, who felt that it was one thing for BSC to be in Latin America, quite another for them to be openly operating on his home turf, not helped, Kim Philby noted, whenever 'Stephenson's strong boys beat up or intoxicated the crews loading Axis supplies'. As a result, the following month Stephenson agreed to transfer the entire US side of the operation to Hoover, leaving JBW to hand over to his FBI colleagues in San Francisco.

With Admiralty in London finally confirming that they would not be requiring JBW's services, he confided to Vera Corda that instead there was talk of a possible posting to Bermuda. Perhaps she might like to join him there? Bermuda was not as far-fetched as it might seem; BSC had set up a huge operation in the basement of the island's Princess Hotel, intercepting clandestine radio traffic and suspect mail, with hundreds of handlers sorting through any post bound for Europe, courtesy of the Pan-American Clipper service who used the island as a stop-off before heading to Lisbon. Intercepted messages, sometimes just a micro-dot (a recent Abwehr invention) concealed underneath a stamp, would then be relayed back to New York and Hoover's FBI. But BSC was not about to let someone with JBW's WT skillset, let alone his fluent Spanish and passable Portuguese, see out the war sifting through stamps in a hotel basement. Nor, despite the Foreign Office's continuing attempts to find a suitable role for him, would JBW be returning to Britain.

Instead, with little or no warning (certainly not enough to

let Vera know that they would not be eloping to Bermuda), he found himself heading up to a military camp on the northern shores of Lake Ontario, so that instructors could properly assess the twenty-four-year-old vegetarian pacifist's suitability for 'work in the field'. And where better, given that as yet BSC had no proper training facilities of their own, for the young Norwegian-speaker to be put through his paces than 'Little Norway', a training camp set up by and for exiled Norwegians – allowing him to perpetuate the myth that he was one of their fellow countrymen. Though the camp was primarily a school for would-be naval pilots, using a fleet of thirty-six Fairchild PT-19 trainers purchased from the United States with the aim of one day spearheading moves to reclaim their homeland, the basic training course was testing enough. The camp's instructors duly recommended JBW's suitability, and with that T. Ifor Rees was able to cable London:

June 4th 1941: From His Majesty's Consul-General, Mexico City.

Volunteer from Mexico Mr J. B. Wood.

Refers to Foreign Office telegram No. 113 of 13th May (W5504/19/49)

States that Mr Wood first offered his services at the Consulate General in San Francisco on or about the 10th April 1940. The matter was later referred to the Consulate at Los Angeles. Mr Wood now prefers to take up the question of possible service in Canada. Registry Number: W7516/19/49

Only this being wartime, Canada was not in Canada. It was in New York.

*

Arriving by train from Toronto at the beginning of July, he made his way across town to Fifth Avenue, for the first time in a while without having to look over his shoulder or constantly change transport, walked down to the Rockefeller Center, passed the statue of Prometheus (the supreme trickster), before taking the elevator up to the thirty-sixth floor for his appointment at the suitably anonymous Room 3603, headquarters of British Security Coordination. Though BSC had originally been intended as a propaganda exercise to try and win American hearts and minds to Britain's cause through newspapers and radio, by the time JBW walked through its doors it had grown to become a fully-fledged intelligence operation with its focus increasingly centred on Latin America.

Giving his address as c/o the British Consulate, 25 Broadway, he spent the next two weeks finding his way around Head Office, attending briefings and meetings, liaising with FBI counterparts and, more significantly, taking the train down to Washington to meet BSC's radio communications expert Pat Bayly, recently recruited from Toronto University. Bayly is quietly credited as the brains behind BSC's success in this field, all but nullifying the Abwehr's Latin American threat, much as his better-known colleagues Alan Turing and Gordon Welchman are credited with breaking the Enigma code at Bletchley (both men were houseguests of Bayly in New York during the war).

At the end of his second week, likely spent getting up to date with the latest WT technology (much of it developed by Bayly himself), JBW learnt that he was being sent down to Panama. Unlike Bermuda, this was no holiday destination. Nowhere in Latin America was more crucial to America's interests, or more potentially vulnerable to Axis sabotage. As the US's most important strategic artery, the Canal was seen as more liable to attack than Pearl Harbor, ensuring that Latin America was often the first item on the agenda at meetings of the US War, Navy and State Departments.

And with that Stephenson's new man in Panama collected his visa, was issued with an advance copy of journalist John Gunther's *Inside Latin America* by way of background reading, then on 21 July 1941 headed out to LaGuardia Airport. With no night flights over Latin America, he made an overnight stop at the border town of Brownsville, Texas, where his career as an intelligence officer – 'spy' if you must – got off to a less than auspicious start. Clearly the sound of an English accent in Brownsville (which back then JBW still had) was rare enough to attract the attention of the local newspaper. 'British Worker Here', the *Brownsville Herald* reported. 'John Bryan Wood of San Francisco, California, arrived at Brownsville Airport Friday morning on his way to Panama City to assume duties as clerk at the British legation there. Mr Wood left here via Pan American Airways' morning plane.'

Lesson learnt – this would be the last time JBW's name appeared in print, at least for a good few years.

JBW contravening
Sufi Vow 5a (I will not
drink), Panama, 1941.

Diary record of April 1942 visit to Camp X,
courtesy of ' रानी ' – erstwhile girlfriend of JBW
smuggled into a nearby apartment.

JBW (seated left of table).

8.

Panama

'The female staff in our office often talked about an absent officer who was undergoing instruction near Toronto at Camp X, the British training centre for secret agents. An untidy redhead, he was a mysterious figure, of unknown nationality, described as being brilliant but eccentric. For instance, he had been seen sitting Buddha style for long periods under a tree.'

Dorothy Maclean, *To Hear the Angels Sing* (1980)

On Monday, 28 July 1941, JBW reported for duty at BSC's Central American station (code no. 72000) on Panama City's Avenida Perú, a mile or so east of the Canal Zone.

Panama's distinctive geography, 'like an elephant's raised trunk stretching out from mainland Colombia', Gunther's *Inside Latin America* began, meant that 'as everybody knows, the canal cuts crosswise through the peculiar configuration of the isthmus, and the eastern end is on the Pacific side, not the Atlantic'.

Certainly the Japanese knew. As far back as 1930 their agents had been photographing Panama's shipping and defence systems; so too the Germans, who retained 'two splendid boys' in place supplying detailed specification reports and photographs of its locks, installations and equipment, enabling the Abwehr – it was later discovered – to construct an exact replica of the canal beside Berlin's Lake Wannsee, with the aim of pinpointing exactly where and how they could inflict the most damage. 'Two of my bombs,' Hermann Goering boasted, 'dropped on the Culbra Cut would render the entire waterway unusable in ten minutes.'

To add to Washington's jitters, the country had recently elected the staunchly pro-Hitler President Arias, who in his inaugural address had threatened that just as 'Panama has ceded its territory to the United States to construct the Canal, Panama also can cede territory to the Germany of Adolf Hitler, so that they can construct here what they wish and can help us against Imperialism'.

As a result the Canal Zone itself was now as heavily defended a strip of land as anywhere in the entire continent. Despite thick jungle in places stretching almost to the banks of the Canal, it concealed some of the world's most powerful defensive batteries ('I saw enormous guns – some are 16-inch, some are 14-inch, hidden along the fringes'). Any ship hoping to pass through was required to undergo a full inspection by the US military, who, if in any doubt, would wrap the entire vessel in netting as a precaution against explosives or bombs being dropped over the side.

With some 65,000 American troops and support workers stationed there, you'd have done well to spot any of the dozen or so BSC staff, operating under the cover of the Economic Attaché of the British Legation, headed up by a Squadron-Leader Peter Wood (no relation), a relaxed figure for a military man, doing his bit to counter the oppressive heat by handing round iced pink gins at eleven o'clock every morning. However, BSC's real head was the Legation's Second Secretary, twenty-seven-year-old Peter Dwyer. Dwyer's staff consisted of just three intelligence officers (including the new 'assistant commissioner', JBW), a courier and half a dozen secretarial staff drafted down from Canada, whose duties included everything from typing to sorting through the mail – other people's mail – looking for any mention of known Axis sympathizers or letters that simply didn't make any sense, suggesting they might be written in code.

Freed up from his previous posting in Paris by Hitler's invading forces, Dwyer had been in Panama for over a year by the time JBW arrived. His proficiency in French, German, Italian and now Spanish ensured that, much like JBW, he had spent most of his time at Oxford studying anything but his chosen subject (Modern Languages), preferring instead to devote his time and talent to producing and directing amateur theatre, which explains both his third-class degree and subsequent fledgling career with Fox Films and Movietone News – before being invited in for a chat at the offices of the Minimax Fire Extinguisher Company at 54 Broadway, long known to London taxi drivers as MI6.

As a photograph from his time in Latin America suggests – cocktail glass in one hand, cigarette in the other, cane suitcase at his feet, propping up a bar in Panama City – Dwyer's easygoing manner, affable charm and sharp sense of humour quickly endeared him to his American hosts, so much so that his next posting would be as BSC's liaison officer to J. Edgar Hoover and he would end up as SIS station chief in Washington. Viewed as one of SIS's most talented young officers, not least for having identified the atomic bomb spy Klaus Fuchs, he was tipped for high office, only to unexpectedly throw in the towel in the late 1940s and return to his first love as head of Canada's Arts Council, before going on to become 'perhaps the best-known person in the Canadian arts community'. As his replacement in Washington, a certain Kim Philby, conceded in his memoir *My Silent War*: 'I knew him for a brilliant wit, and was to learn that he had a great deal more to him than just wit.'

Coming from an artistic background, Dwyer rather enjoyed JBW's oddball nature and various eccentricities, cross-legged under palm trees or otherwise (to the Canadian secretarial staff 'he was definitely odd') and was only too happy to find someone with an equivalent education washing up in such an unlikely setting. Doubtless he was also glad to have someone with JBW's WT skillset and fluent Spanish (and by now passable German) on board, arriving as he did at a time when Admiral Doenitz's U-boats were seemingly able to pick off British-registered vessels at will as soon as they cleared Panamanian waters.

To help counter the threat, Allied shipping had taken to passing through the Canal after dark with all lights extinguished, much to the local Abwehr agent's frustration: 'Impossible to see anything of the Canal as they admit no one to that part without a pass with full details of what they are there for [. . .] and most of them pass late at night after dark.' This meant that JBW was having to work nights – in a shuttered, airless spare office tucked away on the American air base, with banks of electronics and telegraph equipment humming away, hardly helped by the tropical climate and absence of air-conditioning.

As in Mexico, intercepts largely relied on any mistakes that the Abwehr's Latin American operators were apt to make – being either poorly trained, failing to use the more advanced ciphers or else having never received the codes in the first place. Though the immediate requirement was for any indication of U-boat numbers or advance warning of impending attacks, careless operators would sometimes inadvertently reveal details of the Abwehr's Bolivar network or contacts within the United States itself, which would then be relayed back to Bletchley Park using the FBI's communications network. Such was the success of BSC's eavesdropping that by the time the United States entered the war the FBI had all but wrapped up the Nazi network operating north of the border, with no less than 'thirty-six of the forty-two German agents arrested by the FBI in 1941 and 1942 identified with the help of information from Rockefeller Center'.

If any of BSC's staff on the thirty-sixth floors of the Rockefeller Center were still labouring under the impression that they were working for the British, Stephenson's Latin American operatives had no such illusions: 'All BSC's work before Pearl Harbor had one thing in common: it proved as useful to the United States as it did to Britain. [. . .] In Latin America, where United States security was particularly vulnerable, it would have had to contend with an enemy holding virtually unchallenged sway.' And as Hoover was only too aware, 'because legally he had no authority to employ agents outside the United States proper; the British, therefore, could carry out some of the unpleasant or illegal chores in that region'.

For now though, the Abwehr's dominance was exacerbated by the dearth of Spanish-speakers in BSC, leaving Dwyer's three agents – quite possibly the only three Spanish-speaking agents available to Stephenson at the time – to cover the whole of 'Mexico, Central America and all South American countries lying north of Brazil and Peru'. JBW's own field of operation extended to Colombia, Guatemala, Ecuador, El Salvador – with particular emphasis on Venezuela, at the time the world's leading oil exporter. (Coincidentally the very same countries he had been granted visas for back in Paris – make of that what you will.)

Stephenson had given his agent's licence to operate as, how and where the need was greatest, a step up from JBW's WT role in Mexico (assuming his role in Mexico *had* been largely confined to WT duties): he was now a fully-fledged frontline agent in one of the few areas of the globe where he would be operating in close proximity to his opposite numbers, who – as Captain Wiedmann's agents in San Francisco had made only too clear – were unlikely to share his pacifist beliefs, still less to start each day with a list of daily vows, other perhaps than to Der Führer.

On 21 September, little more than a month after arriving in Panama, he was boarding the short Pan Am hopper flight to Colombia – Pan Am was the carrier of choice for BSC agents, Latin American airlines being mostly operated by Axis-friendly companies and flown by ex-Luftwaffe pilots – touching down in Barranquilla, Colombia's main northern port, and returning there the following week. This was followed on 1 October by a meeting with the suitably mysterious Señor César Dugada in a Guatemala City hotel, sandwiched in between regular commutes to Venezuela, no doubt to check out whose oil tankers were harboured in the country's main port, La Guaira. With as yet no transmitters up and running in either country, his initial task was to roll out BSC's successful Ships' Observers Scheme, given the U-boat threat and the limitless opportunities South America's endless coastline afforded Doenitz's fleet to refuel and resupply. As in San Francisco, successful implementation relied heavily on the shipping companies themselves – many of whose crews were ex-Basque and only too willing to keep a log of which flags were fluttering over the bows of which

152

ships, where they might be heading and who or what they might be carrying.

However, it was one thing to set up a Ships' Observers Scheme in California, quite another to operate as a frontline agent in Latin America.

And so sometime in early November JBW found himself heading 2,500 miles north, to the familiar surroundings of Whitby on the northern shore of Lake Ontario. This time, however, he was not going to Little Norway but four miles further along the shoreline, where BSC was setting up their own camp, better known as Camp X. It was the first dedicated training camp for spies anywhere on the continent and run along much the same lines as SOE's Beaulieu training camp back in Britain, even down to importing some of its instructors and using the same manuals – with the young WT operator from Panama among the first to attend.

Other than a single wooden hut, little remains of the camp itself, though a small band of enthusiasts keep the flame burning with fundraising, tours and a dedicated website. 'Is your relative in this picture?' a caption optimistically asks above some grainy photographs of men in uniform. Highly unlikely. Known officially as Special Training School 103, to the instructors and recruits it was simply 'The Farm', being on the site of a 260-acre farm. Not exactly the type of Farm that Shabaz Best and Murshida Martin had had in mind back in Rio de Janeiro when first elevating the young JBW to the status of Farmer, certainly if BSC's own account of what went on there (published some fifty years after Camp X closed) is anything to go by. But it was perhaps rather better suited to his talents.

The first groups to train there consisted largely of

resistance fighters, special forces and intelligence officers of various nationalities, with the aim, as at Little Norway, of then parachuting them back into their homeland. However, William Stephenson's ultimate aim was to provide a proper facility for his American hosts, who as yet had nowhere for specialist training, let alone experience of covert warfare and special operations. As they themselves would later acknowledge, back in 1941 'they were still green and in awe of their British tutors, yet within a decade they had lifted intelligence work to unheard-of levels of technological perfection'.

Various legends have grown up around what exactly went on at Camp X, fuelled by the likes of Ian Fleming (though there is no evidence he so much as set foot in the place) with tales of initiative tests involving dummy explosives being placed in Toronto's power station, trainees assassinating supposed German agents or, as in *Live and Let Die*, swimming underwater to attach limpet mines to the hulls of offshore tankers. The cover story fed to local journalists and residents of the neighbouring towns was that it was a test-ground for explosives training – to the delight of Camp X's British demolitions expert in Canada there was no shortage of explosives: the only reference JBW ever made to his time there was supplementing his diet with a few fresh fish courtesy of a spare stick of dynamite lobbed into Lake Ontario.

Given that, unlike the vast majority of those who went through the notoriously tough courses at Camp X, he had no military experience or background, his initial training was doubtless intended to toughen him up, with his instructors all hardened SOE veterans. They clearly did their job: for all his pacifist beliefs and enlightened spiritualism, my mother would always retain a visceral, physical fear of JBW throughout their marriage and beyond.

Understandably so, given that – as BSC's *Official History* recorded – recruits were taught 'how to shadow a man and how to escape surveillance, how to creep up behind an armed sentry and kill him instantly without noise, how to evade capture by blinding an assailant with a box of matches. In the unarmed combat course [recruits] learnt many holds whose use would enable [them] to break an adversary's arm or leg, or knock him unconscious or kill him outright. [They were] given weapons training, learning how to handle a tommy-gun and use different types of revolvers and automatic pistols, firing them from a crouching position either in daylight or darkness. [They were] instructed in the use of a knife, which killed quickly and silently if driven upwards just below the ribs. Much of [their] time would be spent mastering the art of sabotage: the simplest way of putting a car out of commission without leaving any trace of [their] interference; how to attach explosives to a railway track or oil tank to cause the greatest damage; how to make simple grenades and incendiary devices using materials that could easily be purchased. Before the course was finished, [they] could make and write with secret inks, use different kinds of codes and cyphers for communication with agents and interrogate prisoners to best effect. [They were] trained in parachute jumping [and] took part in night exercises in which one group of students would set out to sabotage a specific target, while others were allocated the job of stopping them.'

Though the courses varied in length, JBW likely stayed no longer than two or three weeks, given the dearth of Spanish-speaking BSC agents in Latin America. On 13 November, relying as ever on intuition, he had sent a telegram from Whitby to congratulate Erica on the birth of her first child

('I'll know when the baby arrives' – or perhaps not: the young Michael Hathaway had arrived on 11 November) before making his way back down to Panama and returning to his apartment in the City's Quarry Heights district – to judge by his photograph, beer bottle in hand, noticeably fitter than the JBW of two years before.

On 4 December 1941 he bought a ($143.10) Pan Am round-robin ticket, once again calling in at Barranquilla before heading on to Venezuela, returning to Panama two days later, on 7 December. He retained his ticket, to be filed away in amongst all his Sufi paperwork, most likely as a souvenir of the events of that day – a day that for Peter Dwyer and his team in the Avenida Perú would be remembered as the day the Japanese did not attack the Panama Canal. Both there and on the thirty-sixth floor of the Rockefeller Center, the attack on Pearl Harbor was if anything a cause for (discreet) celebration: 'white-faced Americans stopped in the street, utterly unnerved and incredulous. In contrast, we were jubilant to realize that we would no longer be alone in fighting the Nazis.'

In some respects America's entry into the war made little difference to Dwyer's station, other than that they were now working hand-in-hand with their FBI colleagues officially rather than unofficially, and it made even less difference to JBW, tasked with training up their WT operators to a level where they could run and maintain their own monitoring posts. As far back as Mexico City, it had been standard practice to share any intelligence gained through wireless intercepts with Hoover's FBI. As a result JBW had built up a close working relationship with his American counterparts, furthered by Hathaway Snr's regular invites to high-society dos and diplomatic functions in San Francisco – cemented by his involvement with the Ships' Observers Scheme. These officers would now form the backbone of their own intelligence agency, the Office of Strategic Services (OSS), and in turn its post-war successor, the CIA – and would continue to cross paths with JBW through the next few decades and beyond. (They included a thirty-three-year-old volunteer, Edward Lansdale, destined to become perhaps the CIA's best-known if somewhat controversial officer.)

This connection, aside from contributing to JBW's transatlantic accent, explains how and why those self-same former FBI colleagues would continue to grant JBW the benefit of the doubt in years to come, no matter what.

All of which would have been news to Samuel Lewis, still with no reason to think that his friend was anything other than Norwegian and that, like many of his countrymen, he was simply working alongside their British allies: 'I am interested in news of your trip,' Lewis wrote – in amongst several pages of wazifas and 'higher thoughts' – 'here they're saying that there are British Secret Service agents in many places. A few years back and no one would dream that we Americans would help the British.'

Unfortunately, his old friends Mr Mynors of His Majesty's Treasury and Mr Allchin of His Majesty's Foreign & Commonwealth Office were under no such illusions as to his nationality. And were still very much on his trail – in spite of T. Ifor Rees's continuing efforts – with Mynors firing off telegrams to the Bank of England demanding that 'a firm line be taken with Mr Wood' and that 'he should be sent a copy of the Defence (Finance) Regulations'. His name remained on the 'Quitters' list 'in view of refusal to return from the United States', Allchin clearly unaware that JBW

157

was working for BSC or in Latin America – such was the need for wartime secrecy.

In early 1942 BSC and Pat Bayly finally managed to track down and purchase a ten-kilowatt transmitter from a Philadelphia radio station, which was then transported up to Lake Ontario and installed at Camp X. It was powerful enough to form the basis for BSC's own transmitting station (called 'Hydra'), which would soon grow in size to house three separate transmitters working ten hours a day sending some 30,000 message groups, mostly across the Atlantic, with their antenna passed off to locals as part of the Canadian Broadcasting Corporation's transmission station.

Among the first recruits sent up to Lake Ontario to familiarize themselves with the new system was Stephenson's young WT operator from Panama. With commercial flights being all but unobtainable following Pearl Harbor, he'd hitched a lift with the US forces as far as New York, reported in to the Rockefeller Center for his briefing, then taken the train to Toronto, stopping off on the way to spend the Easter weekend skiing in Quebec, arriving at Camp X on 7 April 1942 to spend three weeks getting to grips both with Hydra and with Pat Bayly's latest invention, the 'Rockex'.

Rockex was a One-Time-Tape cipher system, which finally allowed operatives to write a tape message in plain text. The tape would then be fed into a transmitter terminal with a special 'scrambler', providing a one-off encoded message which would then be reversed or unscrambled by the receiving terminal. The real value for agents in the field was that from now on messages could be sent straight to Camp X from anywhere in Latin America that BSC had listening posts.

Unlike on his previous visit to Camp X, he was lodged in a downtown apartment – possibly because a fire had burned down some of the accommodation huts – with his evenings and weekends spent cramming up on the various cipher codes and systems, Rockex, Playfair, Double Transposition etc.

But clearly not all his evenings and weekends.

Back in New York he had met up with a fellow Sufi who, having done away with her Western name, simply signed herself रानी (which translates as 'Rani' or 'Hindu Queen'). He and रानी had travelled up to Canada together and were now ensconced in Apartment 615, 64 West St Clair, twenty miles from Camp X. To her credit, unlike her fellow Sufis, in the short time she had known him, रानी managed to work out that his name might not be Jøn and that he might not be Norwegian after all.

In her 'Scrap Book for Bryan – The desire of the moth for the star', she recorded in detail her week of passion with her 'eater of grass in a world of torn flesh', not least where and when it was consummated (on the overnight train to Toronto), before going on to shine an unlikely light into what he was up to at Camp X: 'Monday, April 13th 1942. Today you are having the exam for which you studied with such quiet concentration yesterday – turning the long slippery pages of the Radio Handbook, and when you catch my gaze and glance at me your extraordinary eyes were full of diagrams and your features were like figures – 9s and 4s.' For his part, when not cramming up on ciphers and codes, JBW did his best to teach रानी a little of his Spanish, possibly with a view to her joining him in Latin America. 'Coffee on the propped-up pillows in our nice huge bed – your radio book – my Spanish grammar. You try so patiently to teach me, making the language have meaning & relation to other tongues – not just rules & I try to behave like a good obedient pupil in my white Chinese pyjama top but the button is missing and I put your hand on my breast. You tried to demur, very Puritan. It was two in the afternoon & we weren't up yet "but you're having a Spanish lesson". Everything I love best of you was gone and you were only English.'

But for whatever reason रानी never did make it to Panama, leaving her eater of grass, scrapbook in hand, to return to his Quarry Heights apartment alone.

With Hydra up and running, he spent the next few months setting up a series of monitoring stations from Ecuador across to Venezuela's eastern seaboard and all the way up to Guatemala, a far-from-straightforward task given that the Abwehr already had their own network and accompanying agents in situ. True to his beliefs, if against Camp X's training, he went about his business armed with nothing more than his copy of *Inside Latin America*, which, aside from providing an insight into the politics and make-up of each country (John Gunther had interviewed the leaders of sixteen of the region's twenty countries), also contained a surprisingly informed assessment of the threat posed by Fifth Columnists, even going so far as to provide a breakdown of whom he could expect to encounter on his various travels: 'There are 443 Germans in Honduras, of whom 177 live in the capital Tegucigalpa, 199 Italians and 2 Japanese.'

By October the first monitoring stations became fully operational, and by the end of the year the network covered Barranquilla, Caracas, Montevideo, Lima, Quito, Santiago, Trinidad, San José and São Paolo, all of which could now safely transmit encoded material directly to Camp X. With the help of the cryptographic section of the FBI's Technical Laboratory (and a German double agent), this ensured that virtually all radio traffic between Latin America and Germany could now be read, finally giving BSC the edge over Canaris's Bolivar network.

For his own part, JBW was almost a victim of his own success, his WT skillset sufficiently valuable to both the British and his American hosts for him to be tied to his desk perhaps more than he would have liked, the WT operator's lot being a lonely one, working long, often fruitless hours, headphones clamped to ear scanning the airwaves, almost invariably at night.

With a coup d'état putting an end to Amulfo Arias's Panamanian presidency, JBW was earmarked for a move down to South America, most likely to Rio de Janeiro, given that it was one of the only two existing Latin American SIS stations. Quite likely his favoured option, given that it was home to South America's Sufi movement, but it was not to be. Instead he received a telegram from Room 3603 informing him that he was being transferred to Buenos Aires. A rather more testing post than Rio de Janeiro, certainly one that was unlikely to see him sitting cross-legged under palm trees for hours on end on his days off – Buenos Aires was now the epicentre of Abwehr activity in Latin America and as dangerous a place for a British intelligence officer as anywhere in the entire continent.

Only this time he would not be travelling alone.

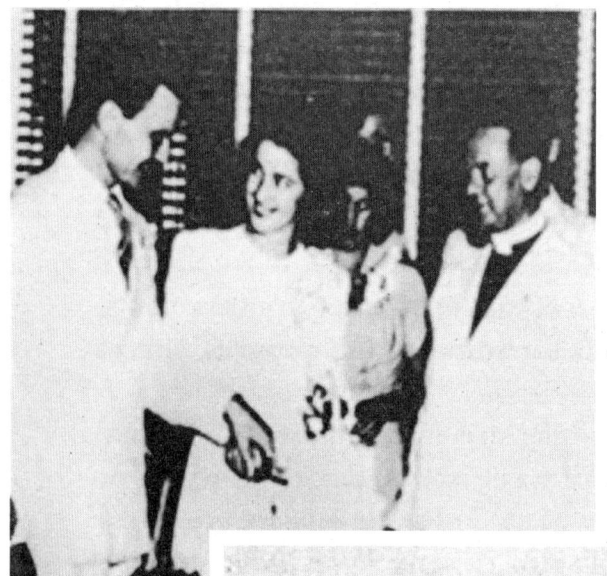

'When he stopped by my desk waving a telegram posting him to Buenos Aires, I instantly knew I had to marry him,' Dorothy Maclean, November 1942.

Número de Orden __58538__

Nacionalidad __Inglesa__

Núm. Cédula Ident. _____

Edad __22__ Color __Blanco__

Pelo __Castaño__ Ojos __Azules__

Dirección __Bellavista #__

__Panamá, R.de P.__

New York
November 19th 1942.

My dear Don Juan,

Congratulations from Gladys and myself and Ariadne. I hope it keeps fine for you both. Best of luck.

Regarding your letter, don't bother your head about the MT stuff. We transferred you to B.A. because you were required there much more than for the MT job in Panama. I understand that it was found unnecessary to continue it there. I am certain you will like the job in B.A.

The delay in fixing up Dorothy's movements is not due to us. We asked B.A. to hasten. (By the way, Joseph Schaeffer envies you very much!)

Tell Dorothy the wedding does not upset our arrangements at all. If necessary we shall have to replace her. I am waiting to see F.O. about this.

All the best. Pat joins me in wishing you a merry new marriage, and the best of everything.

Buenos Aires: 'happy hunting ground to numberless Axis agents.'

9.

Buenos Aires

'After the wedding we flew south. It was
only when he produced a British passport at
the airport that I learned my new husband
was not, after all, Norwegian.'

Dorothy Maclean, *Memoirs of an Ordinary Mystic* (2010)

On 17 November 1942 JBW married Dorothy Maclean
in Panama City's Catholic cathedral. A smattering of BSC
employees were on hand to witness, with both bride and
groom wearing white. Since JBW was yet to become the
obsessively camera-shy figure of later years, here at least
there is a wedding photograph: Dorothy with her trademark smile that seemed to involve the whole of her face (a
smile which many years later I would come to know well),
JBW – no doubt pleading poverty – sporting the same white
double-breasted jacket he wore back at the Mullsjö language
school. The brief ceremony was overseen by the city's Angli-
can bishop, likely drafted in to please unavoidably absent
parents (Anglicans on both sides), who in any case would
have had no inkling of JBW's Sufism.

Much like his bride.

Given that he was being posted to Latin America's most
Axis-friendly country – and according to one OSS officer,

by far the most dangerous, 'much worse than Casablanca', with some 12,000 paid-up members of the Nazi Party – wedding bells may not have been what his Rockefeller Center bosses wanted to hear. If so, they remained cheerfully polite about it. 'My dear Don Juan, Don't bother your head about the WT stuff. We transferred you to BA because you were required much more there than for the WT job in Panama. I understand that it was found unnecessary to continue there. I am certain you will like the job in BA. The delay in fixing up Dorothy's movements is not due to us. We asked BA to hasten. (By the way, George Schaeffer envies you very much!) Tell Dorothy the wedding does not upset our arrangements at all. If necessary we shall have to replace her. I am waiting to see P. D. [Peter Dwyer] about this. Pat [Bayly] sends his regards.'

Clearly BSC were rather better informed about JBW's revised marital status than his longtime girlfriend Cil Egeberg. Though his planned 'gap year' in Latin America was now in its fourth year, a regular 'From your Cil' letter, along with photos of her and her Oslo garden, was still managing to reach JBW every few weeks, despite the German occupation of her homeland and his nomadic existence. And yet for all his WT expertise, from an early age having managed to communicate with the furthest corners of the globe, news of his revised marital status somehow failed to make it back to Norway.

Cil could perhaps count herself fortunate, certainly by comparison to Vera Corda. Just as his Cambridge friends had taken it for granted he would end up with Cil, so too the Sufi community assumed he would end up with Vera, more or less his constant companion back in California ('I was always with him and he was always with me') – just as soon as she could arrange a divorce from her US Navy husband. Hatha-way Snr, however, had other ideas. Meeting Vera for the first time when she and JBW arrived to spend a weekend at his Santa Barbara home, he had felt obliged to undiplomatic-ally intervene, telling JBW in no uncertain terms that 'she'd be a disaster as a diplomat's wife'. The following morning JBW had quietly departed, 'explaining that he felt uncom-fortable accepting our hospitality after what had happened'. More uncomfortable still, he'd all but persuaded Vera to up sticks and join him in Bermuda, at the time pencilled in as his next posting. 'We really planned on my getting to Bermuda and [. . .] were planning to be married there, I don't know – things were cut off so suddenly.' Only for JBW to head up to Toronto with रानी. Six months on he was now heading off into the sunset with Dorothy Maclean, who, up until he'd had to show his passport as they were boarding the plane to Buenos Aires, had no idea he was even English.

'You'd think,' a bemused Harold Shergold would reflect half a century later, 'the first thing anyone would want to know about the person they're marrying would be their nationality. Aside, perhaps, from their sex.'

In Dorothy's defence, it was a spur-of-the-moment deci-sion. True, they'd dated once or twice, but with a ratio of 500 men to every woman in the Canal Zone, she was not short of dates. 'As a former wallflower I very much enjoyed my new-found popularity.' Besides, intriguing as JBW might be, by common consent he was 'definitely odd': 'He spoke of the lost continent of Atlantis as if it were a vital part of the history of our planet.' For JBW the attraction was perhaps a little easier to understand: he was something of an outsider, whereas Dorothy was very much the carefree, popular insider. She'd already turned him down once, 'because I could see his faults, and because people were warning me against him, suspicious of his oddity', but then one morning he'd stopped by her desk waving the telegram from BSC New York confirming that he was being posted to Buenos Aires and – for better or (as her fellow Canadian secretaries warned) for worse – 'I instantly knew that I had to marry him'.

Not her first leap into the unknown, nor her last. A graduate of the University of Western Ontario, Dorothy had taken a job with an insurance office in Toronto, until a family friend had dropped by one day and enigmatically suggested she might want to try for something a little more adventurous. A month later she was boarding the overnight train to New York, chaperoned by a Scottish woman, Sheena Govan, who then shepherded her from Union Street Station to the Rockefeller Center, where she was briefly introduced to a fellow Canadian – BSC's chief William Stephenson (a disarmingly short man as she recalled). 'Secretarial' was as much as she was told about the job, and only when she was asked to sign the Official Secrets Act on her first morning with a warning never to discuss her work with outsiders did she realize she was working for British Intelligence. Looking back on her time there, and whenever she watched later television documentaries on BSC, she'd always be surprised how little her fellow secretaries knew about what BSC was really up to – with the intelligence work proper left to a coterie of imported ex-Oxbridge types, quietly going about the business of obtaining essential supplies for the British war effort, investigating enemy activities, taking measures against sabotage to shipping and property and trying to get American public opinion on Britain's side. But BSC's most enduring legacy was in helping its hosts create their own dedicated intelligence service – as Dorothy witnessed firsthand, with small groups of Americans regularly trooping past her desk on their way to William Stephenson's office, among them Bill Donovan, head of the Office of Strategic Services (OSS).

Exciting as Manhattan and the likes of Radio City, Greenwich Village and Coney Island might be, hearing tales of tropical climates, glamorous lifestyles and that the BSC station in Belize operated from a yacht moored offshore on the edge of a coral reef, she'd volunteered her services, only to be told: 'This is not, repeat not, a travel agency.' But it soon would be.

'They need secretaries in Panama,' someone had mentioned in passing, and with that Dorothy was on her way – via Houston, Brownsville, Mexico City and Costa Rica, as was then the hop-on hop-off way of airline travel. A few months later and the newly married Dorothy Wood was on her way again, this time boarding a Pan Am DC3 en route to Buenos Aires, crossing over the Andes – 'we seemed to almost touch the sides of the mountains' – stopping off in Lima, then heading down the coast down to Santiago, before skimming back over the Andes a day or two later, thence to Buenos Aires, to be met by traffic that 'churns, roars, grunts, seethes on shining boulevards [. . .] with not a single traffic light in all of Buenos Aires, not one flicker of red or green or amber from dusk to dusk. Reason: the Argentines experimented with traffic lights, and then gave up the idea, because no one would obey them.'

Certainly for the first few weeks Buenos Aires was very much the honeymoon that her husband had promised (but which, needless to say, had never quite happened). 'We stayed in a small hotel, ate our meals in the many wonderful restaurants and learned to drink wine noon and night as the locals did.' The standard of living was such that they could easily get by on their salaries – or to be more exact, on Dorothy's: 'I continued to receive the equivalent of my New York salary, which was lavish by Argentine standards, so we lived on my earnings while John put his in the bank.' At weekends, when not exploring the *barrios* or staying in *estancias*, they took to the water, waving to their opposite numbers from the German and Japanese delegations on the River Tigre, the latter recognizable by the rising sun on their oars. For Christmas they took the ferry across the mouth of the Rio de la Plata, sunning themselves on the beaches of Uruguay, with the only hint of trouble a dressing-down for JBW from the local police for not wearing a bathing top.

Of rather more concern to JBW (or rather BSC agent 75703), Buenos Aires was home to some quarter of a million German-Argentines who, between them, controlled the bulk of the country's shipping, many of its newspapers and two of its banks, and was by now very much the epicentre of Germany's smuggling and espionage operations in Latin America. Not that this stopped Camp X recruits from seeing it as a plum posting: 'I was pretty excited, since I was told Buenos Aires was a hotbed of German agents,' one such graduate enthused. As, some forty years later, sometime during that long, rainy weekend following his mother's funeral, JBW recalled only too clearly. He'd been telling my brother and me about his time in Saigon, which had led on to some of the close calls he'd had there. So I'd asked, being just about young enough to get away with it, whether Vietnam had been his most dangerous posting, thinking he might say Berlin. 'Oh no, that would have to be Buenos Aires,' he'd replied without a moment's hesitation, though true to form he didn't go into details.

In the end it was Harold Shergold who explained the discrepancy between Dorothy's memories of 'BA' and her husband's. Spouses, Shergy told me, would always be the last to know what their partners were up to, as much for their own sake as anything. As my own mother could readily attest, claiming to have had no idea what operations JBW was working on most of the time in Berlin, and certainly knew better than to ever ask. OSS went even further, with all married officers automatically barred from Latin America.

Given the posting's 'degree of difficulty' and the continuing shortage of Spanish-speakers, let alone experienced WT operators, the Buenos Aires station numbered just four officers, with a support staff of half a dozen, Dorothy included. Unlike in Panama, they worked out of the Embassy building itself (not that you'll find any of them listed in the Official Register of Foreign Office employees), headed up by Sir David Kelly, an old Argentine hand, and his charismatic wife Marie-Noële de Jourda de Vaux, one of the 'grande dames' of British diplomacy.

For all Marie-Noële and Sir David's best efforts, endless drinks parties included, and despite the two countries' long-established commercial ties – from a local branch of Harrods to ownership of the railways – President Ramón Castillo's idea of neutrality was heavily tilted in favour of the Axis. Though he had banned the wearing of uniforms and regalia at the pro-Nazi 'Ausland Organization' marches and gatherings, little attempt was made to close down the organization itself – or the Abwehr's formidable espionage network and smuggling operations. Raw materials and desperately needed commodities, especially black-market platinum, palladium, drugs and other chemicals, were still being secreted on board neutral shipping to Spain or Portugal while, in the opposite direction, everything from electronic equipment – including an entire wireless transmitter disguised as a piano – to numerous Abwehr agents skulking out of sight on the lower decks headed back across the Atlantic to Argentina (had they but known it, dry runs for the post-war ratlines).

To help stem the tide, BSC continued with its tried-and-trusted Ships' Observers Scheme, with JBW again looking to the local Basque and Spanish Republican community for recruits, their numbers boosted by the sizeable ex-pat Italian community, many of whom had no great love for Mussolini's fascism. Having long since graduated from his purely WT role to fully-fledged frontline intelligence operative, JBW was now also very much expected to get his hands dirty. Or certainly his feet wet.

Offered, as a British Embassy employee, honorary membership of Buenos Aires's Hurlingham Club – closed even to Argentines – he had (predictably) instead chosen to join the city's small but dedicated Norwegian Rowing Club, not least since his presence there was less likely to attract the attention of his Abwehr counterparts, given that 'he spoke Norwegian so perfectly that the Norwegians there, mostly captains and crews of whaling ships, accepted him as one of their countrymen'. Of an evening he would quietly help himself to one of the club's single-scull boats and slip out into the Buenos Aires estuary – his student rowing days on the River Cam not entirely wasted – silently gliding under cover of darkness among the various ships at anchor, hoping to eavesdrop on the crews – or more especially the passengers as they came out on deck for a smoke or to stretch their legs. Not that such night-time forays were entirely successful: amongst the passengers who managed to slip past him was the newly appointed commander of the Abwehr's entire South American network, Johannes Becker, who arrived in February 1943 concealed in the bowels of a cargo ship from Spain. Becker's orders, issued in person in Berlin, were to concentrate all espionage activities in Latin America on radio communication, with Buenos Aires the focal point for all such contact.

For some months BSC and their American Radio Intelligence Division partners had been logging a steady increase in radio traffic to Hamburg, with a network of up to ten transmitters suspected to be operating in Argentina – reason in itself for Pat Bayly to have dispatched JBW down to Buenos Aires at short notice. Though unable to decipher much of the contents, the Government Code and Cipher School (later GCHQ) were being fed enough raw material (via Hydra) to have a clear picture of the more important parts of the German intelligence set-up in Argentina. However, the sheer size and strength of the Abwehr in Buenos Aires meant that the presence of Pat Bayly's young WT operator did not go unnoticed, even without bumping into him on the River Tigre of a Sunday. 'Argentina was a happy hunting ground for numberless Axis agents,' BSC's own historians wrote, though for their quarry it was not such a happy experience. As one of Stephenson's own officers noted following a brief visit to the city: 'The Argentine was very pro-German. We were trailed everywhere. It was most uncomfortable. Our rooms were searched every day. It was horrible. I was very glad to get out of there.'

Not that the newly arrived Johannes Becker had it all his own way. With the tide of war beginning to turn in the Allies' favour following the defeat at Stalingrad in February 1943, the signs were that some of the Abwehr's network – particularly the non-Germans – might be looking to hedge their bets. Attempting to turn an agent was a hazardous undertaking, even for someone who spoke fluent Spanish and with a network of '*exiliados*' and Basques to fall back on. It was also expensive. In early March a typed note from '48976' in New York to '75703' (JBW) confirmed that he was 'authorized to cash sterling cheques to the extent of £500 a year from official funds. The cheques should be forwarded to London with the accounts for the period in which they are cashed.' Even so, the most valuable resource for BSC remained the ex-pat community, with senior employees of the Argentine railways, meat-packing firms, hydro-electric companies and suchlike forming their own network to counter Abwehr attempts to sabotage their own particular enterprises. Many had not seen Britain since childhood but were still keen to do what they could for the war effort, and by March 1943 nearly all British-controlled railways, power firms, mining companies, oilfields and merchant houses were part of the scheme. Some volunteers even found themselves heading up to Camp X for the same two-week induction course that JBW himself had been through, with lectures on codes and ciphers, techniques of trailing suspects, and not least how to use a revolver.

Exactly how much of this was put into practice remains a moot point. Though BSC agents were permitted to use force where necessary, and sometimes where not – be it 'hastening the journey into the next life' of an American businessman in Mexico supplying petroleum to Germany, taking a baseball bat to the Abwehr's radio transmitters in Ecuador, or going over a few dockyard workers in San Francisco – acts of sabotage and the use of (overt) violence were largely discouraged in Argentina, in case public opinion forced the government or, more worryingly, the local police (neither of whom needed much excuse) to weigh in on behalf of their Axis friends.

Certainly the only violence Dorothy recalled seeing was in June 1943 when President Ramón Castillo was forced out of office. By Latin American standards it was a tame affair. The largely unopposed rebels had simply marched across town to the Casa Rosata (Presidential Palace), taking control with a minimum of fuss. Castillo had already slipped out of the back door and across to Uruguay. JBW had stood amongst the watching crowds as the rebels marched past, joined when safe to do so by Dorothy, whose main memory of the coup was 'the youths who put out their hands to stop the streetcars, ordered everyone out, toppled the cars over, and then set them on fire. After I had watched one boy do this, I looked him straight in the eye as his mother might have done. He had the grace to look ashamed and turn away.'

Castillo would be followed in quick succession by Presidents Ramírez, Farrell and Perón, whose interpretation of neutrality proved rather less nuanced than Castillo's, and before long Argentina would break off diplomatic relations with both Germany and Japan. That same month the American Radio Intelligence Division had started deciphering the Abwehr's wireless traffic between Buenos Aires and Hamburg, with direction-finders pinpointing the location of one of their main network transmitters just outside the city. As a result William Stephenson took the decision to start winding down BSC's operations in Latin America, looking to hand them over to Hoover's FBI.

Not that any of this made much difference to the way Becker and his men went about their business. If anything, Castillo's demise only stiffened their resolve: over the following twelve months Buenos Aires became the most active station in the entire network, sending over a quarter of a million messages back to Hamburg. Nor did it make much difference to the way the Argentine police went about their business.

Soon a nervous FBI, conscious of Roosevelt's Good Neighbour Policy, was flagging up 'the tremendous danger of one of our agents being picked up in Argentina and tortured into a full confession, with consequent publicity throughout the world'. BSC was similarly alarmed. Though JBW had been in Buenos Aires for less than six months, he was coming under ever closer scrutiny by Becker's men, leaving Dorothy to wonder why her husband insisted on changing hotels every few days, never ate in the same restaurant twice and always sat with his back to the wall. Much as he had done back in San Francisco, only more so.

They managed to get out just in time, his FBI counterparts fleeing by boat across the River Plate to Uruguay, JBW and Dorothy jumping on the next plane to Montevideo. Others were not so fortunate. Six days later the Argentine police began to round up virtually the entire network of American and British informants and agents, twenty-one of whom ended up in Buenos Aires's Villa de Voto jail.

Not that Montevideo would turn out to be any less dangerous, though for very different reasons.

Transport official with the Central Uruguayan Railway Company –
JBW's (unlikely) cover occupation, July 1943.

JBW returned to England aboard the SS *Rippingham Grange*, along
with several hundred tons of Argentine beef, June 1944.

10.

Montevideo

'Strange, all the suspicion of JBW. Hugh Grindley,
our boss in Montevideo, had written something
negative about him to HQ. I guess we will never
know, but that report may have started things.'

Dorothy Maclean, letter to the author

On 15 July 1943 JBW managed to escape the Buenos Aires
traffic – and quite possibly a worse fate – the short flight
to Montevideo passing directly over the scuttled Graf Spee
battleship, still visible above the waterline, before touching
down in a city with rather more traffic lights and appreciably
fewer Abwehr agents.

'With broad boulevards, neat suburban homes and an
informal social life, emotionally and spiritually it is the Left
Bank of Buenos Aires,' his trusty *Inside Latin America* guide-
book reassured. More reassuring still, the population was
largely sympathetic to the Allied cause, Uruguay having
long since severed diplomatic relations with Germany.
Even the constant stream of propaganda directed across
the water from Buenos Aires was somewhat muted now
that BSC had blown up the pro-Axis Radio Continental's
transmission mast.

Following his experiences at the hands of Johannes

Becker's henchmen in Buenos Aires, it was perhaps understandable that the newly married JBW might want to opt for a rather more conventional and less fraught occupation. Hence his new job with the Ferrocarril Central del Uruguay, the Central Uruguayan Railway Company.

Given that JBW had seldom if ever travelled by train – a Hudson Tourer being his preferred mode of transport – this was something of a departure. Or as cover stories go, something of a stretch. However, aware that a railway employee's salary was unlikely to cover a city-centre apartment, still less a hotel, he and Dorothy settled for a suburban bungalow in Colón, a half-hour bus ride from the Ferrocarril Central's office, situated over the entrance to Montevideo's Estación Central, and from there a short walk to BSC's office (code no. 75000) on the floor above the Montevideo Stock Exchange.

BSC's small workforce of seven belied its strategic importance. Situated at the mouth of the River Plate, it was ideally positioned to monitor the ever-present U-boat menace still threatening the flow of goods and materiel to North Africa, jumping-off point for the invasion of southern Europe which had begun that same month with the Sicily landings. In the previous year alone some 6.2 million tons of Allied shipping had been lost, with the waters off the neighbouring Brazilian coast providing the easiest pickings. Fortunately, at the start of the war Hitler had ordered that U-boat commanders report their positions twice daily. With BSC and America's Radio Intelligence Division increasingly able to break their codes, Pat Bayly and his team were now able to triangulate the positions of the U-boats JBW was listening in on and alert any nearby shipping – often within just ninety seconds.

As in Buenos Aires, with Axis hopes of winning the war looking ever more remote, within a few weeks of arriving he had successfully managed to turn two of Becker's men, who were soon feeding back a steady stream of planted information, mostly prepared by BSC in New York, such as lengths of runways, false shipping statistics, etc. – everything except, as one of JBW's fellow Montevideo WT operators recalled, 'the one thing their German masters back in Hamburg were most interested in, details of the Allies' sonar submarine detection system'.

One of only two SIS stations covering the whole of Latin America, Montevideo was headed up by Hugh Grindley, the epitome of the old-school type favoured by its pre-war head, Admiral Sir Hugh 'Quex' Sinclair. And a world away from William Stephenson and his clever Canadians. As President of the Uruguayan Polo Association, before the war Grindley would typically work any visit to Head Office and Broadway around the polo season or, on one occasion, around securing grounds for a divorce (in the usual way, with the help of a Miss Roberts in Jermyn Street's Jules Hotel). Dressed in impeccably tailored tweed suits, giant Great Dane at his feet, generous glass of Napoleon brandy to hand and wreaths of smoke from his expensive Havana cigars curling up to the ceiling, Grindley was as different from Peter Dwyer, Pat Bayly et al. as it was possible to be, with a no-nonsense manner and reputation for dealing decisively with those who rubbed him up the wrong way, making him 'a feared and respected figure among the Camp X wireless operators in the region'. 'El Dictador Ingles', as Dorothy and others called him.

Grindley made little attempt to disguise his feelings about now having to answer to BSC New York rather than his old school chums in Broadway, and he certainly resented the arrival of a husband-and-wife team – unheard of back then, SIS's house rule being that women were required to resign the moment they married – even though Dorothy's duties largely 'consisted of taking dictation and typing letters or reports based on the intelligence'.

Grindley's modus operandi owed more to Raymond Chandler than Camp X; one BSC agent recalled him turning up to meet a double agent with a 'fedora pulled low over his eyes and a trench coat turned up at the collar and with the side pockets of his coat bulging ominously'. Though happy enough to accommodate (and claim credit for) the successes of his BSC eavesdroppers, the arrival of a vegetarian, pacifist WT operator of seemingly no fixed nationality and showing few if any detectable signs of patriotism was unlikely to cut much mustard with Grindley, even without JBW being blacklisted as a 'Quitter'. And with an unhealthy back catalogue of currency violations to boot (though Grindley was himself no angel in this respect).

Or perhaps it was simply JBW's mutter and his secretive nature that troubled Grindley, just as it increasingly troubled Dorothy Maclean.

True, Montevideo was a welcome chance to enjoy at least a semblance of normal married life. Rather than constantly changing hotels and in contrast to the hustle and bustle of central Buenos Aires, they now had a house of their own with a garden – complete with gardener and cook – could swim in the ocean at weekends or explore the country – albeit not by rail (fellow passengers might reasonably question why a Ferrocarril Central employee knew nothing about gauges or rolling stock). JBW even made it home in time for dinner of an evening (eavesdropping duties permitting) – the only dark cloud on their domestic bliss being when Dorothy found she was pregnant, which neither she nor, more emphatically, her husband wanted, and 'so we found a clinic and I had an abortion. Though I disliked the process, I never regretted the decision,' she said, before adding, tellingly perhaps, 'an office member told me that John was the most selfish person she had ever met'. Equally tellingly, more than a year into their marriage she still knew next to nothing about her husband, other than his curious belief in the existence of Atlantis and (belatedly) his nationality. On more than one occasion she had 'found him sitting cross-legged on the floor of our sitting room in the middle of the night. I had no idea what he was doing and he explained nothing.' Nor would he, certainly for a while yet, and then only reluctantly.

They'd taken what was billed as a 'holiday' in Brazil, cover for a visit to BSC's São Paolo monitoring station, followed by a week with SIS's Rio de Janeiro station (code no. 75200), which, like Montevideo, was now reporting directly to BSC. Rio de Janeiro was also home to Shabaz Best and the Sufi Lodge at 579 Rua Julio Ottoni where, four years earlier in a parallel existence, Ploughman Wood, yellow cord draped over his left shoulder and tucked under his right arm, had been elevated to the position of Farmer. Having a rare free afternoon, JBW had suggested they visit one of Rio's public parks, only to matter-of-factly abandon Dorothy there 'while he went to visit some friends' – which likely had something to do with his BSC work. Or so she had supposed, though by now she was aware that 'withholding information was more than a professional necessity with him, it was part of his character'. His 'friends' were, of course, Shabaz Best and his fellow Sufis, the reason for his reticence being that Dorothy still had no idea of his Sufi past – or present. However, the following day, at Shabaz Best's insistence, she found herself being welcomed through a doorway topped by a symbol of a winged heart and gently introduced to the teachings of Hazrat Inayat Khan.

Dorothy could at least console herself that she had some idea as to her husband's true nationality and, by definition, his marital status. Unlike the Sufi community back in California.

Not before time, this had finally come back to bite him, albeit several thousand miles away, in the unlikely setting of a San Francisco business convention. The guest of honour was Carl Hambro, Norway's representative in the United States (and President of the League of Nations no less), whose quick thinking in the first few hours of the German invasion of his country had resulted in the leading government members and the royal family managing to escape from Oslo and make their way to Britain and Canada. As protocol demanded, he had been seated next to the chairman's wife at the convention, who happened to be a (closet) Sufi. And who, by way of small talk, had happened to mention that she had met one of his fellow countrymen, a highly-thought-of young man who had attended the Little Norway training camp and had been working in the Norwegian Consulate in Mexico City.

Unfortunately for JBW, aside from being the most important Norwegian in the United States, Hambro was also amongst the best informed, as a perplexed Samuel Lewis hurriedly reported back. 'It seems that during the course of the dinner [she] mentioned your name and said you had been connected with the consulate in Mexico. Hambro said he knew practically everybody connected with every Norwegian consulate and that there was no "Jøn Wood" there, or anywhere, so far as he was concerned. I told her that I doubted very much if [Hambro's] statement was true for even if a man was prime minister and possibly minister of state he might not have this information at his fingertips.'

Hambro, alert to the possibility of Quisling-like Nazi infiltrators, was not the type to let matters rest. 'But it did not stop there. Hambro began corresponding with the ministries at Washington and Mexico City and the report came through that there was no record of any "Jøn Wood".' Before long Lewis was being asked to help the Norwegian Consulate in San Francisco with their enquiries. 'I could not swear under oath that your name was "Jøn Wood" in your native land. But I did tell them that I heard you speak in Norwegian, that you had called upon certain of your nationals whose addresses had been obtained through the International Institute [. . .] There was a letter on his desk which could not be opened then, which referred to your case.'

If the Head Gardener at Kaaba Allah (and future King of the Hippies) was not the most obvious choice of character witness, then the same might be also said for Lewis's fellow Californian 'dunist' Bryn Bjorset, who, still prevented by the war from returning to his native Norway, also found himself being summoned by the consulate – though Bjorset could at least vouch for JBW's fluent Norwegian and confirm his having lived in Bergen. In the end it required a visit from the former US Consul to Munich, Hathaway Snr, to finally put the consulate's fears at rest – and presumably Carl Hambro's.

But clearly not Hugh Grindley's.

While JBW had come across as 'decidedly odd' to Dorothy's fellow Canadians in Panama, the mere fact that he had been through the Cambridge of the 1930s was probably enough to set off Grindley's social and intellectual prejudices, given that 'almost all the intelligent and bright young undergraduates had become Marxist under the impact of Hitler coming to power'. And though Grindley knew nothing of Kaaba

Allah or JBW's visits to Spain during the Civil War or of his having been a near neighbour of Trotsky, his suspicions were sufficiently aroused for him to formally record his concerns and the reasons behind them, which he then forwarded via diplomatic bag to BSC in New York. Fortunately, Grindley's reputation went before him; JBW was not the first BSC agent he had tried (and sometimes succeeded) to have dismissed. In any case, BSC were evidently quite relaxed about having a few left-leaning or communist intellectuals about the place, as the Soviets' own wireless decrypts would later happily confirm – the Rockefeller Center was revealed to have been home to several Soviet sympathizers during the war. No doubt Grindley's concerns were duly noted before being filed away in (if their Broadway counterparts in London were anything to go by) an unmarked folder somewhere at the back of an already overflowing cupboard.

As it turned out, it was Grindley who would end up hauled before the authorities, rather than JBW, for – ironically – currency violations, put through the books of his Central Uruguayan Railway Company, a serious enough matter to merit the attentions of both a Uruguayan parliamentary investigation and of Ernest Bevin back in London. Accused of effectively trying to defraud the Uruguayan government, Grindley continued to be attacked both in the Uruguayan press and parliament itself, and the case was never fully resolved. Not that this prevented him being awarded OBE in 1947 . . . for 'services to the Railway Industry'.

By the end of 1943 Stephenson had begun handing over BSC's Latin American operations to his American hosts, who had set up their own parallel Central Intelligence Service to cover the region. With Hydra fully up and running and with the successful cracking of the German naval codes, the U-boat threat was finally beginning to wane and the focus now shifted to the coming European war. 'John and I longed to be in the thick of things,' Dorothy wrote, but there was little chance of a straight transfer across to Broadway given they had already turned him down, in spite of T. Ifor Rees's telegrams of recommendation. Instead he would have to formally resign from BSC and make his own way back, with no guarantee of a job at the other end. A risky move – and his prospects were hardly improved for having Hugh Grindley's report hanging over him and his old friends Mr Mynors and Mr Allchin still hot on his tail.

In early June 1944 JBW, Dorothy and several hundred tons of Argentine beef boarded the SS *Rippingham Grange*, at the time the largest refrigeration unit afloat. Given the still potent U-boat threat, the voyage was not without its dangers – on one convoy the previous year just one out of eight ships had arrived safely. As a result ships tended to opt for the shortest route, sailing straight across to Sierra Leone before heading up the west coast of Africa and eventually to Britain. Thankfully, Dorothy's husband knew better than most how to while away the hours on long ocean voyages: 'We would get up early to exercise, arranged useful classes such as Morse code, taught by John, and games to be enjoyed by ourselves as well as the crew.' Arriving safe and sound in Freetown, to Dorothy's annoyance she was told that women were not permitted on shore, so by way of compensation JBW fetched a bag of earth, which he spread out on deck so she could say she had walked on African soil. They then set off under a cloud of black funnel smoke at a steady eight knots, heavily protected by a submarine, several destroyers, a cruiser and an aircraft carrier.

Back in New York, BSC had started to wind down its

operations and was preparing to vacate Rockefeller Center, with Stephenson handing over to Pat Bayly. Camp X had held its last training course in April, and Hydra was set to be run as a Canadian Signal Corps listening post (it remained in operation until 1969). It appears unlikely that either Stephenson or Bayly took much notice of Grindley's report. Not that it mattered. At the end of the war Stephenson ordered that all BSC's files were to be destroyed. 'We set up a furnace of sorts,' one of its officers recalled, 'a concrete block affair at the camp, with a grate in it and a screen over the top to keep any large pieces of charred paper from floating away in the draught [. . .] Various trusted people watched the fire and fed it from time to time.'

One way or another, JBW would do rather well out of bonfires in the years to come.

Alongside his SIS duties, JBW somehow found time to edit the *Sufi News*, 1946.

All but sidelined by his Section IX boss (Kim Philby), JBW headed back to Kaaba Allah, November 1947.

11.

Broadway

'A V1-bomb exploded behind us just as our train
was entering Penge tunnel. We were in the last car,
which got the worst of it. All the glass shattered,
including the lights, and for three minutes in
complete darkness we could feel blood trickling
down our faces from where the flying glass had hit
us. John was upset that his intuition had not warned
him to take a car further along in the train.'

Dorothy Maclean, *Memoirs of an Ordinary Mystic*

In late June 1944, as Hitler was beginning his V1 rocket campaign, JBW and Dorothy arrived in London with no job and
still no access to his Cambridge bank account. As ever he
wasted no time in falling back on his Sufi connections, bor-
rowing the Pimlico apartment of a fellow spiritualist, Sheena
Govan – the self-same Sheena who had chaperoned Dorothy from Toronto to New York – while she headed down to
Somerset to spend the summer camped out in her Glastonbury caravan.

Despite their work for BSC in Latin America there was
no guarantee that either would be taken on by its parent
organization, but thankfully experienced frontline intelligence operatives with fluent Norwegian were few and far

between, still fewer those with in-depth knowledge of both the country and its coastline, and soon JBW was making the twenty-minute walk up from Sheena's Lupus Street flat to 54 Broadway and the Minimax Fire Extinguisher Company, taken on without so much as a cursory background check either with BSC New York or elsewhere.

Norway had long been a likely entry point for any Allied return to mainland Europe and for several months a huge 'Fourth Army' had been assembling and training up in Scotland. But it was all a bluff. There was no Fourth Army, only an elaborate signals operation filling the air with contrived radio traffic to simulate the communications of three entire – and entirely imaginary – corps. After D-Day it was if anything more, not less, important that the deception be maintained, with an advance south through Denmark offering a far more direct route down the North German Plain to Berlin than having to battle hedge by hedge across northern France – the Germans were convinced and committed close on 400,000 troops who might otherwise have been diverted to Normandy.

Both SIS and SOE had been carrying out clandestine operations almost from the day Germany had invaded Norway, greatly helped by being able to call on a local force of some 20,000 patriots, which now included JBW's Sufi mentor Bryn Bjorset, who had recommended him for Suresnes and then Latin America – and who had finally managed to make his way back to his homeland from California. Agents and commandos would head up to Scotland to board one of the fishing boats (known as the 'Shetland bus') which would ferry them across the North Sea then drop them off under cover of darkness in amongst the endless inlets, islands and waterways of Norway's rugged coastline. SIS were given priority on Norway's western coast, something of a home from home for JBW and where his single-masted 'Oselvar' boat was set to remain moored for the duration of the war, smuggled from under the Germans' noses by his Bergen friends: 'still in excellent condition, the engine never faults, and now it's placed in the Stolmen Boat Club newly painted and treated, awaiting your return'. This return now seemed all the more possible, the lengthening autumn nights providing welcome cover for both the Shetland bus and parachute drops, weather permitting.

If, despite his having kidnapped my brother and being the cause of our somewhat straitened circumstances, our father managed to retain something of a glamorous sheen as we were growing up, this was in no small part down to his wartime service in Norway where, legend (and John Wyke) had it, he'd taken part in various behind-the-lines operations. And so we'd sit down to watch *The Heroes of Telemark* whenever it came on TV, trying to figure out which of the white-ski-suited commandos carving their way through the snows of the Hardanger Plateau to Hitler's heavy-water factory in Vermork might be him, possibly on the self-same light-blue Telemark skis that he'd left behind in our garage. Was it him who had laid the explosives charges, or had it been him who tried to usher the children to safety as they boarded the ferry transporting the barrels of heavy water across the fjord.

Unfortunately, the famous Telemark raid took place long before his return to Europe, back when he was sunning himself in Buenos Aires. Not that he'd ever claimed to have been involved, only that he'd parachuted into Norway during the war, which true to form was as much as our mother had been able to wheedle out of him – leaving a vacuum into which, in the absence of hard facts, Messrs Kirk Douglas and Richard Harris had parachuted from Pinewood Studios.

Dorothy Maclean was not much better informed, believing that JBW spent most of the remainder of the war tied to his desk. Par for the course: what little she knew about her husband – such as his being John rather than Jøn – had been gleaned more by accident than by design, be it having to show a (British) passport as they were leaving Panama or Shabaz Best's insistence that JBW introduce her to Sufism back in Rio de Janeiro. But then his 'enigmatic quality had at first been part of his glamour', just as she had always allowed for the fact that 'working among spies in wartime, in countries where I didn't speak the language, I was accustomed to not really knowing what was going on and to assuming that nothing was quite as it seemed'. However, it was when she finally got to meet his parents that the full extent of his obfuscations became apparent.

They were still living in the same ramshackle house on the Surrey–Hampshire border where JBW had spent his teenage years, complete with radio hut and Marconi wireless, though no Hudson Tourer (long since sold off, petrol rationing to blame). His much-travelled, orchid-growing, beekeeping father – 'the most erudite person I had ever met' – she remembered fondly. His mother possibly less so: Dorothy had arrived sporting a pair of wide-leg slacks à la Katherine Hepburn, which Gladys unceremoniously removed from the end of the bed the following morning with no explanation.

Hepburn slacks apart, she did at least come away having finally learnt something of her husband. 'During these visits I learned a few things about John that he had never mentioned: that he was an only child, that he had refused to go to school at Winchester, where his parents had enrolled him, and that he had a substantial private income.' The fact that her husband had taken a lease on a comfortable furnished apartment on London's Chelsea Embankment should have been a clue, Mr Mynors of His Majesty's Treasury having finally agreed to unfreeze his Cambridge bank account now that he was on Broadway's payroll. And with every cloud a (solid) silver lining: the account had continued to accrue funds in his absence, to the tune of some £3,000 (over £170,000 in today's money). Not that Dorothy need ever know it.

Waiting for the green light to head off for Norway, JBW used the time to reconnect with the Sufi community, several of whom had ended up in similar wartime roles: 'I was never more excited to hear of your arrival,' wrote one from Hut 147, RAF Church Green (Bletchley Park). 'Shall we say Piccadilly Circus tube station, column 4, at 3.30 p.m., Thursday?' Before long his Chelsea flat had replaced column 4 as meeting place for the 150 members of the Sufi 'family', including his friend from Paris, Vilayat Khan, who had fled the advancing German armies with his sister Noor and was now an officer with the Royal Navy – and leader of the Sufi movement in England. Noor's story, of course, had an unhappy ending. She would have been a familiar face to JBW back in Suresnes, not least from all those summer garden parties. Ex-Sorbonne herself, she too had trained as a wireless operator (with SOE) and, under the codename Madeleine, was the first female agent to be dropped into France – only to be betrayed and taken to Dachau, where she was executed by firing squad just a few weeks after JBW arrived back in Britain. 'Given her international background, she was,' her brother said, 'someone who belonged nowhere. She gave her life for a universal ideal.'

Thanks to Samuel Lewis's endless, voluminous letters (most of which he admitted to having thrown in the bin unread), Vilayat was aware of JBW's Monday-night lecture spot at the Sufi Centre in San Francisco, and when away on active service would sometimes ask JBW to stand in for him and address the faithful at church halls and assembly rooms in and around London. And though the entrance to Penge railway tunnel might be a far cry from the bright lights of Mexico City, Buenos Aires and Montevideo, it proved only marginally less dangerous – that V1 rocket attack resulted in JBW appearing before the Bromley faithful 'head turbaned in bandages', no doubt still castigating himself for not having seen it coming.

With the Wehrmacht forces in retreat, Eisenhower launched an intensive behind-the-lines operation aimed at tying up, damaging or destroying as much of the German war machine as possible, with a large-scale sabotage campaign against the Norwegian railways aimed at hampering the German withdrawal. In February 1945 alone there were over a hundred successful sabotage attacks on transport being used to ferry troops down through Denmark to the western front. However, given that was largely SOE's remit, the likelihood was that JBW would instead be posted up to the Russian-occupied Helsinki – he'd already made a start on Hugo's Russian-language course, along with rudimentary Finnish, by his own admission not the easiest of languages ('studied this and came to conclusion Cantonese is easy').

In the event it was Dorothy not JBW who headed up to Finland. She had also been taken on by SIS, resuming her former secretarial duties, albeit spending most of her time navigating Broadway's labyrinthine corridors of wooden-partitioned, frosted-glass offices as she hot-desked between senior officers. On the understanding that JBW would follow on as and when, she'd jumped the gun and accepted a post with the British Military Mission in Helsinki. Shortly before Christmas 1944 she found herself in a blacked-out landscape, arriving in torrential rain to a country where everything was rationed – even water, ironically – as one half of the standard two-'man' team (most stations had just an officer and a secretary, sometimes shared with a neighbouring country), working alongside the station chief, Rex Bosley.

But if JBW was needed anywhere, it was not Norway or Finland but at 70 Grosvenor Street, Mayfair W1, where Bill Donovan's OSS had set up their first offices outside the United States. Having worked cheek by jowl with them in both San Francisco and Latin America – back when the OSS was 'scarcely more than an arm of BSC' – few were better qualified. And so, come VE day JBW was free to celebrate back in London, while Dorothy remained stuck in Helsinki – 'hard to celebrate in a country where people had a pathological hatred of our Russian ally and were mourning the victory' – where she was set to remain for several months yet.

However, with its then chief Sir Stewart Menzies (pronounced 'Mingis') facing a 50 per cent post-war budget cut, SIS's future was far from certain – as was JBW's. All the more so as Central Europe was now the focus to the exclusion of all else: overnight JBW's fluent Spanish and Norwegian were relegated to 'additional languages' on his CV, replaced by a working knowledge of German but as yet little in the way of Russian, well-thumbed copy of Hugo's notwithstanding.

As it turned out, Counter-Intelligence was the one

department to emerge relatively unscathed, on the basis that 'if MI6's reputation was to survive into the post-war world, Menzies knew it would all depend on the development of Section V – the brightest feather in C's cap'. Part of his reasoning was the growing awareness that the Soviet Union, Britain's ally for the past four years, was anything but, a suspicion confirmed within three days of the end of the war when Igor Gouzenko, a cypher clerk in the Soviet embassy in Ottawa, defected with a lengthy list of his country's covert operations in the United States and elsewhere – along with the revelation that Soviet Intelligence had managed to infiltrate both the Foreign Office and SIS itself.

Given JBW's experience with Hugh Grindley, it no doubt came as something of a relief to hear that one of the more recent intake of SIS officers, the highly regarded head of its Iberian section, had been appointed head of Counter-Intelligence. Kim Philby wasted little time in getting rid of 'the duds', along with older officers nearing retirement, determined to start shaping a more youthful (and intelligent?) intelligence department. 'Finally, there was a score of younger men about my own age, give or take five years, who had acquired a taste for intelligence work during the war and were keen to make it a career for life.'

Having acquired just such a taste in Latin America and being five years younger than Philby, JBW fitted the bill. Like many younger officers and Cambridge graduates, he was probably rather pleased that 'at least one communist should have broken through and that the social prejudices of our superiors had, on this occasion, triumphed over their political prejudices'. Philby's charm and easy-going manner – to which several members of my own family could happily attest – must have seemed like a return to the halcyon days of his former station chief in Panama, Peter Dwyer, though whether he ever mentioned having lived on the same street as Trotsky seems unlikely – in all probability he had long since learnt that his past was best left unvisited. Much like Philby himself.

As a Production or 'P' Officer, JBW was responsible for gathering intelligence from abroad and channelling it back to the department's controllers in Broadway. With SIS hurriedly having to reorientate itself to the Soviet threat over the winter of 1945–6, Counter-Intelligence began rapidly expanding 'with a headquarters staff of sixty officers and another sixty officers overseas, equipped with personal ciphers for direct communications to Philby'. Though some saw this as a golden age for SIS, with 'a well-trained corps speaking every known tongue and a few unknown ones, experienced in separating fact from forgery, and with specialist qualifications in the professional crafts ancient and modern', for JBW and others it turned out to be not quite so golden. Tied to his desk for the most part, with just the occasional visit to Germany, it was a far cry from his free-wheeling adventures on the front line in Latin America; over the coming months he found himself one of a number of young officers left wondering whether they weren't being slightly sidelined at the expense of other, perhaps less able recruits – and in JBW's case, certainly less gifted linguists. To Philby's credit he would occasionally stop by JBW's desk of an evening, if only to ask what he was up to, during which he taught him a form of patience (the card game, not the virtue) which JBW would play ad infinitum while absorbed in his Russian- and Finnish-language tapes.

On the other hand, this left him free to pursue his extra-curricular activities – editing the *Sufi News*, giving talks to the faithful in and around London, along with vetting new recruits, one recalling how 'the evening was interrupted by the arrival of a rather mysterious man by the name of John Wood, who appeared to possess great knowledge and wisdom, though he didn't talk much. I assumed John had been asked to come and vet me.' Soon enough JBW's 'parish' extended to southern France, Germany and Holland, which in turn meant having to circumvent still-draconian currency restrictions – of which he had more experience than most – even persuading Dorothy after her return from Finland to secrete bundles of cash about her person as they headed across the channel. With the Dutch Sufis in The Hague still surviving on a post-war diet of potato and gravy, JBW's visits – for which he prepared in the usual way, by learning Dutch – were as much humanitarian as spiritual. Sixty years later one of its members recalled him as 'thin, medium height, laconic, stiff-lipped but what emerged always was worthwhile or witty', before adding, 'but I must not forget a remark John Wood once made to me – he said that with foreign names and terms, he often found it easiest to write them down in the Indian "Nagari" script with its wide choice of consonantal and vowel sounds'.

In early 1947 'F. J. Wood' (F for Farmer, presumably) was elevated to General Secretary of the Sufi movement in Britain, complete with a further embossed certificate from the San Francisco hierarchy and an invitation from Murshida Martin to visit. He arrived in mid-June, landing first on Vera Corda with no warning, as was his way, then on Erica and Bill Hathaway with no warning, as was his way (their son remembered him 'appearing on a motorbike sometime in 1947 when we lived out in the desert hills east of San Diego. Quite impressive to a seven-year-old boy'). Murshida Martin, nearing the end of her life, was in the process of finalizing her succession plans. With his friend and mentor Samuel Lewis the obvious choice to take her place as head of the San Francisco movement, who better to take over from Shabaz Best – as Martin had always envisaged – and help kick-start the Sufi movement in Latin America, much as she herself had done in California, not least by purchasing the plot of land in Marin County on which Kaaba Allah was built.

Given the seemingly becalmed state of his SIS career – no business for an enlightened pacifist Sufi at the best of times – on his return to Britain JBW dipped into his Cambridge bank account to the tune of £333 (over £16,000 in today's money) for a ticket to Rio de Janeiro along with the necessary *atestado de saúde para temporarios* (health certificate), arriving in time to spend Christmas in a hotel on the Rua Paysandu, a two-minute amble to the Praia do Flamengo seafront and a taxi ride away from the Sufi Centre at the Rua Ottoni. Where Shabaz Best broke the news that on her deathbed Murshida Martin had decided against Samuel Lewis succeeding her. In the ensuing fallout Lewis had left the movement to go his own way, and with him went any prospect of JBW moving to Rio de Janeiro.

And so he returned to Broadway, where, thankfully, a rather different path was starting to be mapped out for Farmer Wood.

In early 1947 Philby had been transferred to head of station in Istanbul and, coincidence or not, JBW's SIS career had finally started getting back on track. Up until now his visits to Germany had largely been confined to helping the Allied Control Commission deal with the huge backlog of displaced persons – some 2 million of whom were camped out in and around Berlin, having fled eastern Europe in the face of the advancing Russians, many with just the clothes they stood in. Some had walked from as far away as Croatia, Romania and eastern Poland, and the numbers were swelled by returning prisoners of war (POWs). The process was originally designed to weed out any Nazi sympathizers, but increasingly SIS focus was on anyone with firsthand knowledge of Soviet factories, ports, airfields and suchlike, with their official release papers, passes and travel vouchers providing a treasure trove for SIS's forgers.

While the Allies were stretched to the limit simply trying to preserve law and order, the Russians had enjoyed a two-year head start, most of it spent recruiting informers and setting up clandestine radio posts, their transmitters tuned to the Soviet military administration's Karlshorst headquarters, a 160-acre complex just outside Berlin's centre.

Like many of the younger, more ambitious officers, JBW had hopes of a permanent posting but Berlin was still the preserve of the military rather than SIS, who at the end of the war had (mistakenly) based themselves some 300 miles to the west in the quiet spa town of Bad Salzuflen rather than Berlin, partly for fear of antagonizing their Russian allies.

It would be several months before he finally got his wish – thanks largely to Dorothy. She'd returned from Finland to a much-altered, slimmed-down SIS, and but for the decision to disband SOE a few months earlier, she too would likely have found herself out of a job. As it was, SIS had been keen to acquire some of the so-called Ministry of Ungentlemanly Warfare's specialist skills, including its training instructors and research staff, which was how Dorothy came to be working as secretary to Colonels Philip

Rea and Dennis Ambler (brother of the spy novelist Eric Ambler).

Colonel Rea – later the Hon. Lord Rea, Liberal leader in the House of Lords – was wrestling with the problem of how best to stem the rising tide of communist influence in the Middle East. Despite having shared his concerns with Philby's Counter-Intelligence team, little progress had been made, frustrating for someone who'd previously worked alongside the head of SOE, Colin Gubbins, a man of action if ever there was. He had shared this frustration with his secretary, though he probably shouldn't have, who in turn had mentioned it to her husband, though she probably shouldn't have.

A few days later JBW's (anonymous, for obvious reasons) thoughts on the subject – 'Ideological Answers to Communism' – landed on Rea's desk, with faintly comic results: assuming Dorothy to be the author, Rea immediately offered her a promotion (declined).

It was not hard to spot the hand of the committed pacifist at work. Alarmed at how 'America and Russia give every appearance of settling down to a "slugging match" which is bound to lead to war', over the course of several thousand words and some sixty recommendations it set out the need to win over hearts and minds to combat the 'glamour' of communism, detailing 'how this alternative ideology might be developed and applied, first to halt the progress of Communism, and later to eliminate it'.

As Rea was quick to appreciate, 'Ideological Answers to Communism' was 'not necessarily pro-British', nor was it virulently anti-Russian, other than to recommend publishing a populist version of the defector Igor Gouzensky's revelations, 'not as an attack on Russia but simply to illustrate

Soviet methods and to make people realize their existence'. Rea was initially reluctant to circulate it within Broadway and elsewhere, on the basis of: 'A). The difficulty of persuading a Foreign Office to accept an ideology. I can't find any precedent in modern history for that, though the latest JIC [Joint Intelligence Committee] paper shows that the awareness of the need for it is much greater than I thought. B). Cowardice.'

Fortunately, Ambler had no such qualms. After suggesting to Dorothy that the author might want to edit out its more flowery passages ('If it is true that reason is deafened by the clamour of emotion, it is also true that emotion can be deafened by the clamour of the spirit or a high ideal . . .'), he forwarded all fifty-plus pages higher up the chain, attaching a prefacing note to say that 'the author is P.6 and, if you are interested, he can answer questions much better than I can. Note: he would prefer to remain anonymous.'

A few days later Ambler received an urgent telegram from BAH/51: 'I have read the paper with considerable personal interest and should like to know a little more about the background of it. Will you drop me a DO [demi-official] line at your convenience.' BAH/51 was the head of the SIS station in Berlin, which before too long would find itself entirely cut off from the outside world.

That same week JBW tidied up his Broadway desk and was on his way. Given the rapidly deteriorating situation in Berlin, wives, Dorothy learnt, would not be allowed.

PART THREE

Berlin, 1948, caught off guard.

I.

Berlin

'Each officer was issued with his own
Volkswagen Beetle. These were embellished in
various ways, either by painting them a colour
other than black, or by fitting badges, spotlights,
radios and so on. A wide selection of different
number plates was also available to us.'

Anthony Cavendish, *Inside Intelligence* (1987)

In a three-piece suit, with no military record and no accompanying chestful of medals, JBW probably felt somewhat out of place reporting into Berlin's SIS station, staffed as it was almost entirely by ex-Army Intelligence Corps officers. But the rapid deterioration in relations with the Soviets meant that by 1947 the station was embarking on a correspondingly rapid expansion, which would see it grow to become the largest intelligence station anywhere across the globe, with over fifty officers and countless support staff working out of the former House of German Sports, a four-storey building situated directly behind the Olympic Stadium.

My father's cover was Political Officer with Allied High Command, a role he would later describe – if only for the benefit of his cleaned-up, post-SIS CV – as 'more academic than administrative, in that I was involved in the interesting exercise of forecasting Soviet political intentions in Europe on the basis of the ideological and theoretical statements appearing in Russian and East German party material'. Not that there was much need to scour the small print of Russian or East German party material to forecast Soviet intentions – he need only look out of the window.

The thinking in Whitehall and Washington was less if Stalin would make a move on the city but when; the American military governor telegrammed the Pentagon to warn that 'war may come with dramatic suddenness'. The best SIS could hope for was to obtain some sort of early warning of an imminent attack, if only to buy time, but even this was hampered by the dearth of reliable intelligence, with not a single agent in place behind the newly christened Iron Curtain.

Tensions came to a head when Stalin imposed road and rail restrictions on all Allied military and supply traffic into Berlin, in the belief that a blockade would force the West to abandon the city altogether. Cut off by road, rail and canal with barely enough food and fuel to last a month, Berlin was relieved by the famed airlift, with, at its height, a conveyor belt of over a thousand flights a day landing at Tempelhof Airport, some dropping chocolate bars into the streets below as they made their landing approach, others making a point of flying low over the Soviets' Karlshorst headquarters 'to impress them'. If anything, the Soviet stranglehold succeeded only in uniting the local population behind the occupying British, American and French forces, as JBW wrote to Dorothy Maclean back in London: 'If you thought the spirit in the Blitz was good, you should see Berlin.'

Morale within SIS's headquarters in Bad Salzuflen had also received a timely boost with the appointment as head of station of John Bruce Lockhart, a name not unfamiliar to the Russians – Lockhart's uncle had done time in Moscow's Lubyanka Prison (along with Sidney Reilly) for plotting to assassinate Lenin. His first success was to charm the various armed forces intelligence units into working for SIS, which meant that 'civilian' officers such as JBW now found themselves operating alongside the pick of Army Intelligence.

Given the pressure to try and figure out Moscow's next steps – which, according to one SIS officer, 'none of us there at the time would claim that we had the success in meeting' – Lockhart encouraged his staff to put caution to one side, allowing them a more or less free rein – 'sometimes leading to embarrassing consequences, but throughout all of these he never lost his cool or his ability to encourage others to try again'. Having been all but sidelined back in Broadway, JBW needed no encouragement: from here on in his work would be neither 'academic' or 'administrative', though it might reasonably be described as 'interesting'.

The city's four sectors (French, US, British and Russian) were marked out here and there by a line of white posts, not that anyone took much notice of them, least of all JBW, who was soon fully immersed in the 'agent-swamp'. With (as yet) few restrictions on venturing across to the Russian zone, Berlin was almost an echo of Buenos Aires, where he'd bump into his opposite numbers in the street on an almost daily basis. For some it was simply an opportunity to stock up on discounted East German goods – the Kaufhaus des Ostens store a particular favourite, 'each parcel wrapped in the red-and-white striped paper of the store, decorated with little red stars and the initials KO'. For anyone in the business of obtaining classified information (which just about everyone was), the numerous cheap coffee bars were an added attraction, with the Café Warsaw the rendezvous of choice – 'a sort of stock exchange for secrets, with half the tables taken up by Soviet, Czech, Polish, British, American, French and East and West German agents. The going rate for a scrap of negotiable information was five pounds. A few dollars were enough to make many of the boys change sides between cups of coffee.' *Mischkaffee* (half coffee powder, half 'other stuff') aside, such trips were not without their dangers. In just the first six months of JBW's posting it was reported back to Moscow that some 549 people had been arrested for espionage in Germany, 391 of them American, 121 British, 31 French and 6 from other services. Even so, most SIS officers felt that the chances of being picked up were slim so long as they stayed within the central Mitte district. Needless to say, JBW did not confine himself to the central Mitte district.

Despite the blockade the city's elevated railway system, the S-Bahn, continued to operate much as before, allowing relatively easy access to the Russian sector and beyond, and soon enough JBW's walkabouts were extending to the Pots-dam, Weimar, Dresden and the annual Leipzig state fair, held every September to showcase East European goods to the West, where business reps and factory managers might be gently persuaded, over a few beers, into parting with rather more than hydraulic presses and tractor parts.

Not that it was all one-way traffic. With no let-up in the air-lift and the growing realization that the blockade was unlikely to succeed, the Soviets' actions became ever more brazen, with kidnappings by Russian and East German agents in West Berlin becoming commonplace. It wasn't long before their attention turned to JBW, his cover as political researcher for Allied Command unlikely to have fooled Karlshorst even without the assistance of his former Broadway boss, Kim Philby. Back in

San Francisco, Erica Hathaway was surprised to receive a call from a 'German friend' of JBW's who wondered whether she might happen to have an address for him in Berlin. The unlucky caller was not to know that despite her surname Erica was, of course, German herself and knew a Russian accent when she heard one. A few days later JBW rang to explain: 'My old apartment in Berlin was raided. They must have found your letter amongst other things. So please, don't ever give my address to anyone, and never use headed stationery.'

However, not everyone in SIS's Olympic building shared JBW's penchant for going walkabout in eastern Germany or a thirst for questionable coffee at the Café Warsaw.

A few months before JBW's arrival, perhaps the most highly regarded of Bruce Lockhart's Army Intelligence officers had transferred across from Bad Salzuflen to head up the Berlin station. Generally described (if described at all) as a self-effacing, almost shy man, Harold Shergold had little if any military bearing and none of his future Foreign Office colleagues' airs or graces, despite having attended both Oxford and Cambridge. He was as far removed from the popular image of a spy as it is possible to be.

Born and brought up in Winchester, he'd attended the local Peter Symonds Grammar School (I'd once made the mistake of presuming he'd attended Winchester College, only to be matter-of-factly corrected). After Oxbridge – in its truest sense – he'd taken a teaching post at Cheltenham Grammar School, signing up with his local Hampshire regiment when war was declared, only for his fluent German to see him swiftly moved to Army Intelligence and North Africa, where Field Marshall Erwin Rommel was sweeping all before him.

If ever anyone was curious as to what exactly marks out a future SIS intelligence officer, they could do worse than look at the young Shergold's guile during the Second Battle of El Alamein. In what threatened to be a rolling, drawn-out engagement, much depended on when and where Rommel planned to commit his Panzer brigades and the more battle-hardened, elite divisions. As a forward interrogator, Shergold was tasked with questioning captured German and Italians, with little success, most giving just the obligatory name, rank and number. Frustrated, he delegated the task of removing the POWs from the battlefield to a regular Army NCO and left him to it. However, he'd given the (unknowing) NCO a list of Rommel's various regiments and units, suggesting he allocate a truck to each. As the several hundred POWs waited for their unit to be called out, they unwittingly revealed which troops Rommel had committed to the battle – and, more importantly, which ones he was holding back – allowing General Montgomery to plan accordingly.

But it was in the later, decisive stages of the battle that Shergold's aptitude for a career in the dark arts truly came to the fore, when two mortally wounded German officers were brought into the field hospital. Suspecting they might be from Rommel's crack regiments, Shergold – as he cheerfully admitted – quietly helped himself to a surgeon's gown, slipping on a pair of Red Cross armbands. Holding each officer's hand in turn, he carefully noted down any last wishes (dutifully forwarded to their respective families after the battle), at the same time gently coaxing out the necessary information; outside the tent a staff officer held up a telephone link, with Montgomery himself on the other end.

Shergold stayed with the Eighth Army all the way to Tunis, took part in the Sicily landings, then crossed over to the mainland, continuing all the way up through Italy via Monte Cassino, ending his war in 'a muddy field in northern Italy filled with half the German chiefs of staff, all camped out in tents in front of me'.

In the summer of 1948 he returned briefly to London to watch the Olympics – or more especially a member of Britain's shot-put team, Bevis Reed. She too had served in Egypt and Italy, between them forming something of a double act (Bevis interrogating Italian POWs, Shergold interrogating German POWs).

Shergold was always reluctant to venture into the Russian sector for no good reason, on the basis that it was only likely to invite trouble. Nor did he place much faith in the hundreds of low-grade agents and informers who made up the 'agent-swamp'. Faced with a dearth of solid intelligence and the improbability of any high-level defectors – certainly no one on a par with the cypher clerk Igor Gouzenko in Canada – SIS fell back on more reliable methods of gauging Soviet intentions; the best they could hope for now was to try and glean whatever they could from the Soviet communication lines, with JBW working alongside Army Intelligence's operators in a cramped shed behind Tempelhof Airport. Given the reliance on Signals Intelligence (SIGINT), it was inevitable that Shergold would end up working closely with JBW, possibly more than he might have wished.

As Shergold remembered all too clearly (dropping into German every now and then, as if reliving the pain), clever though JBW might be, he was oh so *pedantisch* with it. '*Nach links zeigen, rechts abbiegen*' – 'always indicating left, turning right'. Obsessed with the need for secrecy, with a fear (not entirely misplaced) that he was under constant surveillance and unable to give a simple answer to even the most straightforward question (nationality and marital status included). Shergy recalled how even the simplest cross-town journey with JBW at the wheel would involve doubling back on themselves and weaving in and around and about the French, American or British sectors – sometimes all three. '*Warum einfach, wenn's auch umständlich geht?*' Shergold summed up. 'Why do things the easy way when you can do them the hard way?'

Then again, given the tinderbox atmosphere of Berlin, likely flashpoint for a Third World War, in the grander scheme of things these were minor irritations. And no one in SIS's Olympic Stadium building had more experience of working hand in hand with their CIA counterparts, the majority of whom had been recruited directly from the OSS. Some of them knew JBW personally from his time in Latin America and San Francisco, others by reputation; JBW's transatlantic accent only confirmed to Shergold and others his feet-in-both-camps status. And though the Americans might be relatively new to the murky world of espionage, they were to all intents and purposes bankrolling much of it.

The transition from Farmer Wood to frontline officer in Berlin at the height of the Cold War had necessitated a degree of sacrifice. His Norwegian nationality had long since been dropped, his devotion to Sufism – which not so long ago had seen him on the cusp of moving to Rio de Janeiro – was now hidden out of sight. The transition was made easier both by William Stephenson's decision to burn all BSC's records at the end of the war (Hugh Grindley's suspicions included), followed by Kaaba Allah accidentally burning to the ground, taking with it his voluminous correspondence with Samuel Lewis and conveniently wiping the slate clean of past eccentricities. Not that he had completely abandoned his Sufi beliefs in the aftermath of Lewis's split with the movement. Aside from the occasional cross-legged contemplation at the bottom of the Blau-Weiss (Blue-White) Club swimming pool, he was still somehow finding the time to edit the *Sufi News* and continue his role as National Secretary – up until he was caught using the SIS 'diplomatic bag' to post his articles back to London, for which he duly received an official ticking-off, (as yet) the only blot on his SIS record. A setback, but one which failed (along with the Penge railway tunnel bomb and the Kaaba Allah fire) to lessen his belief in the power of *murāqabah* to give him a premonition of what was to come, even to warn him of impending danger. Useful as this might be in his present line of work – nowhere more so than in Berlin – it would prove to be his undoing there, certainly so far as Harold Shergold was concerned.

And then there was Dorothy.

Having returned from Finland to find JBW and periodical flatmate Vilayat Khan playing host to what seemed like London's entire Sufi membership in their Chelsea apartment, she came to realize before long that her husband, 'probably enjoying the freedom of being a bachelor again, did not truly welcome [her] return'. To add to her problems, shortly after submitting 'Ideological Answers to Communism' on his behalf, she'd left SIS, victim of the post-war winding-down of the service, signing up for a fine art course on Regent Street along with a series of talks given by the Indian philosopher Krishnamurti, with the result that a spiritual gap now also opened up between her and her husband. Soon she began to wonder whether they might be better off going their separate ways, a thought that (according to her memoirs) had first occurred to her at the point of orgasm during sex with JBW (too much information?), concluding that his eagerness to go to Berlin was just part of a 'long pattern of simply running away when relationships became difficult for him'.

He had form on this front. His German friend Erica (Hathaway), stopping off at Chelsea Embankment on her way over to Munich to visit her parents – who had survived the war unscathed, despite their antipathy for Hitler and in spite of nightly bombing raids – was surprised to come face to face 'with a tall woman' who JBW, 'with a mischievous smile', introduced as his wife. '"You scoundrel," I thought. "Vera is still waiting for you in San Francisco."' Even his first love, Cil, had yet to hear full confirmation of the end of their relationship, though she probably knew better than to ask: 'What about you? Here rumours have it that you got married in South America.'

Having been told by JBW (not entirely truthfully) that wives were not allowed in Berlin, towards the end of 1948 Dorothy decided to head back to her native Canada, booking a passage on board Cunard's RMS *Media*. Which, blockade or no blockade, had her alarmed husband hurrying back to their London flat, waving two last-minute BOAC airline tickets. Not to be dissuaded, Dorothy insisted on continuing by sea and by herself, only to find JBW waiting to meet her at the quayside in New York. They spent a happy enough Christmas with her parents at her childhood home in Guelph, Western Ontario, after which JBW headed straight back to Berlin.

Except that, true to form and unbeknown to Dorothy, he had not headed straight back to Berlin. Instead he'd stopped off in Ottawa to formally apply for Canadian citizenship on the basis that his wife was Canadian, even putting his name down for a Canadian Civil Service competition for the role of Foreign Service Officer in the Department of External Affairs – if only to add a little weight to his application. As with many of JBW's sleights of hand, this too would one day come back to bite him.

Dorothy meanwhile headed down to California and ended up living in a spiritual community in Ojai run along similar lines to Kaaba Allah, founded by the self-styled Vitvan, a devotee of Shakti yoga taught to him by an Indian mystic. Despite his name and for all his devotion to Eastern mysticism, Vitvan could not have been more American – he was originally Mr Ralph DeBit from Kansas City – just like his overriding mantra: 'Act, don't react.' And so, after travel restrictions were finally lifted, Dorothy duly summoned up the courage to head out to Berlin, sending JBW (aka Mr J. Williams, c/o No. 4 EAD attached BTB, Berlin, BAOR) a postcard to let him know she had arrived: 'I'm here, though I shouldn't be.'

If JBW was caught off guard by her unexpected appearance (he was in Vienna at the time), so too was the rest of the Berlin SIS station. 'I was a surprise to them, for he had told nobody that he was married.' Even so, it turned out to be an amicable parting of the ways, with one of JBW's German agents doing the (pretend) honours in a Berlin hotel, 'believing the set-up was just another part she had to play in gathering intelligence', and a lawyer on hand to witness (burst in on) their supposed adultery (still the preferred method for obtaining a divorce). Following which, in lieu of the honeymoon he had promised at the start of their marriage (but which, needless to say, had never happened), he and Dorothy 'motored through Germany, Luxembourg, Switzerland, Italy and Liechtenstein, having a wonderful time together', the only blemish for her being a four-hour wait outside a bar in eastern Switzerland as JBW listened in on a group of native Romansh speakers, hoping to pick up a few words of a language that up until then he had only known from textbooks. At the end of the week he dropped her off in the picturesque Bavarian Alpine town of Oberammergau in time for her to catch the famous passion play, held once every ten years.

Leaving JBW free to return to Berlin and pursue a passion play of his own.

The SIS women's hostel.

New girl Margaret Miller
(my mother), 1949.

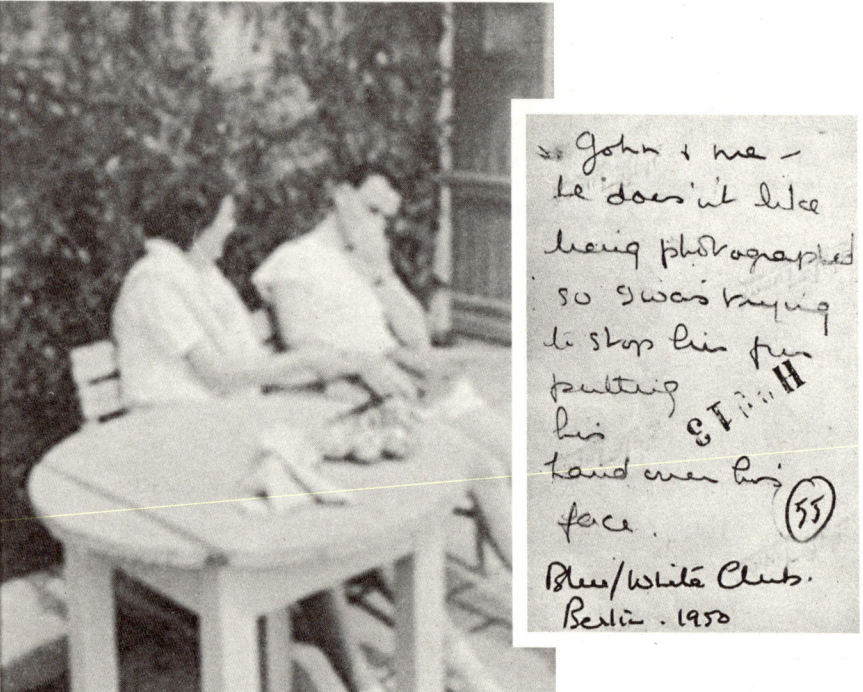

» John & me –
he doesn't like
being photographed
so I was trying
to stop him from
putting
his
hand over his
face.

Blue/White Club.
Berlin. 1950

Photographed (or not) with JBW: 'John & me – he
doesn't like being photographed so I was trying to
stop him from putting his hand over his face.'

2.

No. 12 Bettinastrasse

'Berlin in the late 1940s was a dangerous city.
It was the meeting place of East and West, a
divided city, and one in which completely
opposed ideologies played sinister games of
espionage and intrigue as they strove to exploit
the instability of those early post-war years.'

Felicity Gray (aka my mother), *The Decoy*

Judging by the sheer volume of laughter permeating up
through the floorboards of our old Woking home whenever my mother's Berlin friends were down from London,
life for the small band of women in the SIS women's hostel
at No.12 Bettinastrasse was, as her Box Brownie prints seem
to confirm, a constant merry-go-round of ballgowns, cocktail parties, boating on the Havel and Lake Wannsee, tennis
and swimming at the Blau-Weiss Club, cantering through
the Grunewald, skiing and hot glühweins in the Austrian
Tyrol, even the occasional donkey ride across the floor of
the Golden Horseshoe nightclub. Otherwise all I had to go
on was a B film I saw on a Saturday-morning cinema visit,
about a group of orphaned children scouring the ruins for
whatever they could find, during which my mother kept up
an intermittent commentary whenever she recognized a

particular landmark or street – the first time I heard her even mention Berlin. (We left when the main film came on.)

None of which quite tallied with the Cold War Berlin that Len Deighton et al. conjured up. Nor, come to that, the Berlin and Vienna that John Wyke, Peter Lunn and Shergy described.

At one minute past midnight on 12 May 1949 the Berlin blockade ended and the first train rumbled across the border from western Germany, arriving at 5.32 that same morning. Celebrations in SIS's granite building were rather muted, given that the first indications of the climbdown had come not from its own sources but from TASS, the Soviet news agency.

A few months before, in SIS's very own Black Friday, the Soviets had changed their cipher systems in favour of unbreakable one-time keypads; overnight both SIS and the US Army's team of crypto analysts in Virginia – who up until then had been able to read enough wireless traffic to be reasonably sure of Soviet intentions – found themselves completely in the dark. At the same time Soviet military, diplomatic and intelligence headquarters in East Berlin and Vienna halted all ultra-high frequency (UHF) radio communications with Moscow and switched to landlines – as JBW would have been among the first to know, UHF intercepts being something of a specialist subject for him ever since Mexico City.

The abrupt cut-off was, as some suspected, down to Soviet moles in the West alerting their controllers that their communications were compromised. Given the failure to recruit any double agents of their own – certainly no one prepared to stay in place and supply information – SIS had to make do with whatever Army Intelligence, in their anonymous cramped quarters behind Tempelhof Airport, could glean from Soviet troops and pilots dropping their guard and gossiping in Russian 'plainspeak', though this was largely just small talk. Otherwise, it was a matter of going back to scouring Soviet and East German party material for scraps, both in Berlin and elsewhere – JBW even resorted to thumbing through his old Norwegian address book for possible leads: '*Kjære Jøn, Hvad Russere angår – så kan jeg ikke hjelpe dig . . .*' ('Dear Jøn, As for the Russians, I can't help you. I am living next to the embassy, but I would never dare enter without introducing myself.')

Or, failing that, it was simply a matter of heading across to the Russian-controlled half of the city, as Bruce Lockhart had long encouraged.

Aside from endless *Mischkaffees* with the *Hundert Mark Jungen* ('hundred-mark boys') 'who were offering to lay bare the innermost workings of the Kremlin, Whitehall or the Pentagon for the price of a good dinner', more usefully JBW was ferrying a steady flow of two-way radio sets and spare parts over to East Berlin in the hope that any signs of unusual activity or military build-up for a possible invasion could be reported back. As a fellow officer recorded, 'smuggling two-way radio sets into East Berlin was enormously risky and complicated. And training agents to operate these radios was difficult – most of them were simply unable to master it.' His all-too-brief on-the-spot training sessions on how to set up and use the transmitters inevitably resulted in more failures than successes, while even those who managed to master the basics were prey to the attentions of Soviet eavesdroppers. As was standard practice on both sides, the Soviets would often hold back from making an arrest in the hope of uncovering the entire network – a calculated risk, given that an operator might close down the network altogether if they got wind they were being watched, or simply arrange to be exfiltrated before they were rounded up.

Which in a roundabout way was how JBW came to be working alongside my mother.

Within a few weeks of arriving in Berlin the twenty-one-year-old Margaret Miller had found herself being 'borrowed' for just such an operation, involving the leader of one of the cells JBW was running in East Berlin. As was often the way, 'Frieda' had been recruited via a relative living in the western half of the city – in this instance her sister. Given the shortage of German men (for obvious reasons), not to mention the treatment many women had suffered at the hands of the Red Army at the end of the war, most of JBW's recruits and contacts were female. Frieda had been running a small though highly successful cell, but via a prearranged signal was now warning her sister that she suspected the East German authorities were onto her and her apartment likely under surveillance. The idea was that a suitable 'double' would head across and swap places, allowing Frieda to make her escape. Frieda was slightly taller than the average German. As was my mother.

Harold Shergold, as head of station, was always reluctant to involve the younger, more innocent members of his team in frontline operations. Still less someone who just a few weeks before had never been abroad. Then again, needs must. Waving away suggestions that she might want to obtain the permission of her Aunt A (her SIS guardian, my mother having joined SIS before she was twenty-one) – 'I don't think she would complain, she spent a lifetime doing this sort of thing' – from time to time she would be asked to put her typewriter to one side for the greater good, her only reward a lifelong bond of loyalty from Shergy.

The plan was that she tag along with an American news unit who were putting together a report on life in the Soviet sector and who, slightly surprisingly, had been granted permission for a day shoot in the Unter den Linden, the wide boulevard on the eastern approach to the Brandenburg Gate – the Soviets were apparently keen to showcase the restoration work being carried out on its bombed-out buildings and the replanting of its famous lime (linden) trees. A few days later, drably dressed with a 'blondish wig, under a dirty cap', clutching her forged identity papers, my mother was squeezing her 5 ft 10 frame into the back of one of the film trucks for what would be her first such operation behind the Iron Curtain. No sooner were the cameras set up than the usual crowd of curious onlookers gathered round to watch them film, allowing her to slip away, 'heart racing with excitement', to take the U-Bahn across town to the 'quiet, sunlit street' where Frieda lived, all but empty bar the usual bockwurst stand. She entered 'jauntily through the entrance of the back of the flats and, as instructed, climbed to the second floor' where she changed into a summer dress and broad-brimmed hat, and exited the building through the front door. As planned, she spent several hours joining the endless food queues ('never did an afternoon pass so slowly') before heading back, only to be stopped by a besuited man hovering beside the bockwurst stand, her SIS minder, who drove her back to the Brandenburg Tor checkpoint crossing (British 'BZ' number-plated cars were still permitted to cross into the Russian sector), arriving just in time to see 'the tail-end of the film unit disappearing through the barrier to safety [. . .] carrying a similarly fair-haired young woman, sitting silently in the back of one of the equipment vans'. She was then instructed to join the long line of bar workers and waiters waiting to cross into West Berlin to begin their evening jobs in the Kurfürstendamm and elsewhere, only to be met at the sector dividing line by JBW, who 'spoke confidently to the East German guards as they checked a set of very competently forged identity papers and raised the barrier'.

Or at least that was the story as her old Berlin friends recounted it.

Listeners to her hospital radio plays three decades later would be treated to a rather more colourful version (*The Decoy*), in which she was employed as a research assistant to an 'author of best-selling spy thrillers', with the SIS minder upgraded to the role of bockwurst-seller and JBW – or rather 'Desmond Savage' – taking on the guise of a flower-seller, tucked discreetly out of sight behind the rows of azaleas across the road from Frieda's apartment, keeping watch on her every move.

When her hospital radio plays – certainly those with any hint of her former occupation – were outed and abruptly taken off-air, *The Decoy* was reworked and retitled *A Summer in Berlin*, a (slightly toe-curling) romance – 'Could she really trust this enigmatic young man who had won her heart so completely?' – and entered for a *Woman & Home* short story competition. The judges noted that it 'feels like a true story! The writer knows the setting, or seems to, which is just as good.'

Certainly the romance was true enough. Mission accomplished, she and JBW had gone their separate ways (he to Vienna), but then one evening he phoned her out of the blue, not at the SIS Bettinastrasse women's hostel but from across the floor of one of the bars she and her fellow secretaries had stopped off at on a girls' night out (most likely the famous Resi in Hasenheid), where 'every table had a telephone and any admirer was free to ring and ask for a dance'. By way of a first date, they drove out to Lake Tegel, where SIS's French counterparts in the SDECE (Service de Documentation Extérieure et de Contre-Espionnage) were holding a candle-lit dinner dance, her Institut Français evening classes finally paying off, if rather overshadowed by her date's near fluency and casual 'gesticulating in true Gallic fashion', which made it 'difficult to realize that he was English, if in fact he was'.

She hadn't read too much into their evening by the lake – unsurprisingly, the handful of female staff in the Berlin station were not exactly short of dates – but returning from Bad Salzuflen on the overnight military train a few weeks later she found her 'mysterious friend from the night-club' waiting to meet her on the platform. He took her for breakfast at the American Services Club, flashing the appropriate pass at the entrance, which along with the transatlantic accent made her think he might be American. 'I'm not, but I am partly Canadian,' he told her. 'I was to learn in time that he claimed to be partly a great many nationalities, which accounted for the ease with which he spoke so many languages.'

Partly Canadian though he may have been – certainly was, according to his Berlin Command Ration Card (No: D 008623, Nationality: Canadian) – he was also entirely married. A detail which came as a surprise to Harold Shergold and indeed everyone else in the Olympic Building when Dorothy Maclean put in her unscheduled appearance, though, as Dorothy said: 'His female co-workers seemed quite pleased that I had turned up, perhaps hoping I would keep him in order.' This problem was amicably solved (courtesy of the hotel room, compliant female agent and witnessing lawyer), then sealed by the sightseeing drive through central Europe (he told Shergold that he had been away in Canada arranging a divorce). So JBW could now resume where he had left off: occasional doubles partners at Grunewald's Blau-Weiss tennis club, dinners at the Kurfürstendamm's Restaurant Aben (her favourite), sailing on the Havel – soon enough they were a regular sight at the American Anchor Club and the Stobensee Yacht Club, albeit one seldom caught on film, JBW being nothing if not camera-shy.

Returning from her first home leave in Whitley Bay, my mother sailed into Hamburg to be met at the quayside by JBW, who whisked her up to Copenhagen for a long weekend (all he could manage, having used up his leave allowance on his week away with Dorothy Maclean – which of course my mother knew nothing of, nor ever would). And, improbable as it may seem, neither she nor Shergold was aware that Dorothy Maclean had worked for BSC, having been told by JBW she worked in insurance, which at least had a basis in truth: Dorothy had taken a summer job with a Toronto firm of loss adjusters immediately after leaving college.

However, it wasn't JBW's marital status that was to put a hold on budding romance but events several thousand miles away. In June 1950 the North Korea People's Army – trained by the Soviets – had invaded South Korea, once again catching Western intelligence agencies off guard. The prospect of war with the Soviet Union drew attention to the acute lack of Russian interpreters and translators both in the Foreign Office and in the armed forces, not to mention SIS's Olympic Stadium HQ, where most officers spoke German but barely a handful could muster more than a few words of Russian.

JBW was one of the few who could. He'd made a start on learning the language back in Broadway in the expectation of being posted to then-Russian-controlled Helsinki and had by now what might be termed 'passable' Russian – unless you happened to be Russian. In early October JBW headed back to his alma mater, St Catharine's College, Cambridge (or more exactly to 5 Salisbury Villas, Station Road) for a course in Slavonic Studies. 'I thought you already had so much Russian in Berlin all you wanted was to complete,' his Norwegian friend wrote, and complete he did, with the help of the inimitable Dr Liza Hill.

Born to a Scottish father and a Russian mother in St Petersburg at the turn of the century, the teenage Yelizaveta Fyodorovna Hill and her family had managed to escape the Bolshevik Revolution and arrived in London all but destitute. Despite her father being reduced to working as a door-to-door chocolate salesman, she had put herself through university before embarking on a lifelong career teaching Russian that would culminate in a damehood. Remembered as an inspirational figure by a string of notable ex-students, she also had the dubious distinction of being credited by George Blake with having first enthused him with all things Russian. Most of Hill's intake were would-be translators and interpreters on secondment from the armed forces; JBW was one of only a few SIS officers, enrolled under his official cover occupation of 'Political Officer of the Research Department for Allied High Command in Berlin'.

Courses lasted six months, by which time even those new to the language were expected to speak grammatical Russian. For those who already spoke something of the language, the course was more demanding still, with Hill maintaining that Russians regarded their complex language as part of their defence against outsiders, playing down any thought that it could be mastered by foreigners. The upshot of which was that he and his fellow students were urged to '*rabotat, rabotat, rabotat*' – 'work, work, work' – with the promise that if they did, they 'would fall in love with themselves'. Hill believed that 'Russian is best taught in Russian' and just as the students at Mullsjö had been taught to 'inhabit' a language and its culture, Hill's students were expected to immerse themselves in Russian art, Dostoevsky and Chekhov, and to attend Russian Orthodox Church services, alongside learning a minimum of forty words a day, with the emphasis on correct pronunciation, explaining the healthy extra tuition and excess supervision fees column on JBW's invoice from St Catharine's.

The Slavonic Studies department's reputation as little more than a finishing school for spies would only come later, but not much later. In April 1951 JBW had headed back across the Channel with his 'Certificate of Competent Knowledge', followed a month later by another ex-student, Guy Burgess (who'd only lasted one lesson with Hill), accompanied by a Foreign Office diplomat, Donald Maclean (no relation to Dorothy). JBW struggled to recall having met either man, both having left Cambridge before he arrived, and in any case they were exactly the sort of English public-school types he'd have done his best to avoid. However, rather closer to home, in July his former Broadway boss, Kim Philby, was forced to resign from SIS under a cloud of suspicion.

Along with infusing the service with an unhealthy degree of paranoia, the events of that summer only doubled down on the need to keep operations to as small a team as possible. As a consequence, my mother, as *der Notizenmacher* ('the notetaker'), occasionally found herself being roped into work rather more demanding than her pay grade. The small size of the Olympic Building's offices combined with the rapid expansion of the Berlin station meant she had to squeeze in at the back of Shergold's office, legs tucked underneath her or more usually flat up against the wall (a habit she would never quite manage to shake off) as she scrawled her indecipherable – even to herself – Pitman shorthand.

The lack of any successful infiltration in the opposite direction placed an even greater emphasis on trying to decipher the Soviets' next steps after the Korean invasion. As a result of which JBW was once again spending as much time in East as in West Berlin, possibly encouraged by an unwritten understanding that neither the Soviets nor SIS would directly harm each other's employees and, of course, further emboldened by his *murāqabah*-inspired belief in a sixth sense of impending danger.

Even so, after five years of occupation the Russians had grown wise to the SIS officers' constant toings and froings – and to their accompanying paperwork, forged or otherwise. Officers taking both the S-Bahn and U-Bahn ran the risk of being followed the moment they disembarked at any station. To get round the problem, JBW maintained a series of 'safe houses' in the eastern half of the city – which had been what the Russians were really after when they'd phoned his friend Erica in San Francisco, knowing his West Berlin address only too well, having raided it several times.

With the blockade over and construction of the Berlin Wall several years away, the intelligence agencies went toe-to-toe, with abductions and assassinations carried out against a backdrop of wire-taps, eavesdropping, black-bagging, cut-outs, echoing footsteps and figures lurking in the shadows.

For all that, JBW's most fraught mission that summer was quite possibly his visit to Whitley Bay.

On his return from Cambridge he and my mother had more or less carried on where they'd left off – though if she'd missed him, you wouldn't know it to look at her old photograph albums. But in August he took the train up to Newcastle to meet her parents, his divorce to Dorothy Maclean finalized a few days before, though doubtless he knew better than to mention this to his future father-in-law, a devout Scottish Presbyterian – just as he knew better than to mention his Sufism, nationality or indeed pretty much anything else about himself. They spent most of the day in the back garden, JBW keeping his jacket and tie on throughout, along with a fixed if slightly nervous smile.

In December, their engagement was announced in the *Newcastle Journal*, though they would have to wait until the following September to tie the knot in a Tynemouth registry office – following several last-minute postponements by JBW. She'd turned him down twice, and whenever she was asked (not least by her own offspring) why she had agreed to marry him, the best she could come up with was that he had been very persistent. Then again, his star was once again in the ascendant, just as it had been at BSC. For his part, though no longer the oddball of his Panama days, he was still something of an outsider, whereas my mother, like her predecessor, was very much the carefree, popular insider.

If her parents disapproved of their daughter's choice, as surely they did, they were not alone. Though JBW's mother had never entirely warmed to Dorothy Maclean (or her Katherine Hepburn slacks), she was less than pleased to hear that Dorothy and her son had divorced, all the more so because the first she heard of it was when JBW informed her of his engagement to my mother. Unsurprisingly then, his parents failed to make it up to Tynemouth on the day itself, clearly having more pressing matters to attend to: 'September 11th, 1952. Rather cool, mostly cloudy. Finished re-potting down below for present, swept up floor, swept both (green)houses & lit top house fire before tea. Went to Farnham pm, took Mrs H with us. Did some shopping, got some books from Wells, dropped Mrs H home. Sent wire to Tynemouth.'

Allan Batham and (camera-shy) fellow officer on the River Havel, Berlin, 1950.

For any secretary with an eye for a bargain, visits (reconnoiters) to the Russian-controlled central Mitte district were a routine day trip, 1953.

3.

The Russian sector

'It was one of five or six big operations we ran. But
of course it's the one that everybody knows about.'

Harold Shergold, discussing the
Berlin tunnel, 'Operation Gold'

Though Harold Shergold would forever remain 'utterly dedicated to the idea that SIS should sustain the secrecy of its people and its operations beyond the grave', when it came to the Berlin tunnel he was rather undermined by it being perhaps the best-documented of any SIS operation. This was thanks in no small part to the Russians having given the world's press a guided tour of the tunnel itself shortly after it was 'blown', rubbing salt in the wound by opening it to the public – some 90,000 of whom visited – and publishing a full account of its discovery, 'Caught Red-handed', complete with hand-drawn diagrams of the tunnel layout.

Shergold was long gone from Berlin by then, drafted back to Broadway, but he had been very much involved in the tunnel's inception. Not that he made much of it: modest to a fault, he felt that if anyone deserved the credit, it was the Berlin Post Office, who, in the rush to get the city's essential services up and running in the immediate aftermath of Hitler's defeat, had shared a rudimentary map of the city's cable network with the four occupying powers. But with Russia still a close ally – for a few weeks yet at least – and with SIS yet to have properly set up camp in Berlin, the map, Shergy thought, had 'simply ended up on a shelf somewhere gathering dust'.

Three years later it was a very different matter. With the city surrounded and cut off from the West, the thinking in Whitehall and Washington was that it was only a matter of time before Stalin made his move. 'All I want is 24 hours' notice of a Soviet attack,' US Secretary of State George C. Marshall had pleaded. Given that neither SIS nor the CIA had a single reliable intelligence source behind the Iron Curtain, this was a tall order – especially now that the Soviets had switched to one-time pads and had started using landlines instead of UHF radio. 'Agent-swamp' gossip and smuggled two-way radio sets notwithstanding, SIGINT held out the best hope of an advance warning of Soviet intentions. All of which meant that the few frontline officers with anything like the necessary technical knowledge or experience over and above basic radiocraft – and who also spoke both Russian and German – found themselves very much at the sharp end of the Cold War. This was how Shergy came to be working cheek by jowl with JBW, and why JBW was soon having to divide his time between Berlin and central Europe's other frontline city, Vienna.

He'd always claim to have preferred Vienna, despite (or because of) its reputation as 'the shooting gallery', its bombed-out Inner Stadt familiar to cinema audiences courtesy of the 1949 film *The Third Man*, with bodies still turning up face-down in the Danube or dumped in the rubble of collapsed buildings. Officers were technically barred from entering the Russian-controlled zone, but with a permit could pass through to reach their own zone, a loophole that was there to be exploited. Like the city itself, the SIS station was correspondingly much smaller than Berlin's, with just twenty or so regular staff housed in city-centre hotels, mostly in the faded grandeur of the Sacher (or the Parkhotel Schönbrunn) – but certainly not the nearby Imperial or Grand, which were occupied by the Soviet Kommandatura, with the result that SIS officers were liable to bump into their opposite numbers whenever they stepped out for beer and schnitzel.

The station also kept an eye on the troublesome Balkan region, which following the communist President Tito's unexpected split with Stalin was proving as irksome to Moscow as it was to Whitehall or Washington. The fear was that the 100,000 Red Army troops in eastern Austria might intervene, sweeping down through Hungary or else via the British-controlled southern Austrian provinces of Styria and Carinthia, which bordered Slovenia, then part of Yugoslavia. Judging by the bundle of used railway tickets to border towns such as Klagenfurt, Leibnitz, Föderlach and Viktring (which, for whatever reason, JBW never got round to throwing away), this was undoubtedly – or ostensibly – part of the reason why he was now having to spend as much time in Vienna as in Berlin.

Even so, it's hard to believe that he wasn't there primarily on 'tunnel business'.

The Vienna station was headed up by Peter Lunn, dispatched to Austria by a concerned Broadway just as Stalin was sealing off Berlin and neighbouring Czechoslovakia was falling to a communist coup. Lunn had previously worked in Section VIII, SIS's specialist communications unit, and shortly after arriving in Vienna began leafing through the large pile of documents supplied by the city's Post, Telegraphs and Telephone Administration at the end of the war, which showed that several of the cables linking the Red Army command post to Soviet units and airfields in the east of the country ran through the British and French sectors of the city. Lunn recognized that if he could tap these 'he would be the first to know if Stalin gave the order to invade Western Europe'. A telephone engineer was duly seconded from the Dollis Hill Post Office, along with a specialist mining engineer and SIS's leading technical expert, John Wyke. Between the four of them, they planned and excavated a tunnel leading from a shop basement out under the adjoining road and across to where one of the cables was buried, allowing Wyke to crawl through 70 metres of mud and place the first tap. The 'take' was more than SIS had dared to hope for. Conversations between Red Army HQ and forward units allowed them to gauge both the strength and location of Soviet troops, while even their overheard small talk – plans for the upcoming weekend and so on – proved invaluable, confirming that no Soviet move on either Yugoslavia or Austria was in the offing any time soon.

Additional tunnels were built, including one from the basement of Wyke's rented house in the French quarter, with the waxed recording cylinders spirited away in the back of laundry vans. As was invariably the way with Wyke, there were various Ealing Comedy moments: the Harris tweed shop set up as cover above the initial tunnel proving so popular with the locals that it ended up financing much of the operation; an officer collecting some of the cylinders from a schoolgirl go-between being mistakenly arrested on suspicion of child molestation; tunnels all but caving in under the weight of passing trams. Key to the operation's success was Lunn's insistence that anyone not directly involved be kept entirely in the dark as to what they were up to, not least the Foreign Office itself, which he somehow managed to bypass with the tacit agreement of Harold Caccia, the British Ambassador in Vienna.

How JBW knew or heard about the operation was possibly down to Lunn himself, with half an eye on repeating his success in Berlin, or more likely Wyke, hardly the most discreet of officers, matter-of-factly running JBW through what he had been working on (just as he would later matter-of-factly run George Blake through what he was working on during fishing trips on the Grunewald lakes). This was not the first time he and JBW had worked together – one of Wyke's after-dinner reminiscences was a long-winded tale about them trying to lift a cipher machine from under the Soviets' noses by tunnelling up into the basement of one of their centres via the sewers, though whether this ever came to anything only Registry would know.

Either way, soon enough JBW was back in Harold Shergold's office helping clear the dust off that map supplied at the end of the war by the Berlin Post Office, many of whose staff were still in touch with their former colleagues across the divide, a useful 'in' that paid off when one of the East Berlin communications engineers agreed to hand over an up-to-date, detailed route map of the cables used by both the Soviet military and the intelligence services. (Usual terms of business: safe passage to the West for him and his family.)

As Lunn had in Vienna, Shergold kept the initial discussions, on whether a similar operation could be carried out in Berlin, to as few people as possible – possibly just himself and JBW, with my mother – *der Notizenmacher* – tucked away in the corner of Shergy's cramped office jotting it all down.

The first step had been to carry out a recce of potential sites – ideally those where the cables ran closest to the British zone, most of which were in East Berlin's central Mitte shopping district. It was felt that rather than have an SIS officer loitering with intent, the notetaker might be better casting: being female in the entirely male-dominated world of 1950s espionage was cover in itself – the KGB's Berlin headquarters in Karlshorst didn't have a single female employee. And for any secretary with an eye for a bargain, Mitte was a routine day trip, one my mother had made many times, her secondhand Box Brownie able to do the job just as well as any Minox spy camera – enough to fill several pages of her old photo albums, albeit mostly snaps of ruined buildings, clumps of Russian soldiers and endless queues.

But in the end her various shopping trips came to nothing. The more Shergold and JBW investigated possible locations, the more they came to the conclusion that the idea of excavating a tunnel slap-bang in the centre of the most heavily policed square mile in Europe was optimistic at best, never mind the logistics of removing an estimated 3,000 tons of earth without anyone noticing (the Vienna tunnels were all in relatively quiet, out-of-the-way suburban locations). And though Wyke would always maintain that the idea of a city-centre tunnel should have been kept on the table, the search was widened to include sites further out.

The most problematic if potentially the most rewarding of these was situated some fifteen miles to the south-east of the city centre in the suburb of Altglienicke, where no fewer than three separate cables ran alongside each other.

However, the cables ran next to the main road leading to the nearby Soviet airfield and were several hundred yards inside the Russian zone, far more ambitious than anything Lunn's team had attempted in Vienna. Even carrying out a basic recce of the site was anything but straightforward, as it meant crossing a featureless tract of bare ground with just a bare apple orchard and disused churchyard by way of cover. One thing to have a secretary pop across from the Tiergarten for a day's shopping in Mitte, quite another to have her wander several hundred yards into the Russian zone in a southern suburb for no apparent reason. And so in the end, loath to bring anyone else in at this stage, Shergy reluctantly agreed to JBW's suggestion that they carry out the preliminary recce themselves.

Fifty years later, Shergy recalled the events of that day with a still palpable sense of unease. He was reluctant to cross over to the Russian zone at the best of times, even in central Berlin; here, there was nothing by way of an obvious destination they would be walking towards, still less a credible alibi. Certainly, anyone driving to or from the Soviet air base, or any passing border guard, would likely have raised an eyebrow – or gun – seeing two men wandering several hundred yards from the nondescript suburb of Rudow in the American sector, through a bare apple orchard, past an all-but-abandoned cemetery, then ambling across to the main road, only to turn round and head back again. Let alone the SIS head of station and one of his more senior officers.

For all his North African and Italian wartime experiences and his time with SIS, Shergold candidly admitted to having felt distinctly uneasy throughout. Unlike JBW, for whom it appeared to be nothing more than the proverbial walk in the park. His curious sangfroid irked Shergy at the time, troubled him afterwards and would still trouble him half a century later.

Sheer distance alone would, perhaps should, have ruled out the Altglienicke site, never mind the absence of a Harris tweed shop or a handy villa to disguise what would need to be a colossal tunnelling operation, not least the removal of several hundred lorryloads of soil. But JBW was not so easily dissuaded: though he knew next to nothing about tunnel engineering, he knew that one of his Eardisland uncles, an officer in the Shropshire Light Infantry and an engineer by training and trade, had helped construct a similarly extensive tunnel under the German lines during the First World War. Given the pressing need for hard intelligence on Soviet intentions, it was decided they should press ahead with the site, no doubt for much the same reason that Harold Caccia had given Lunn the go-ahead in Vienna: 'I couldn't look at myself if there had been an invasion and I had denied the chance of getting the information.'

SIS had been urgently exploring plans for an eavesdropping operation ever since the Russians had switched over to one-time cipher pads and landlines, but as yet none were sufficiently advanced to bother sharing with their American counterparts, though the CIA's head of station was aware that the British were up to something, not least since they themselves had been exploring a similar operation. This would all change towards the end of 1952, when a new head of station, Bill Harvey, arrived from Washington. As one of the Agency's foremost Soviet experts, Harvey already knew about the successful penetration of the East German Post Office and had been aware of the plan to replicate the Vienna operation in Berlin ever since it was first mooted – he would now become the driving force behind the proposed

Altglienicke tunnel, to the extent that it would come to be known simply as 'Harvey's hole'.

Harvey observed the need for secrecy to an almost obsessive degree. This may have owed something to the British involvement and his conviction – voiced to anyone who cared to listen – that Kim Philby, his SIS counterpart back in Washington, had been (and still was) a Soviet agent. Unlike JBW, who came highly recommended by Harvey's colleagues, almost all of them being ex-OSS. No sooner had Harvey settled into his palatial Lepsiusstrasse residence than he was asking to see the site for himself. A straightforward request, if one that Shergy recalled with considerable shake-of-the-head bemusement.

Harvey insisted they take separate cars, follow different, zigzagging routes and stagger their arrival times, preferably changing cars en route. For both Harvey and JBW, this was pretty much standard practice, if in this instance slightly impractical: by the time they arrived in Rudow it was already mid-afternoon. Once there, they crowded into the one car as JBW took Harvey through the pros and cons of the site, pointing out likely routes a tunnel might take to reach Altglienicke and the airport road, just about discernible in the far distance, and, 28 inches below ground, the Soviet cables.

To avoid hanging around longer than was necessary, the plan was that they stop off on the way back into town to discuss next steps and the practicalities of building a tunnel there, given the distances involved. A simple enough plan, but one which failed to take into account JBW's by-now well-established reputation for overcomplicating – *Warum einfach, wenn's auch umständlich geht?* 'Why do things the easy way when you can do them the hard way?'

As agreed, Shergy and Harvey pulled over at a suitable

spot, only for JBW to draw up alongside in his regulation VW Beetle, wind down his window and insist that they should try further into town, just to be on the safe side. Which they duly did, only for the same thing to happen again. And again. Until finally, after various leapfrogging stops and starts, to Shergy's exasperation they ended up outside 'quite possibly the most heavily watched place in the whole of Berlin' – JBW's own apartment.

If this had rankled with the secrecy-obsessed Harvey – hard to imagine otherwise – it didn't appear to do lasting harm: Harvey agreed to Shergold's suggestion that JBW caretake the British side of the operation until Lunn finished his current posting, still some months away.

On paper, they seem a most unlikely pairing: the hard-drinking, gun-toting, larger-than-life (physically and otherwise) legend that was William King Harvey and the pacifist Farmer Jøn of the Kaaba Allah collective. JBW drank the occasional beer or (Norwegian) aquavit; Harvey's standard lunchtime intake was four or five straight Martinis before getting back to work. JBW was a Cambridge-educated polyglot who had travelled the globe, while the 'rough upstart from Indiana' had never been abroad until he arrived in Berlin and once there would make no attempt to learn a single word of German. And whereas JBW rarely (if ever) carried a gun, Harvey was a one-man walking armoury, never without a shoulder holster, another firearm tucked into his waistband, a smaller pistol strapped under his trouser leg for back-up. And, in contrast to JBW being pulled up for smuggling Sufi literature back to London in the diplomatic bag, Harvey was caught smuggling home a cache of some forty-two revolvers, pistols, rifles and shotguns aboard a CIA courier flight.

For all their apparent differences, they did have something

of a shared history. After graduating from the FBI training academy with a perfect 100 score – on the machine gun – Harvey had been heavily involved in the Bureau's efforts to close down the Abwehr's clandestine communications network, working alongside BSC in the burgeoning field of electronic communications, where the British 'aimed for 100% co-operation with the Americans on signals intelligence'. Much to his frustration, as a married man Harvey had been turned down for 'special assignment', a euphemism for the FBI's operations in Latin America, instead spending the rest of the war focusing not on the Abwehr's activities but the Russians', with the result that his knowledge of communist activities was second to none. Much like his alcohol intake. Found slumped over his steering wheel by a passing patrol officer early one morning, he was dismissed from the FBI – only to turn up a few weeks later at the newly formed CIA, much to Hoover's annoyance. And so to Berlin.

However, for all his faults, Harvey 'had a basic trait of being able to admirably and accurately define and illuminate [. . .] talent or character in an individual, and then he would stick with that person forever'. With their shared habits of always sitting with their backs against the wall and speaking in code over the phone, in the years to come Bill Harvey would continue to give JBW the benefit of the doubt, no matter what. And it would be a very big what.

My mother with SIS minder 'Peter D', spring 1953.

Working holiday: Cakor Pass, Albanian border, June 1954.

4.

Altglienicke

'I left JBW in charge of the tunnel operation.
Yes, now that I think of it I suppose he was –
up until Lunn could get there.'

Harold Shergold, on
'Operation Gold'

As was now standard practice, plans for a possible Berlin tunnel
were kept to as small a group as possible (initial discussions
were likely confined to just Shergy and JBW). With the result
that the notetaker was asked to put down her pen and notepad
for the cause – along with her wedding ring – and head out to
Rudow in the American-controlled sector of Berlin.

In the grand scheme of things it was, she would always
maintain, just a walk-on part.

A survey of the site was needed, in the first place to work
out whether a tunnel on this scale was feasible, then to plot
the likely routes and distances involved. The survey team
needed a 'point man' – or 'point woman' – so that they could
take some initial readings. Though JBW was handling the
British side of the operation for the time being (somewhat
against Shergold's better judgement), the idea of having a
senior officer only too recognizable by the 'other side' wander
around a nondescript patch of ground some fifteen

245

miles from the city centre for a second time risked putting an end to the operation before it had even begun. Whereas *der Notizenmacher* was a stranger both to the area and to the Russians, and – better still – strictly speaking no longer employed by SIS now that she was married.

This still left the problem as to why a lone young woman would be traipsing across to the main airport road several hundred yards inside the Russian zone for no good reason, and several times – mapping out a tunnel on this scale would likely require her to make more than one visit.

The solution was that she and an accompanying officer pose as a romantic couple, not the first time SIS had employed this cover. The lucky man selected for the task went by the name of Shoebottom – destined, inevitably, to be referred to simply as 'Shoebum' forever after. (I'd almost certainly unknowingly met Shoebum at one or other of my mother's various drinks dos at the training camp, given that he ended his career in charge of the nearby Fort Gilkicker.)

With the construction of the Berlin Wall and its accompanying watch towers still a few years off, the divide between the American and Russian zones was marked out by nothing more than a few white posts here and there, and this far from the city centre was only lightly patrolled. The hope was that any Volkspolizei driving along the airport road would be unlikely to take too much notice of a young couple sat on the cemetery wall facing back towards the American zone rather than the Russian zone, still less suspect that they had strategically positioned a metal disc against the wall or one of the apple trees – as several hundred yards in the distance Wyke's surveyor got down to work.

Possibly to settle her nerves or simply to pass the time, she upped her occasional smoking habit, useful cover given that pretty much all East Germans chain-smoked – East German brands only of course, which (as with the local *Mischkaffee*) meant she could count herself fortunate if she came across any tobacco in her tobacco. To help Wyke's team make their calculations, she might stoop occasionally to tie a shoelace or whatever, in the process scooping up a handful of soil, which turned out to be not dissimilar to the pale-grey sandy soil of the Surrey heathland near to JBW's parents' home.

This was not the first time she had been called into action, whether to serve as a decoy in SIS's various people-smuggling operations or to recce potential tunnel sites. But this was one of the few times she had ventured beyond the central Mitte district – for good reason: in one of her rare hints that her Berlin days might not have consisted entirely of ballgowns and horse-riding, she'd recalled how, when she first arrived there, officers would hop on board the city's elevated S-Bahn and get off pretty much as and where they pleased. But before long they found they were being tailed from the moment they got off the train; to get around the problem, a few friendly S-Bahn drivers were persuaded to slow their trains at various points, allowing their 'passenger' to reach out and grab hold of one of the stanchion bars of the signal points that ran alongside the track, then simply climb down unobserved. This proved successful for a while, until one or two failed to make the return journey. The reason for which soon became clear in daylight, when it was discovered that the Russians had coiled thick razor wire round all the stanchion bars.

The biggest fear at the Altglienicke site was that a passing border guard or Volkspolizei, or possibly even the apple orchard's owner (a Farmer Noack), might stop for a chat only to then question her less-than-fluent German. It was never clear what she and Shoebum should do if the worst came to

247

the worst, other than make a run for it – not entirely practical given that they were several hundred yards away from the American zone and safety.

And, as she could be forgiven for thinking, a very long way from Whitley Bay, with gruesome tales of fingernails being pulled off, cigarettes stubbed out on skin and eyes poked out, even if by and large such 'encouragements' were not meted out to their SIS opposite numbers. Nevertheless, it was something that every officer was prepped for when venturing over into the Russian zone.

Less so the secretarial staff.

At Camp X, as her husband knew only too well, foreign nationals had been supplied with cyanide pills before being dropped into their German-occupied homelands, and this was still common practice in Berlin, as one of her SIS contemporaries noted in his memoirs: 'Agents who were in a position to be caught were issued with an L [lethal] tablet. These were concealed either in a hollow tooth or in a ring and when swallowed resulted in instantaneous death.'

For all that, I never (over)heard any talk of L-pills or lethal tablets either by her or anyone else in the training camp, not even John Wyke. Then again, somehow I can never quite erase an early childhood memory of the single large, pale-coloured pill that my mother once briefly flashed in front of me, tucked away inside the same small velvet box that had once housed her wedding ring. 'Both equally deadly,' she'd remarked, or something just as pithy. Which I remember for no better reason than, like most young children, I'd always baulked at having to swallow even the tiniest pill – aspirins or whatever – and couldn't imagine how anyone might be expected to deal with anything that large.

*

While his wife was heading across to Altglienicke, JBW was enjoying a rather less fraught journey to work, returning to London once or twice a month to update SIS's Section Y, who had handled the Vienna eavesdropping operations and were now handling Berlin's. Overseas visitors sometimes stayed at the suitably nondescript United Services Club a few yards up from Marble Arch (Aunt A would occasionally run into JBW there), but just as often he'd head back to his parents' house, an hour's train ride from Waterloo. His impromptu visits – with a few hours' warning at best – were duly, if perhaps unwisely, logged in his father's garden diaries alongside his orchid chores, Fahrenheit readings and the usual bee stings: 'JBW came early afternoon, packed hurriedly, left on 6pm train Vienna'; 'left about 9.30 by car and left his overcoat, much phoning, posted coat to Dover'; 'JBW rang up from Cologne late evening'; 'JBW did bees & finished just before rain about 1pm, left 3pm train'; 'JBW did bees on Sunday and got a bad sting beneath the eye'.

His visits were not entirely apiary-related. The house, tucked away in a tree-covered valley on the Surrey–Hampshire border, was a few minutes drive from Longmoor Army Camp, unlikely setting for what would be the first stage of the Berlin tunnel operation proper. Though no structural or civil engineer, JBW was aware that Altglienicke's sandy grey soil had much the same consistency as the sandy grey soil of the Surrey heathland. Hence the indifferent quality of Farmer Noack's apples; hence also the regular visits back to his parents.

A team of Royal Engineers had been assembled at Longmoor under the command of a Major Robert Merrell, and they now began an exploratory tunnel in the vertical face of the camp's demolition pit, normally used for explosives training. What quickly became clear was that the sandy soil was likely to prove far more problematical than anything Wyke had to deal with in Vienna. Merrell's team tried various different techniques at varying depths before then excavating upwards to the depth at which the Soviet cables were buried. All attempts ended in failure, the surface soil all too often collapsing, until eventually the team's sheet metal workers and carpenters assembled a hollow steel box which became known as The Mole.

At the same time Bill Harvey – being the archetypal American 'full-speed-ahead type of guy' – was pressing on with plans for a similar test shaft at White Sands Air Force base in New Mexico. He was also attempting to address Rudow's major flaw: unlike the sites in Vienna, there was nothing to disguise the entrance to a tunnel. This would eventually be solved by the construction of an entire radar station, ostensibly focused on the nearby Soviet air base but which housed a basement large enough and deep enough to hide both the tunnelling work and the thousands of tons of sandy soil that would need to be removed.

Once the initial teething problems had been solved and planning was fully underway, in early June 1953 JBW was finally able to hand over to Peter Lunn, newly arrived from Berne, thanks to his two-year posting having finished – or, just as likely, the Alpine snows having finally melted away. Given a tour of the possible sites, he agreed to press ahead with the Altglienicke proposal, which in turn allowed the notetaker to put her wedding ring back on and put a stop to her apple-orchard romance. JBW's contribution to Operation Gold was over before the first spade had even hit the ground.

Though marriage had put an end to my mother's SIS career – for the time being at least – by way of compensation it

250

came with a ground-floor apartment in leafy Douglasstrasse, complete with a Frau Margaretha to keep house and a part-time gardener, all just a short walk from her friends in the Bettinastrasse women's hostel and from John Wyke's house in Grunewald – allowing JBW to brief him over the kitchen table rather than in SIS's Olympic Building headquarters, where the presence of its leading technical expert would not have gone unnoticed. The end of the Berlin blockade and a return of sorts to civilian life also meant that my mother could finally have visitors to stay – younger sister Sheila was among the first to arrive, playing tennis at the Blau-Weiss and sunning herself at the American Anchor Club on Lake Wannsee before heading off to begin a new life in Canada.

By August the team of Royal Engineers had finished excavating their dummy shaft at Longmoor, ready for Lunn and Harvey to inspect, and that same month the CIA's head of operations arrived in Germany for a final run-through before presenting a detailed plan of the operation to the head of the CIA, Allen Dulles. JBW and my mother could finally take a few days' holiday – a short road trip (by his standards) down through Switzerland and the Italian lakes, across to Elba and then on to St Tropez, before heading back to Berlin via the Alps, his beloved Hudson Tourer having long since given way to a pale-blue secondhand Vauxhall Wyvern, anonymous enough not to attract attention – British Zone (BZ) numberplates aside – and small enough to be winched on and off the small cargo ships taking them to Elba, then on to Marseilles.

With his two-year Berlin posting now well into its sixth year, he had been told to expect a new assignment on his return, only to find that he was set to remain where he was for a further year, likely at the request of his American counterparts, given Bill Harvey and Peter Lunn's initial, undisguised loathing for each other. Lunn, at one point, was heard to say to Harvey, 'I respect you as a professional intelligence officer, but as a man, I hate your guts.' They ended up close friends and mutual admirers.

Harvey would keep detailed notes throughout the operation, typed up every night and all carefully locked away in his safe – these too would end up on a bonfire, courtesy of a routine office clear-out in the early 1960s, and with them JBW's contribution. Though no longer directly involved in the operation, he was still having to report back to Carlton Gardens every few weeks, as recorded by his father: 'November 22nd. JBW doing bees, cut down tree fallen over footpath & extracted honey, left for London about 10am.' But neither he, nor Lunn, nor Harvey was among the five CIA and nine SIS officers present at the first tunnel meeting proper in December, where it was agreed that the British would supply the technical equipment and handle the eavesdropping side of the operation while the Americans would carry out the construction of the tunnel itself, all carefully noted down by the official notetaker at the meeting, one George Blake.

In January 1954 the plans were signed off by Dulles, then given the final go-ahead at a joint CIA/SIS conference in Carlton Gardens, and US Army Engineers began construction of the radar station, excavating a basement large enough to disguise the tunnel entrance. Harvey would continue to visit the site throughout, always after dark, returning home in the small hours covered in mud (and reeking of whisky), unlike Lunn, who kept well away, his one and only visit spent largely out of sight in the basement without so much as getting his shoes muddy, as my mother would occasionally remind him in the years to come.

As in Vienna, it was left to John Wyke to deal with the business end of the operation, accompanied by a team of six sappers. He'd sensibly kept away from SIS's headquarters behind the Olympic Stadium, given that his presence was unlikely to go unnoticed by the hundred or so staff, few of whom (if any) knew anything about a possible tunnel operation. Nor would they. When George Blake turned up in Berlin, he was slightly baffled to find they were still none the wiser, despite the tunnel being fully operational by this time, with a small army of transcribers back in London already hard at work on the avalanche of resulting 'take'.

JBW's initial involvement in and knowledge of the operation – by far the biggest in SIS and CIA history – meant that there would be no more walkabouts inside the Russian-controlled half of Berlin, for fear of his being grabbed off the street by the KGB or Volkspolizei. Not that this put too much of a brake on his clandestine activities, if John Wyke's after-dinner tales were to be believed, or as my mother's younger brother Gordon witnessed firsthand. Fresh out of Newcastle Art College that summer, Gordon spent most of his first-ever trip abroad traipsing round various Bauhaus landmarks and pre-war artists' haunts – those that were still standing – returning every evening to Douglasstrasse for dinner, where they would sometimes be joined by JBW, now a more avuncular host than the introverted mutterer of earlier years. But one evening JBW had sat by the phone playing endless hands of patience, barely saying a word. Only for – as in all the best espionage thrillers – the phone to 'suddenly' ring and, as they say, all hell to break loose as several men burst in, one with a blanket over his head, then just as suddenly disappeared off into the night, JBW included, having successfully 'sprung' a senior East German police official.

Not an everyday occurrence perhaps, though par for the course for JBW who was still continuing to smuggle both operatives and whole families out of East Berlin – ironically, often by tunnelling through the basements of collapsed buildings – as much for humanitarian reasons as for any useful information they might impart. One such newly liberated East Berliner told Gordon that he could never thank JBW enough for what he had done both for them and their country.

By early summer 1954, with construction of the radar station warehouse well underway and Lunn having settled his differences with Harvey ('Once you had come to like and trust him, you couldn't have a better friend'), JBW was finally able to catch up on a three-year backlog of unused holiday. There were vague plans to drive down through Italy, stopping off in Trieste, where Aunt A had been stationed for the past year (second only to Venice in popularity with SIS staff, all the more so because the British had managed to bag the majestic clifftop Duino Castle at the end of the war, leaving the Americans to 'doss down' – as Aunt A drolly recorded in her diary – in the even more impossibly glamorous waterfront Miramare Castle).

But they would not be driving down through Italy, nor would it be a holiday.

As promised, her husband made an overnight first stop in Trieste for a catch-up dinner with Aunt A (while he attended to 'other business', Trieste being home to the various Yugoslav factions opposed to President Tito), only to turn the car south rather than west the following day and drive down into Croatia. Two years into her marriage, she knew better than to ask where exactly they might be heading. (On their honeymoon – billed as a road trip along the Mediterranean coastline – seemingly on a whim he had boarded the ferry across to Tangier, taking a ten-day tour round the mosques of Morocco and Algeria.)

From Trieste they followed the idyllic Adriatic coast road, down to Igrane and then on to Dubrovnik before continuing on to Montenegro, cooling off along the way at the then entirely deserted beaches of Budva, Bar and the Bay of Kotov – squeezing in a rather less glamorous side trip to Petrovac's oil wells, Minox photographs included. Having booked into Herceg Novi's bougainvillea-clad Park Hotel, first thing the following morning he'd driven down to the small border town of Ulcinj, with its largely Albanian population, whose language he had spent the past twelve months getting to grips with in the usual way, headphones clamped to ear, tuned into Radio Tirana, dictionary by his bedside.

Needless to say, he was there on business. Six months earlier, on New Year's Eve, Radio Tirana had announced that the state police, the Sigurimi, had arrested a team of CIA-trained Albanian agents. This was only the latest in a long line of disastrous attempts to infiltrate exiles into the country in the hope of seeding some sort of opposition to the country's communist dictator, Enver Hoxha. Though the blame would later be pinned on Kim Philby, SIS had showed themselves more than capable of screwing up without Philby's help, as their American counterparts needed no reminding. That *New Statesman* article on Maurice Oldfield that my mother had cut out and kept included a CIA officer's account of Broadway's approach to Albania at the time. 'After sitting around a table in desultory fashion for an hour or two, one

Englishman finally said, "I say, why don't we get old Henry up here, he knows about this." A day or two later old Henry finally showed up from down in Sussex and agreed to undertake the task, although as he said, "This will wreak havoc with the garden, you know, just getting into trim."'

Though ostensibly an SIS initiative, once again it's difficult to imagine that Bill Harvey wouldn't have known about JBW's trip south, possibly even instigated it, hoping he might gain at least an on-the-ground insight, over a beer or two, into what was happening inside Albania, as opposed to what was broadcast on state radio. Basic fieldcraft, as even I had witnessed more than once during my years at the SIS training camp, when John II had studiously avoided nearby drinking holes for fear of running into trainee officers who would be 'dropped off at a pub and instructed to persuade an unsuspecting drinker to reveal personal details [. . .] which would later be checked to determine whether the trainees had succeeded'.

So JBW would leave my mother to her own devices and head off to a local bar – just as he had done all the way down the Adriatic coast – hoping to put his (presumably rather basic) Albanian to good use and glean a little intelligence or gossip from the small band of Albanian exiles who had made it across the Buna River, which doubled as the Albanian–Yugoslav border. Unlike in Berlin, he decided against attempting to ford the river and going walkabout in Albania itself, possibly put off by the Sigurimi's impressive track record of executing infiltrators and then liquidating their entire families. Instead they drove back up to Bar and then Budva, JBW having told the hotel – and my mother, sat beside him – that they would be heading back to Trieste. Only to then head up into the mountains, hugging Albania's northern borders as close as roads would allow, snaking their way up to Andrijevica and then by way of light relief heading down the vertiginous Cakor Pass into Kosovo, JBW at one point stopping off without warning and disappearing for several hours to meet someone, once again leaving his wife to her own devices, though as ever she knew better than to enquire where he'd been or what he'd been up to. They then motored back down to Northern Macedonia and Skopje before crossing into Greece, mission accomplished, holiday resumed.

At the end of August JBW paid a final visit to the Olympic Stadium headquarters, where he was informed that he had been awarded an OBE, rarer than one might think in this particular branch of Her Majesty's Service, markedly so for someone just thirty-seven years old. As a certain Ian Fleming noted, 'British spies hardly ever receive decorations.' His star very much in the ascendant, for a few months yet at least.

My mother (heavily pregnant) on her Vespa, December 1955.

5.

Helsinki

'His cover had been blown. Once that
happens, you're not much use any more,
so they had to pull him out.'

John II on the 'official' reason
for JBW's dismissal from SIS

Ten years late, JBW finally made it to Finland. In some respects the country hadn't changed since Dorothy Maclean's time there: caught between East and West politically, with a more or less open border with Russia, only now there was an upcoming election that, like the country itself, could go either way.

Up until a few months beforehand he had more or less assumed that he would be posted to Vienna, given that the station's remit also included Albania. Though Vienna was a city my mother knew well enough, judging by her photograph albums its main draw lay in its proximity to the Austrian Alps, SIS having 'appropriated' one of the better ski runs for the use of its staff at the end of the war. However, as with Berlin, the only time she mentioned Vienna to my brother and me came courtesy of the cinema again, this time a Saturday-morning trip to see *The Sound of Music*, which had 'at long last reached Woking. Lovely scenery. Renewed my urge to go back to Austria.' Possibly not the best window into life as a frontline agent in the Cold War Vienna of Graham Greene's *The Third Man*.

Despite having spent July skirting around Albania's borders via Croatia, Montenegro, Kosovo and northern Macedonia, and despite her husband's ongoing attempts to master the language, she knew better than to take anything for granted. 'I never knew the reason for our moves but the build-up was always the same, lengthy enigmatic phone calls, hours spent away at "meetings" and JBW, who loved change, wearing an air of suppressed excitement. When the time was ripe he would tell me where we were going and when, usually in a few days or even hours, so we kept our possessions minimal.'

But to everyone's surprise Moscow had suddenly begun pulling Red Army troops out of the city, hoping to persuade the Western allies to do likewise in Berlin (and within a year would agree to Austrian independence), making any Soviet military move on Albania highly unlikely – and JBW's move to Vienna redundant. Added to which, the feeling was that Albania was perhaps best left to its own devices, given that all SIS's infiltration operations had ended before they had barely begun, its agents picked up the moment they stepped ashore, as JBW's circuitous fact-finding journey round its borders had likely confirmed. Philby to blame, of course.

There was talk of a possible move to South Korea, but when this too was put on hold JBW used the time to head off to Leipzig for one last visit to September's annual trade fair, still the venue of choice for anyone hoping to do business with Eastern Europe, clandestine or otherwise. Not the wisest of moves for someone so closely involved in the planning of the proposed tunnel operation, and certainly not one that the Berlin CIA station chief, Bill Harvey, would have sanctioned.

That same month my mother learnt she was pregnant with my elder brother (Jonathan – soon to be shortened to 'J') and so with SIS's blessing they headed back to London, returning overland via northern Italy – belated compensation for her cancelled summer holiday in Lake Como. With no definite word on his next posting, they rented a cottage in Walton-on-Thames, a half-hour train ride up to Waterloo and from there a brisk walk up to Broadway and Carlton Gardens.

Christmas was spent in Walton-on-Thames, during which JBW announced that he would be leaving for Helsinki in a few days' time. This was not entirely unexpected, given the scarcity of Finnish speakers within the Foreign Office, let alone SIS – so few that the resident station chief Rex Bosley had been obliged to remain at his Helsinki desk for over a decade.

In some ways Bosley was a hard act to follow. 'A garrulous bon viveur whose indiscretions went hand in hand with his clowning', like many from the pre-war era, he believed that the Service's best work was done after 6 p.m.. Espionage-wise, Bosley was a rather easier act to follow. Despite its cheek-by-jowl existence with the occupying Russians, the Helsinki station had produced little, if any, information of use – not altogether unsurprising, given that 'on introducing himself at parties, the SIS agent would lift his collar, dart his eyes, and growl sotto voce, "Don't tell anyone but I'm a spy."'

Meanwhile, with the due date of her first child only three months away, my mother agreed that JBW should go on ahead by himself. Never a good idea, as Dorothy Maclean could have told her.

After seeing in New Year in the usual manner – head

buried in his well-thumbed copy of Hugo's Finnish–Russian dictionary and headphones clamped to ear, as per Mullsjö's tried-and-trusted *direkt metod*, JBW flew up to Helsinki, giving his address as Norra Esplanadgatan, one of the city's more imposing streets, though this was likely just an office of the British Legation or similar while he looked for somewhere to stay.

Thick snow aside, the first thing he would have noticed was that all the airport taxis, as with the vast majority of cars and manufactured goods, were Eastern European. Barely a quarter the size of Vienna and one tenth that of Berlin, Helsinki had escaped being divided up between the Allies, which in practice meant that the Russians more or less had the place to themselves. Finnish politicians of whatever persuasion were still obliged to cultivate a *kotiryssa*, or 'home Russian', within the vast Russian embassy. Aside from being the only European country bordering Russia that hadn't – as yet – fully fallen under the Soviet yoke, the Finns' stubborn resistance to Stalin's invading Red Army over the winter of 1939–40 had hardly endeared them to their neighbours, who at the end of the war had imposed heavy financial reparations, land-grabbed some of the country's eastern territory and arranged to 'lease' its main naval base just to the southwest of Helsinki. Ten years on, Finland found itself in the crosshairs, as much a Cold War hotspot as Vienna and Berlin, if slightly less bombed-out and with fewer bodies turning up here and there. But the intelligence war being played out against a backdrop of the upcoming election was no less intense, if far less well documented. With much riding on its outcome, the CIA and SIS were actively supporting the Social Democrats' Karl August Fagerholm, while the KGB backed his opponent, Urho Kekkonen, reason enough for

JBW to be dropped at short notice into a Helsinki that was fast becoming the new 'agent-swamp'.

The local KGB station was far larger than all its Western counterparts put together and they would have had no illusions as to the true nature of JBW's job, even without *The Times* (un)helpfully listing his OBE award with the job descriptor 'research sec., Polit Br Mil Gov, Berlin'. Being an altogether different class of operative to Rex Bosley, he would have been under surveillance from the moment he stepped off the plane, easily done in a city this size and in the depths of winter. After spending his first few weeks in city-centre hotels he returned home to Walton-on-Thames for my brother's birth – if only briefly – 'he was in Finland when I went into hospital and was back in Finland when I came out of hospital' – heading back to Helsinki the next day.

He didn't last long.

If our mother made only the occasional passing reference to her time in Berlin, whatever it was that occurred in Finland was never mentioned, not least because she herself was never entirely certain what exactly happened there, her only comment being: 'No sooner had I let him out of my sight than everything just came crashing down.'

Nor were the instructors at the training camp, my usual source, much better informed – not even John Wyke, normally the most reliable fund of unreliable information. Not that this stopped both him and others offering up versions of what they *thought* had happened, though even these varied with every telling. Nor, needless to say, is there anything to be had by way of official records. Armed with a visitor's pass to the National Archives, anyone can access pretty much everything to do with Finland all the way back to Viking times, courtesy of the Freedom of Information Act – except for the year 1955, which, for whatever reason, remains off-limits with no signs of being declassified any time soon.

And so once again it was left to Harold Shergold to fill in the blanks. Or in this case, the void. Shergy had returned to London in early 1954, his field of operation now extended to the Baltic States – Lithuania, Estonia and Latvia – all of which had remained under Soviet control at the end of the war. Various local resistance movements had sprung up, some managing to remain active for several years before being closed down. Their survival was hardly helped by the majority of SIS's Baltic operations, which included landing operatives and equipment ashore by FPB launch (possibly the self-same FPB that ended up all but mothballed at the training camp) had met much the same fate as in Albania: 'No sooner had the agent clambered into a dinghy for the final stage of his journey [. . .] than two patrol vessels arrived on the scene and opened fire.'

Though this was not viewed as any great cause for concern within Broadway, Shergy thought otherwise. 'Shergold was seriously alarmed by what he found and quickly came to the conclusion that these networks were, in fact, under KGB not SIS control, so thoroughly were they penetrated by Russian Intelligence. There was great resistance in Broadway Buildings when Shergold proposed that the Baltic networks be closed down.' It wasn't long before the network in Poland was found to be similarly compromised (as Aunt A could have told them), lending ever more importance to SIS's efforts in Finland, just across the water from and within easy radio transmission reach of the Estonian capital, Tallinn. A city and a region that JBW knew well from his regular summer drives up to Norway in years gone by, reason enough in itself for Broadway to have posted him up to Helsinki at such short notice. If rather against Shergy's better judgement.

Credited by his fellow officers as having an almost sixth sense for whether a defector was genuine or an officer was telling the truth, Shergy 'had the nose', as one colleague later told John le Carré. And Shergy's nose had first begun to twitch several years before, during the Berlin airlift, when JBW had disappeared off to Canada on 'urgent family business' (trying to save his marriage to Dorothy Maclean – and apply for Canadian citizenship while he was at it). It wasn't so much the last-minute flight across the Atlantic – on JBW's salary? – more that he had managed to bag himself a seat out and then, more improbable still, *back* into Berlin's Templehof Airport at a time when every last inch of aircraft space was desperately needed, the city's very survival hanging in the balance. JBW's explanation that a pilot friend had owed him a favour hadn't quite rung true.

However, it was during their joint recce of the proposed tunnel site that Shergy's doubts about JBW really took hold. The prospect of the Berlin station chief and one of his senior officers being spotted wandering across several hundred yards of open ground in an out-of-the way location for no apparent reason made it a highly hazardous undertaking, enough to set anyone's nerves jangling – and Shergy didn't mind admitting that his had jangled. But what really unnerved him was that JBW hadn't shown the slightest hint or twitch of anxiety – he might just as easily have been heading out to pick up the morning papers.

These doubts had never fully gone away, and following the events in Helsinki, never would.

Over the years I heard several versions, for want of

a better term, of JBW's 'Helsinki incident'. The gist of which would be familiar to anyone who's ever picked up a spy novel in an airport bookshop: deserted street, screech of tyres, KGB snatch squad spills out, victim is bundled into back of waiting car, spirited off to who-knew-where, interrogated, agrees to be 'turned', is released, only to renege on the deal. Soon afterwards is lured into meeting with possible double agent, only to be ambushed in a hail of bullets, lucky to survive. Cover blown, he is recalled to London.

But in truth there was no screech of tyres, no KGB snatch squad, no bundling into the back of any car, no kidnapping in fact. Far from it, Shergy revealed. More disturbingly, much more disturbingly, my father had simply walked into the KGB's Helsinki headquarters entirely of his own free will.

Back then SIS's R5 section were responsible for investigating communist influence within the intelligence services – very much a full-time job in the 1950s, one would think. The section was headed by Charles Ransom, who had personally conducted JBW's questioning, an indication of the seriousness with which the incident was viewed within Broadway. Almost certainly he would have consulted Shergold, as JBW's erstwhile Berlin station chief, though Shergy made no specific mention of it – instead he pointed to the low settee slung against the wall to one side of his desk, where only a few months before his former colleague and longtime friend had been sitting, and told me, but for the inconvenience of Ransom having died in the intervening period, 'you could have had it straight from the horse's mouth'.

For a relative outsider such as Ransom to navigate the labyrinthine 'agent-swamps' of Berlin, Vienna and Helsinki would itself have been a daunting task, let alone attempt to winkle the truth out of someone as talented (and trained) in the art of obfuscation as JBW.

He didn't get off to the best of starts. Asked to hand over his passport – as much for administrative purposes as anything – to the consternation of Ransom and his team, JBW had matter-of-factly produced a Canadian rather than a British passport. As Shergy drolly reflected: if SIS could not even get his nationality right, the chances of obtaining a successful prosecution were finished before they'd even begun.

Ransom took what at the time was the standard interrogation approach, trying to trip up the interviewee by running through all the various events and timelines in the hope that somewhere along the line his answers might not tally with the known facts. Beginning with what exactly had happened in Finland, before then fact-checking some of the Vienna and Berlin operations JBW had been involved in, no doubt also probing to try to find out how exactly he had managed to obtain a flight in and out of Tempelhof at the height of the airlift, why he had headed off into East Germany for the annual Leipzig trade fair just as he was being recalled to London, why he had been so unconcerned about the possibility of being spotted when he and Shergy had carried out their initial recce of the proposed tunnel site. For which JBW doubtless had perfectly plausible explanations. Shergy's assessment of his late friend Ransom's chances were blunt: 'Someone of JBW's intelligence would have run rings around him.'

That said, Shergy made no bones about having used Ransom's questioning as the basis for his own questioning of George Blake five years later. Whether he had listened to actual recordings or simply gone through it all with Ransom he didn't elaborate, saying only that both he and

R5 concluded that without a confession the chances of anything standing up in a court of law were negligible. Not that Ransom's efforts were entirely in vain. In what sounds to have been a relatively gentlemanly affair, as much interview as interrogation – certainly no ripping up of floorboards or rummaging through waste bins – JBW was free to head back home to Walton-on-Thames at the end of the first day. The following morning a frustrated Ransom and his team tried a different tack, probing the *motives* behind his actions. Put bluntly, why would anyone in their right mind want to wander into KGB headquarters of their own accord? At which point JBW had suddenly dropped his guard.

Not that it was anything like the sort of confession that Ransom and R5 had been looking for, and not one that Shergy, an uncomplicated man, had felt able to make any sense of. With a look of discomfort almost as pained as when he had nearly expired on me earlier that day, he had paused, gazing up at the ceiling. JBW's explanation had been that he had been acting on 'voices from God . . . or some such nonsense'.

Unsurprisingly Shergy hadn't the faintest clue what JBW was talking about. But I had a fair idea.

Of course, it's not impossible that his unexpected appearance in the foyer of the KGB's Helsinki station was simply the culmination of having spent the best part of the last fifteen years constantly having to look over his shoulder, sit with his back to the wall, have his apartment raided, even pick the occasional bullet out of the plasterboard – perhaps Helsinki was simply the last straw. But more likely, much more likely, his intuition and his belief in the power of *murāqabah* would have told him that there was nothing to fear and that he would emerge unscathed, much as when he and Shergy had blithely wandered across to the Soviet sector in Altglien-icke, seemingly without a care in the world.

Exactly how long he had been detained by his Russian hosts no one seemed to know for sure – some said over-night, others as much as three days, while they attempted to 'turn' him, his value to the KGB being far greater if he were to remain in situ. And if he wasn't defecting, then what was he doing? Wyke volunteered that the whole episode had been told back to front, and that, having gone to meet a potential informer and found himself being shot at, JBW had walked into the KGB offices to question why the Berlin protocol of not attacking one's counterparts didn't apply to Helsinki. But the common consensus was that having – for whatever reason – entered the KGB offices, they needed hurriedly to turn him, likely gently reminding my father that he now had a family, and then, after coming to some sort of 'agreement' with him, had released him.

The terms of the agreement were never clear, if indeed there was one, not that JBW had ever kept to *any* agreement, nor ever would. As both Dorothy Maclean and my mother knew only too well. What isn't disputed is that he did go to meet a contact, out of town in the surrounding forest, not long after his impromptu visit to the KGB headquar-ters (or before it, according to Wyke), a routine enough task for someone with his Berlin experience, if one that always carried a degree of risk. Having driven out to the agreed rendezvous point, no sooner had he stopped his car than he was met with a hail of bullets. Quite how he managed to escape with his life only JBW (and the KGB) will ever know, but escape he did, more or less unscathed – the clunky body-work of his East European-manufactured hire car evidently strong enough to see off East European-manufactured bullets. Hardly his first brush with mortality, though one of the closest.

Aside from the awkwardness of having to return a car peppered with bullet holes, the ambush resulted in Broadway urgently recalling him to London on the basis that his 'cover' had been blown. A moot point: his cover had been blown from the moment he started working for Philby.

With no conclusive outcome from Ransom's questioning, and with no legal grounds for dismissal, JBW was restricted to low-level intelligence tasks, certainly low-level enough for him to have no qualms about bringing his work home with him: years later minute sheets, background enquiry requests and papers marked 'Secret' would continue to turn up under the eaves, stuffed at the back of drawers or even used as lining paper: 'Feb 1st 1956 No: S1/4856. Charles Baskin. Suspected Soviet agent at present in Mexico, born about 1900 in Russia, dismissed from job with Standard Oil of New Jersey for political unreliability, sometime resident of 31 Sloane Avenue, SW3'; 'Letter from RCMP dated March 2nd 1956. Rolf Alexander, originally Hoffman, of the USA, Canada and Mexico, would not surprise me if he has papers to support alias, now living in Paignton, Devonshire.' And so on.

But it was events in Berlin and the resulting overhaul of SIS that would put an end to JBW's career, not Ransom. In April 1956 a Red Army border unit was dispatched to Altglienicke tasked with tracking down a supposed fault on the Soviet cables (heavy rainfall had caused them to short). After digging some exploratory shafts, they came across what appeared to be a covered chamber, which they assumed must be something to do with the sewage system or else left over from the Second World War. But with the arrival of a KGB colonel in the early hours, the tone changed, and the following morning they clambered down into the darkness only to come face to face with John Wyke's handiwork (much of it proudly stamped 'Made in Britain'). After cautiously working their way along several hundred yards of tunnel, they were halted by a handwritten sign in Russian warning that they were 'now entering the American zone', quickly followed by the chilling sound of a .50-calibre machine-gun bolt being pulled back and let go – by no less a figure than the CIA station head himself, Bill Harvey.

Though the Russian unit had seemed genuinely shocked at their discovery, both Harvey and Lunn were (rightly) convinced that the KGB must have had inside information, a suspicion that the Russians themselves made little attempt to dispel, suggesting that they had known about the operation since the previous May – coincidentally round about the time JBW was making his unscheduled visit to the KGB building in Helsinki. And for all the vast amount of American manpower and money spent on the actual construction and running of the tunnel, no one seems to have spent much time investigating whether the leak came from their side. For Lunn, the task of narrowing down a possible source was made all the easier by the small number of officers who had been involved in the operation, most of whom had deliberately kept well away from SIS's Olympic Stadium headquarters. By a simple process of elimination JBW would have been a possible candidate, not least since he had known about the operation from its very inception.

He did his best to defend his corner, detailing his involvement from beginning to end, even suggesting two other possible sources of the leak. Their names were duly committed to paper, only to be (mis)filed along with hundreds of other such papers deep within the bowels of SIS's Broadway head office, never to be seen again.

The Soviets timed the announcement of their discovery of the tunnel to perfection, while the Russian leader Nikita Khrushchev was on a state visit to Britain. Unusually, he'd chosen to travel by sea, arriving with his entourage on board the cruiser *Ordzhonikidze*, whose sleek new propellor design intrigued naval intelligence enough for them to dispatch a diver, a Commander 'Buster' Crabb, beneath the waves of Portsmouth Harbour to inspect it. Unfortunately the ageing, overweight Commander Crabb was not perhaps the best choice to undertake the mission (especially as the SIS training camp – with rather better-qualified divers – was located just around the headland). Crabb failed to return. The Russians rightly complained, leaving a suitably embarrassed – and enraged – Anthony Eden to apologize to Khrushchev, explaining that espionage was 'a fact of life, and a disagreeable one'.

And with that SIS suffered the ignominy of having Dick White drafted across from MI5 to clear up the mess.

White wasted little time getting rid of what he termed the 'dissolute adventurers', as opposed to the modern intelligence officer, exemplified by Harold Shergold. Overnight the business of 'identifying those who would mean to do us harm' became the work of solid professionals rather than gifted mavericks. (Indeed no sooner had White sat down at his desk than Lunn, as he himself would later cheerfully admit, was bounding up the stairs and talking him through the whole tunnel operation from beginning to end and who he felt might be responsible for the leak.)

In what was nothing short of a wholesale overhaul of SIS, there would be no more underwater adventuring, no more going walkabout behind the Iron Curtain, no more fraternizing with their opposite numbers, with instant dismissal threatened for any officer even coming into contact with a KGB counterpart. Unsurprisingly then, JBW was one of the first to have his name green-inked for dismissal by the new 'C'. The irony of this was likely not lost on my father: when he'd arrived in Berlin, SIS had barely known the name of a single KGB officer, and it was very much with the encouragement (orders) of the then station chief Bruce Lockhart that he 'had almost daily contact with a wide range of Soviet personnel, with the result that I feel I gained a greater knowledge of their theories and attitudes than I could have done by any other means'. And while the unveiling of the Berlin tunnel may have been seen as a failure by some – not least the British press at the time – it had more than done its job, providing the all-important reassurance that the Soviets were not about to move on Berlin, and in the process revealing almost the entire make-up of the KGB's Karlshorst station right down to the name of every officer – pretty much down to what each of them had for breakfast. 'For a failed operation, it's funny how everyone tries to claim credit for it,' as my mother would pithily remark.

JBW would forever after protest his innocence, as well he might given George Blake's unmasking some five years later, not that it would likely have made much difference. In the newly reformed SIS there was barely room for the likes of John Wyke, let alone someone as disparate and as duplicitous as JBW – even with a degree of familial bias, both my brother and I have always found it difficult to argue with White's decision.

A footnote of sorts to all this. A few months after his dismissal, SIS had a walk-in visitor of their own, and surely one of the most unlikely, with or without his customary white robes: JBW's fellow Sufi and close friend Samuel Lewis, former head gardener at Kaaba Allah and future King of the Hippies, on his way back from a spiritual tour of India. 'Have done a lot of walking, always interesting and more time in Green and Hyde Parks, but have also spent some time trying to locate my old friend John Wood at the foreign office. It took two hours to locate him and then to learn he has a roving job (just as he always had). If we meet we can do a lot about the world problems. Not just talkie-talky.'

PART FOUR

JBW repairing rigging, Stranford Lough, Northern Ireland, 1957.

Brother (J), shortly after being 'sprung' from Vancouver, January 1959.

Tugboat steering the *Empress of Britain* out of Saint John's harbour on the way back to England, February 1959.

I.

Vancouver

'True to form, JBW at no time took us into his confidence as to his plans, past or future, & from that day to this we have not had a cheep out of him. Later we heard that he had high-tailed it to Canada.'

Jean and Allan Batham, JBW's
business partners 1956–7

No matter how intellectually gifted one might be or how many languages one had mastered, finding work after exiting the Secret Intelligence Service under a cloud was far from straightforward, as a previous ex-employee had soon discovered: 'Lucrative employment remained a distant aspiration since when I applied for work, the first question asked was always why I had left the Foreign Service.' With hindsight Philby could count himself fortunate. Five years on from his resignation there was now something of a glut on the market as a result of Dick White's purge of SIS.

As was the way of things, the terms of JBW's exit were more gentleman's agreement than scruff of the neck. He received a pay-off and retained his pension rights, such as they were, with the understanding that he would look for work abroad, most likely Canada given his – ahem – nationality. He'd joined the Institute of International Affairs, taking the train up to London once a week or so to kick-start the process of finding employment better suited to his talents than was likely to be posted up in the local labour exchange. Using Chatham House's library, he began the slightly dispiriting task of firing off applications to various far-flung teaching and lecturing posts, along with a carefully edited CV, his linguistic abilities now confined to Spanish, Russian and French (no mention of Finnish, Norwegian, Albanian, etc.). To placate his understandably rattled wife, he used his pay-off to put down the deposit on a house in the commuter-belt town of Woking. An improbable choice, possibly explained by the house looking much like the one she had grown up in back in Whitley Bay, but much more likely due to Woking being home to the first purpose-built and, at the time, the largest mosque in the country, a focal point for Islamism. Which was where, having first knocked on the Foreign Office's door, Samuel Lewis finally managed to track down his friend and spiritual protégé, the first time they had spent any time together since JBW visited Kaaba Allah in 1947, shortly before it burned to the ground. Back then he had been plain Farmer Jøn and so far as Lewis knew a bona fide Norwegian, pacifist and vegetarian to boot, pencilled in to take over from Shabaz Best in Latin America, just as Lewis was pencilled in as likely successor to Murshida Martin. But after Lewis was unexpectedly passed over for the leadership role, JBW's spiritualist activities had been largely confined to bouts of cross-legged contemplation at the bottom of Berlin swimming pools.

Prodigious letter-writer and diarist though Lewis was, for once he failed to record exactly what they discussed or just how they intended to solve 'the world's problems', noting only that in 'another of those fairy book experiences' he had finally met up with his 'best friend' before going on to give an address to the faithful 'at the Mosque in Woking on the teaching of Sufism in the Western world'. But as Lewis always preached: 'A Sufi has no home or family or country.' And so it was with JBW.

With no immediate prospects on the job front, at the start of 1957 he teamed up with a former Broadway colleague and sailing companion Allan Batham, who, back in the day, had helped JBW pen his 'Ideological Answers to Communism'. Batham, flatteringly (unflatteringly?) described in an American magazine as 'a large man, his arms and hands are the sort that dock workers need, his calves are the sort often seen in football defense platoons', was a former naval officer, and as such was always more at home on the water than on land – even in Berlin he was more likely to be found on the Havel than in SIS's Olympic Stadium headquarters. Finding himself at a loose end post-Berlin, he had joined his family's engineering firm but was now attempting to branch out on his own, renting a small factory space in Belfast with the aim of 'researching a method of preserving packaged meats in a new form of synthetic material'. Possibly not the line of work JBW had in mind when commuting up to Chatham House, but needs must. A few weeks later – despite a relative of Jean Batham warning her and her husband not to have anything to do with 'their friend John Wood. Would never say why, simply "watch out", I guess he had some inside information' – the Bathams and JBW put to sea in their 36-foot ketch, *The Falcon*, sailing from Tilbury Docks to Northern Ireland via the Scilly Isles, bootlegging whisky along the way before dropping anchor in Stranford Lough, County Down.

A few weeks later JBW was joined by wife and son, the Bathams having rented the top floor of a large country house a mile or so from the shore. Picturesque, but a long way from the nearest shop, let alone civilization – not ideal for a young mother with no means of transport and with JBW disappearing off to Belfast first thing every morning. And so, come autumn, mother and son headed back to Woking, leaving JBW to his own devices. Never a good idea. Reduced to helping develop packaging for preserved meats in a disused factory in Belfast in the middle of winter, through – as he saw it – no fault of his own, no doubt he had reason to feel hard done by. However, it would be hard to blame George Blake for the mess he was about to land himself in.

With the business up and running, the Bathams' secretary, Rita, headed across from London to help out, and was given the bedroom adjoining JBW's – with the inevitable result.

A few weeks later he headed back to Woking in time for Christmas, only to learn on arriving that his wife was now three months pregnant. With the Bathams starting to question the wisdom of their Belfast venture (and hatching an impractical plan to sail to the Virgin Islands and start up a dive school-cum-hotel – duly realized the following year) the prospect of a second child was possibly not the news that JBW wanted to hear, especially given that – as she would ruefully admit – it had been more her doing than his, having persuaded a reluctant JBW into bed shortly before leaving Ireland: 'Thought I'd give it one last go.' Unplanned though her pregnancy might be, there was little chance of her agreeing to his suggestion of a termination, as Dorothy Maclean had back in Montevideo. For which I have always been rather grateful. In common with many a failing marriage, he-said-she-said battle lines were soon drawn up. She said that he was seeing someone else; he said that she had been seeing someone else ('In rural Ireland? In the 1950s? Chance would be a fine thing'). Their stand-off was not helped by the cloud of suspicion that had hung over JBW ever since his dismissal from SIS, a cloud which even her fellow ex-Berliners found problematical, with dinner invites and monthly drinks dos all but drying up. And where Kim Philby's wife Aileen had taken to the bottle under similar circumstances, my mother took to her bed, the doctors advising complete rest for the time being. Or as JBW would later describe it, 'psychiatric care and committed for some months'.

Either way, with or without his wife's agreement (without), JBW decided their three-year-old son would be better off back in Ireland with him – or, more accurately, with Rita – returning to Woking a few weeks ahead of my birth, differences seemingly resolved. But then on that sunny July morning, as I lay on a blanket in the garden next to my mother, he leant out of our upstairs window to say he was 'just heading off for a loaf of bread', before driving off with my brother and my mother's passport all the way down to Southampton to board the SS *Homeric*, which set sail for Canada that evening.

When our pale-blue Vauxhall Wyvern was eventually located in the Southampton Docks car park (clearly the car park of choice for departing diplomats – Burgess and Maclean had left their car there when fleeing the country a few years before), a check through the various ships' manifests revealed father and son as having disembarked in Montreal. But after this initial breakthrough, the trail went cold. Weeks turned into months, and wherever they were by now, they weren't in Montreal.

Help eventually came from an unlikely source: the local conveyancing solicitor who had overseen the purchase of our Woking home, who managed to succeed where the police, not to mention SIS, had drawn a blank. Noting that my brother had started attending a local Steiner school, he got in touch with the Canadian education authorities. Sure enough, a few weeks later back came the news that he was now enrolled in a Steiner school in Vancouver.

Cue a twenty-four-hour dash up to Petty France to pick up a replacement passport, book a passage over to Canada and somehow fit in my smallpox jab, before tramping the mile or so across Horsell Common to Mrs Taylor's (her cleaner and, from here on in, unlikely confidante) to drop me off, then head to the station to catch the boat train. Five days later my mother disembarked in Quebec, stopping off with her sister who – as luck would have it – was now living in Sudbury, Ontario, having emigrated to Canada a few years before, then made her way over to Vancouver.

No doubt there is a proper legal procedure to be followed in such cases, but this was not for her. Preferring instead to bring the full range of her Berlin 'secretarial skills' to bear on the situation, my mother kept her distance until an unknown woman (a redhead like herself, she noted) came to collect her son from the Steiner school. Shadowing them back to where they were staying, she waited until he went for his afternoon nap, let herself in, crept upstairs and snatched him back. Reunited, mother and son then headed back across Canada to her sister's apartment and spent a few days on the ski slopes recuperating, before taking the train to Saint John, New Brunswick, where they boarded the *Empress of Britain*, arriving back in Liverpool in early February.

JBW would forever after insist that my brother's kidnapping had been very much a spur-of-the-moment decision, accounting for the half-constructed wireless sets and shotguns left behind in our garage and the transmitter aerial still slung round our chimney. But as a slew of recently released Canadian government documents reveal, their berths on the

Homeric had been booked weeks in advance and my brother (discreetly) added to his own passport some three years earlier via the Canadian consulate in Helsinki: a relatively straightforward process that JBW had managed with his customary sleight of hand, listing his address as Spring Street, Guelph – the address of his former rather than his current wife.

As it turned out, JBW and son were not short of company on the *Homeric*, despite what he would always claim. Scroll a little further down the ship's manifest and there is the Bathams' secretary, Rita Harris, for appearance's sake (this being the 1950s) booked into a separate cabin. But what the manifest and Canadian immigration records don't record was that Rita was by now nearly four months pregnant.

From Montreal they made their way across Canada, his job search having finally come good with the offer of a post in the University of British Columbia's Political Research Department, 'teaching Russian and Spanish language and history courses [. . .] though my principal interest is in Political Theory and International Politics, with particular reference to Marxist theory and ideology'. About which he had more practical experience than most, it might be said. Almost certainly he'd landed the post with the help of his former Panama colleague and station chief Peter Dwyer, now heavily involved in setting up Canada's own intelligence service, 'whose security and culture briefs coincided perfectly in the induced birth of Soviet studies and Russian-language programs in the Canadian universities'. However, with just a 2.2 to his name (his truncated stay at the Sorbonne had done him no favours), JBW's role was restricted to that of a visiting lecturer, which, combined with a lack of funding, meant that his job description also included organizing UBC seminars and summer schools.

Frayed collars and patched-up elbow holes notwithstanding, he still managed to cut something of a dash with the female staff, one of whom recalled a handsome if slightly dishevelled figure casually wandering past her office on the first day of the new academic year, curious-looking typewriter tucked under one arm. Another recalled overhearing students in the canteen excitedly discussing the new lecturer, whose talks came across more like reports from the front line than textbook readings. As they likely were. His skilful glossing-over of much of his past didn't stop some wondering whether he might be a talent-spotter for Canadian or American Intelligence, suspicions only encouraged by a car he later sold to a fellow tutor continually failing to start, which the garage quickly traced to an over-sized shortwave radio draining the battery. And by how at the very height of the Cuban missile crisis in October 1962 he was to be seen calmly pottering around his garden, insisting there was no cause for alarm. But then again, given that he had turned up with a Cyrillic typewriter and speaking fluent Russian, this was perhaps only to be expected.

And though he might (and did) argue otherwise, his wife's unexpected appearance in Vancouver surely came as something of a relief, allowing him to present a clean slate on the domestic front. With a baby of her own on the way – Sophie, born in early December 1958 – Rita had been understandably reluctant to continue looking after someone else's child, still less to find herself an accessory to kidnapping, with the result that my brother was farmed out to a hapless and unknown (red-headed) carer, who, along with feeding and clothing duties, dropped him off at the Steiner school every morning, enabling a diligent conveyancing solicitor to eventually track him down and his mother to snatch him back.

With his second marriage all but behind him – cause of breakdown: 'my wife having refused to remain in Vancouver' – JBW was able to fully immerse himself in UBC's extramural programme and summer schools, which in time would lead to his becoming a founder member of the Canadian University Service Overseas, a voluntary student organization with the aim of filling skill gaps in developing countries. The first batch of graduates headed off in August 1961 to work as teachers, nurses and agriculturalists. Along with UBC's summer schools, this offered a balm for JBW's endless wanderlust, with visits over the next few years to Costa Rica, Algeria, Strasbourg, India and South America, even a return to Mexico City.

A way of life not perhaps as demanding – or hazardous – as his previous existence, but one that he might have happily continued in for a few years yet, were it not for the head of the Technical and Scientific Department of the Polish Secret Service unexpectedly turning up in West Berlin.

The take that Colonel Michal Goleniewski brought with him included the revelation that Polish Intelligence had an agent inside British Naval Intelligence and that the KGB was running a highly placed officer within SIS itself. It didn't take long for Harold Shergold to pinpoint the likely suspect, with the result that on a bright spring morning in early April 1961 he and George Blake took a leisurely walk across St James's Park to Carlton Gardens, where they were met by a small team of SIS officers. 'There's a few things we'd like to discuss with you about your work in Berlin.'

Aware of the difficulties that his friend Charles Ransom (now station head in Rome) had faced when questioning JBW, Shergold went into the meeting knowing that nothing short of a full confession was needed. Blake was free to return home at the end of the day's questioning, albeit with MI5 tailing him – which, as when Ransom had questioned JBW, made for a more relaxed atmosphere, as Blake himself later acknowledged. Nevertheless, after three long days the team had failed to make a breakthrough. At this point an exasperated Shergold suddenly changed tack, questioning Blake's motives, suggesting that he had been either blackmailed or tortured into working for the Soviets. A suggestion that incensed Blake: he had done it entirely off his own bat, he insisted – it was a decision born solely out of conviction – before proceeding to unburden himself of the full extent of his treachery, Shergold and the team listening in stunned silence until Blake finally interrupted himself: 'Am I boring you?' Once again, not the sort of confession that SIS had been expecting, though unlike JBW's 'voices from God' one that might stand up in court.

Shortly afterwards, Shergy telegrammed Peter Lunn to inform him of the breakthrough, with the name of the traitor to be spelt out in a second, encrypted telegram. Lunn is said to have openly speculated about the likely candidate – later reframed as 'a wild guessing game' – only for the second telegram to contain five coded letters. Not four. B-L-A-K-E. 'It was not what he had expected. He had implicitly trusted Blake and was shattered by the news.'

No such telegram, encrypted or otherwise, would wind its way to Vancouver, even had anyone known JBW's whereabouts – indeed quite possibly the first he heard about Blake's forty-two-year prison sentence was via the newspapers, like everybody else. But he would no doubt have wryly noted that he had correctly identified George Blake as one of two possible Soviet moles during his own questioning six years earlier.

Ironically, it would be Lunn himself who, rummaging through Registry for something else entirely, would eventually unearth the document in question. A few days later, striding down from the Main Mess in the SIS training camp as I was cycling up, he'd turned on his heel and, circling me all the while as he spoke (some sort of advanced skiing manoeuvre, I'd assumed), confirmed that he'd come across something concerning JBW that might be of interest, which he had duly passed on to my mother, who might want to fill me in on the details. Given that the document was written long before Blake's eventual unmasking, this seemed to suggest that JBW might possibly, perhaps, be in the clear, no?

'If only it were all that simple . . .' my mother laughed out loud. With the naivety of youth, clearly I had strayed into the proverbial 'wilderness of mirrors', where nothing and no one is ever quite as it seems. Nevertheless, from then on Lunn, a fundamentally honest man (and devout Catholic to boot), would always make a point of referencing JBW's contribution to the tunnel operation whenever he gave his lectures on the subject – though JBW would remain forever edited out of all SIS's semi-authorized accounts.

With the question mark hanging over him finally resolved, certainly so far as the Americans were concerned, JBW headed down to Florida. Only this was no vacation; he was there on business.

The flight from Vancouver involved an overnight stop in London, Ontario – or so he claimed – the airport coincidentally just a twenty-minute taxi ride from the new home of his estranged wife's younger sister, Sheila. Even for someone with JBW's track record, his unscheduled appearance was

surely the very definition of chutzpah, given that he had kidnapped her nephew four short years earlier.

Nevertheless, Sheila had always got on well with JBW,
having spent a lazy Berlin summer at the Blau-Weiss Club
and on Lake Wannsee back when she was a student nurse,
and when he'd learnt that she was emigrating to Canada he'd
sent a farewell package of 'Canadiana', mostly bits and bobs
he no longer had any use for, including his old North American road atlas. Ironically it was this that had led her – long
before anyone else – to have doubts about JBW, the name
of the atlas's previous owner (inscribed on the inside cover)
being Donald Maclean. But then she was hardly to know that
JBW's first wife, Dorothy Maclean, had a brother with the
same name as the Cambridge spy.

And so, against her better judgement, she showed JBW
in, for what turned out to be something of a cameo performance. True to form, he'd arrived with next to no
luggage, having packed only light summer clothing, so she'd
lent him some of her husband's pyjamas. And though she
knew him well enough not to expect an answer, over breakfast the following morning she'd asked where he might be
heading off to. Somewhere warm she hoped. But instead
of the usual muttered obfuscation, he'd calmly explained
that he was on his way to Florida and that his visit was in
connection with the recent Bay of Pigs fiasco (in which
a ragtag collection of CIA-sponsored Cuban exiles had
stormed the beaches, only to be rounded up shortly after
stepping ashore – echoing what had happened in Albania).
He then spent most of the morning on the phone, though
what the calls were about she had no idea since, as per
usual, he was constantly changing language. Mostly Spanish, she thought. Phone bill aside, she'd fretted slightly

about leaving him alone in the house while she headed off to work, but in the end left him sitting by the fire with the weekend papers, which happened to be serializing the latest Ian Fleming offering, *Thunderball*. He'd lasted a paragraph or two but it was not for him – and promptly used it to get the fire going. As she headed out the door he'd called after her asking if she could book him in for a dental appointment, which she duly did, but when she returned at the end of her shift he had upped and gone, never to be heard from again.

His uncustomary frankness about his visit to Florida was, of course, entirely deliberate. It was simply his way of letting his estranged wife know – via her sister – that he was no longer 'persona non grata', certainly on this side of the Atlantic. Unfortunately, it was a wasted effort. Worried that her elder sister might think she had somehow encouraged JBW's visit and in any case should never have let him through the front door, Sheila decided the whole episode was best kept to herself. Almost certainly the correct decision.

And with that, just as Blake was stepping into Wormwood Scrubs, JBW was stepping off the plane and into the Miami sunshine. In the aftermath of the Bay of Pigs fiasco the Kennedys had set up Operation Mongoose, hoping to rid themselves of the communist threat on America's doorstep and, if needs be, Fidel Castro himself. The men tasked with this thankless task? A former San Francisco OSS officer, Edward Lansdale, and JBW's former CIA station chief in Berlin, Bill Harvey. The self-same Harvey who 'had a basic trait of being able to admirably and accurately define and illuminate [. . .] talent or character in an individual, and then he would stick with that person forever'. For Harvey, who had been the first to point the finger at Kim Philby, Blake's unmasking had come as no great surprise, his reported reaction: 'Here we go again. We should never trust the Brits.' But then, of course, JBW was no Brit, nor ever had been.

Harvey and Lansdale were ostensibly joint CEOs of Zenith Technical Enterprises, the suitably anonymous cover for Operation Mongoose's headquarters, situated in an abandoned corner of Miami State University, its walls cluttered with sales charts, business licences, even an award certificate from the United Givers' Fund. With some 15,000 Cuban exiles connected to Zenith in one way or another, JBW had been flown down to Miami for much the same reason that he'd been dispatched to Panama all those years ago – he spoke Spanish, unlike the vast majority of CIA staffers, Harvey and Lansdale included. It says something about the pressure Robert Kennedy was putting the agency under that the gun-toting, Martini-fuelled Harvey thought to bring in a pacifist, aquavit-sipping, part-time university lecturer who would have advised against any form of armed intervention and was not entirely unsympathetic to Castro's cause. But then Harvey knew JBW well enough, warts and all.

As, in a rather more unexpected way, did Lansdale.

Lansdale was by this time something of a fabled figure, an expert in covert warfare (wrongly) thought to have been the inspiration for Graham Greene's novel *The Quiet American*, in which the protagonist casts off his uniform to live among the local Vietnamese population, much as Lansdale had done both there and in the Philippines, where he was credited with having seen off the communist-led Huq insurgency, marking the start of a career that had seen him rise to become a two-star general in the Pentagon by the time he arrived in Miami.

But this was all a far cry from the Lansdale that JBW's fellow Sufis remembered back in San Francisco in the early 1940s. Back then he was just a thirty-something ex-advertising man, married with children, who in a bout of post-Pearl Harbor patriotic fervour had quit his job, hoping to enlist with the military, only to end up being recruited into the newly formed OSS.

Given their lack of worldliness, OSS recruits were encouraged, not least by Hathaway Snr – as former Consul General in Munich – to hear from those who had witnessed the rise of Nazism at close quarters. As a result his son Bill and daughter-in-law Erica – having lived in Munich for over a decade and, in Erica's case, having (famously) refused to shake Hitler's hand – found themselves being visited by a steady stream of visitors eager to hear firsthand accounts of life in Munich, Erica's Braunes Haus visit included. None more so than Lansdale, whose interest in the Sufi movement is often viewed as an (eccentric) interest in the spiritual – he 'not only interviewed foreign-born students at thirty-seven different universities to obtain information about their homelands, he also talked to a couple of Sufi murshids (or teachers), practitioners of a mystical sect of Islam, to learn about social structures of South Asian and Middle Eastern countries'. In reality, few if any had either the Hathaways' or the local Sufis' experience of, and insight into, what was happening in Germany at the time, furthered by Murshida Martin's and Samuel Lewis's early sponsorship of Jewish refugees. Lewis claimed to have spent the rest of the war working for Lansdale as 'historical consultant and secretary for Army Intelligence', describing his work as 'fighting the war in the inner planes' (though how exactly this might have played a part in Adolf Hitler's downfall remains unclear, Lansdale having ordered him to destroy all record of their work together: 'This was easy because no one believed me anyway').

By the time Lansdale joined the OSS, JBW had already left for Panama – quite possibly they'd never met prior to his trip to Miami – but he would have been a familiar enough name to anyone in the OSS offices at 54 New Montgomery Street, not least for helping implement the Ships' Observers Scheme in the local dockyards and having trained many of its officers, several of whom had followed him up to Camp X and then down to Latin America, before resurfacing as CIA officers in Berlin.

Whether his week in Florida amounted to anything more than giving sage advice and lecturing (in Spanish) to Cuban exiles, after his years in the wilderness it must have felt like a vindication, not to say rehabilitation. And though Operation Mongoose would be wound up within a few months, someone with JBW's experience and know-how was never going to be sidelined for long. If he was not quite 'back in the game', he was certainly back on their radar.

And with that JBW headed back to Vancouver and university life, leaving Harvey and Lansdale to concentrate on conjuring up new and ever more bizarre ways of unseating Castro, exploding cigars and booby-trapped conch shells included.

John B. Wood

Resident Representative a. i.

UNITED NATIONS
DEVELOPMENT PROGRAMME
P. O. Box 2048 Alwiyah
TEL. 84171
BAGHDAD – IRAQ

برنامج التنمية للأمم المتحدة
ص. ب. ٢٠٤٨ علوية
تلفون ٨٤١٧١
بغـداد — العراق

The United Nations new Resident
Representative in Iraq, 1965.

СЛАВА ТРУДУ

ПОЧТОВЫЕ МАРКИ ДЛЯ ТЕМАТИЧЕСКОЙ КОЛЛЕКЦИИ.

Baghdad 'welcome gift' from former Soviet counterparts.

2.

Baghdad

'Somebody from the office travelled on a plane
from Iraq to America with him the other day.
He had been "advising" in Iraq – and a fine
mess we have had in the Middle East too.'

Mother, letter to Aunt A, 11 June 1966

All well and good though a second career in Vancouver might have been, it barely paid the bills, at least not JBW's bills. With a growing family (or families) to maintain – a second daughter, Louise, had arrived in late 1961 – his salary failed to stretch as far as England, even with his quarterly trust fund, while his prospects in the academic world were hampered for want of a first-class degree or equivalent. The solution was for him to return to San Francisco and embark on another degree course.

Unsurprisingly, this cut little ice back in Woking. 'The present lack of funds is apparently due to the fact that he feels all that is stopping him making a fortune is the lack of some degree or other, so he is at Stanford University, California – very nice too, no redbrick for JBW – but has not mentioned what degree it is or how long it is going to take. It seems to me that if you cannot make enough cash with a Cambridge

MA then cash-making isn't in your line and another degree at his age isn't going to make much difference.'

Aside from his Stanford course fees, he needed to find somewhere for himself, Rita and their two young daughters to live for the duration. Thankfully, he still had San Francisco's Sufi community to fall back on, or more precisely Vera Corda. Even by JBW's inimitable standards this was a big ask. After all, the last time he'd been to stay with her, back when she was living on Tenth Avenue, Vera had spent the next morning plastering over a bullet hole in her living-room wall after an attempt on his life by the local Nazis. And then there was the small matter of his trying to persuade her to elope with him to Bermuda, only to then marry Dorothy Maclean and somehow fail to communicate the glad tidings. 'I just couldn't believe it when I heard he'd married someone else.'

A further complication was that his friend Samuel Lewis, having returned to San Francisco from his trip to India via Woking, was under the impression that his wife was called Margaret and that they had two sons. Which did not quite tally with his present domestic set-up. And so the ever-tangled JBW web now became more tangled still. His solution was to pass Rita off as the wife of an (entirely fictitious) elder half-brother who had disappeared off to South America, never to be seen again, leaving him with the responsibility of looking after her and her two daughters. 'He introduced Rita as his sister-in-law, and she always behaved like that.' Given that, after starting out as a ballet dancer, Vera had gone on to become a successful paediatrician with a masters from Columbia specializing in at-risk children, this was surely a bend of the truth too far, even for someone with JBW's track record of duplicity. But seemingly not. 'He was living in my home and I was seeing him every day so closely and not realizing they were his children!'

And so the now Professor J. B. Wood emerged from Stanford, with a string of straight As in Hispanic Studies. Not to discount the possibility that his choice of subject had something to do with his visit to Florida (Cuba was not the CIA's only concern in Latin America), he set about applying to Canadian universities with a Latin-American department, attaching the usual carefully edited career highlights: 'My academic field is in political science where I have specialized in the various international aspects of the theory and practice of Marxist/Leninist doctrine. I spent a number of years in South America in the war, having been sent there on foreign service work. I was in Panama, Argentina and Uruguay, and also had occasion to spend some time in Brazil and Venezuela [. . .] I have taught Russian and Spanish language and history courses. My principal interest is in Political Theory and International Politics.'

In the meantime he remained at the University of British Columbia (UBC), promoted to head of the extramural division as a 'special lecturer', though his focus was increasingly turning to the Canadian University Service Overseas (CUSO), whose hands-on activities in developing countries were very much in line both with his humanitarian ideals and with the career path that Samuel Lewis and Murshida Martin had envisaged for him at Kaaba Allah all those years ago. To the irritation of his UBC employers, he was soon spending almost as much time in airport lounges as on campus, with first-time visits to the Far East and a secondment to India, revisiting old haunts in Latin America and Europe, even managing to find time for the occasional stop-over at his mother's house, arriving, as was his way, without so much as a pre-emptive telephone call.

Since CUSO's work overlapped to some extent with that of the various United Nations agencies, he increasingly found himself boarding planes and sharing notes with UN agency staffers, so it was perhaps inevitable that he would be sounded out for some of the temporary roles that came up from time to time. During a CUSO seminar in Algeria, he was asked to drop by the UN office in Algiers to 'have a look at our operation there' – and to discuss 'your candidature for a post with us', for which JBW prepared in the usual way, headphones clamped to ear and Arab dictionary to hand. And though in the end nothing came of it, his efforts didn't go unnoticed and a few weeks later he was approached for a short-term role in Baghdad, the incumbent having been taken ill. By which time he was in Santiago, Chile, chairing yet another seminar. If he was reluctant to give up the relatively safe pastures of academia, it didn't show. JBW accepted the post immediately without consulting his current employers, to UBC's further irritation. But Baghdad would open the door to a career rather more suited to (the better side of) his talents, with the added bonus that the fast-track nature of the appointment, billed as a temporary post, meant that there was no need, and no time, to carry out the standard vetting processes or background checks. 'Please confirm acceptance our offer and reporting date New York,' the UN cabled urgently. And with that he was on his way.

With little time to prepare, rather than head back to Vancouver he decided to stay over in New York and continue on with the basic Arabic he'd acquired on his Algiers trip. Like Finnish, Albanian and Russian, not the easiest language to attempt more or less from scratch – and as he himself later admitted to my brother and me, one that he never fully mastered. Thankfully help was at hand in the shape of a Ms

Furse Ripley, a recently divorced publishing editor from possibly the shallower end of the Sufi spectrum, who put him up in her Bleecker Street apartment; while JBW buried himself in *Arabic Made Easy* and learning the names of Iraq's cabinet ministers, from the prime minister downwards, Ms Ripley 'made [herself] ugly with the fumes of too much whiskey and far too many cigarettes'. An unlikely relationship if, by his standards, an enduring one – her apartment a home from home whenever he was in New York on UN business, from where she kept up a stream of largely illegible, felt-tip-penned, stream-of-consciousness letters (outdoing even Samuel Lewis for length if not for spiritual content) posted off to wherever in the world he happened to be.

In the meantime there were still one or two hurdles that Canada's newly appointed UN officer in Iraq would need to overcome before heading out to the Middle East, first and foremost of these being that he was not actually Canadian.

Back when he was still (just about) married to Dorothy Maclean, returning from his one and only visit to her hometown of Guelph, he had stopped off in Ottawa to apply for Canadian citizenship, on the basis that he was married to a Canadian and was, ahem, living in Guelph. And was still claiming to be living in Guelph seven years and one marriage later when he'd registered the birth of my elder brother with the Canadian embassy in Helsinki.

Not for the first time, JBW's casual relationship with the truth would cause him problems further down the line. In the tug-of-war over her missing son, my mother's trusty conveyancing lawyer had pointed out that her husband 'was not a Canadian citizen as he claimed to be [. . .] but was of British nationality'. The Canadian Citizenship Court concurred, declaring his Canadian citizenship null and void on the grounds that he had never been domiciled in Canada, let alone Guelph, and in any case was long since divorced from Dorothy Maclean. A series of (costly) legal appeals ensued, contested on the flimsy grounds that he and his parents had arrived in Canada back in 1922 intending to settle there and, flimsier still, that he had subsequently spent several weeks in Ontario at the start of the war (Camp X), having turned down a return to Britain 'to take up the question of possible service in Canada'.

Obliged to dust down his British passport, he wisely concluded that it might be better if he took the overland route to Iraq and enter by the back door, so to speak, rather than fly directly into Baghdad, a journey of well over 3,000 miles from the UK, facilitated by having an experienced map-reader accompany him: his seventy-three-year-old mother. After packing up her husband's old linen suits and what was left of the family silver, which JBW claimed would be needed 'for representational duties', off they set. As always he took the scenic route, through Switzerland then all the way down the Adriatic coastline as far as Montenegro, before cutting across to Sofia and once again skirting round Albania – and a good deal else besides, not least any mention of Rita, his two daughters or that his two sons had been made Wards of Court by the UK authorities and would not be joining him in Baghdad any time soon.

Unlike Vera Corda and others, his mother was not so easily fooled. And though she would never know of the existence of his two daughters, let alone of Rita, she began to have serious doubts about her only offspring, not least how he had managed to be let go by the Foreign Office just a few months after he had collected his OBE from Buckingham Palace, and how someone with a sizeable trust fund and a steady income could not afford to support his wife and sons. Even so, as she told my brother and me, she'd enjoyed every last mile of her unexpected road trip. Or rather every last mile up until they crossed into Turkey, when for no apparent reason JBW had suddenly insisted she fly straight home from Istanbul rather than continue on to Baghdad – where he was due to be joined by Rita and his two daughters.

Which in turn presented JBW with a further problem, given that according to his marriage certificate and his UN personnel file his wife's name was Margaret. And so Rita was now Margaret Rita.

On 1 March 1965 he reported for work in Baghdad, only too keen to share the view from his window with former colleagues back in Canada: 'My office looks over the Tigris River on one side and a nice sunny garden of palm trees on the other. Is it still raining in Vancouver?' A month later, with the incumbent Resident Representative having failed to recover from his illness, he found himself with 'a family of eighty-two international experts to look after as well as conducting all the negotiations and arrangements with the government of Iraq relating to all the United Nations technical assistance; one is also called on to be UN "Ambassador", which fills one's social calendar rather too much'. When not wining and dining, he and his legal team in Vancouver launched yet another appeal to acquire the appropriate passport, his case likely helped by having friends in high places to call on, including his former Panama chief Peter Dwyer, now re-invented as the highly regarded Head of the Canadian Arts Council and the Canadian Film Board, who would have been only too happy to offer JBW similar scope for reinvention. Not that there's any way of knowing: shortly before his early death at the age of just fifty-eight, rather than deposit his personal papers with the National Archives, Dwyer gathered them together in a large pyre in his suburban Ottawa back-yard, BSC-related documents included. Not the first time JBW had cause to be grateful for the slate-wiping benefits of a roaring bonfire.

In the end Canada's representative in Iraq was granted Canadian citizenship on the (questionable) basis that he had been (illegally) domiciled in Canada for the previous six years. And with that, on 26 May 1965, JBW headed west on the Baghdad–Damascus highway on a 'field visit', only to drive past Damascus and on to Beirut and the Canadian Embassy, where Canadian passport No: YT562406 was ready for collection. Finally free of his British nationality, with any trace of his time with SIS, his fluent Norwegian, Finnish, Albanian, etc. long since omitted from his CV, he was now a bona fide frontline aid worker – the path he would surely have followed had various wars, both hot and cold, not intervened, and the path that Samuel Lewis, Murshida Martin and Suresnes had long advocated.

And where better to undergo his Damascene conversion than on the road to Damascus?

PROGRAMME DES NATIONS UNIES
POUR LE DEVELOPPEMENT
BOITE POSTALE 1255
SAIGON

By Airmail
PAR AVION

u Comité du Mékong

(ARTISTA)

● De gauche à droite Mme B. Klausener, épouse du représentant de l'UNICEF, M. J.B. Wood, représentant résident de l'UNDP, l'ambassadeur O.W. Dier, chef de la délégation canadienne près la CIC.

'He said he volunteered [for Vietnam] as he had no ties and was therefore expendable. I should have thought he had more ties than most.' Mother to Aunt A, 1968.

3.

Saigon

'. . . a 122 m/m rocket [. . .] came sailing
through my bedroom window and if it is still
there I would like to keep it as a memento
to my closest contact with socialist realism'.

JBW, letter to his UNDP successor
in Saigon, 18 November 1968

On 1 December 1966, at the height of American military
involvement in the Vietnam War, the newly formed United
Nations Development Programme's first Resident Representative arrived in Saigon.

For someone who had only recently joined the United
Nations – on a short-term, temporary basis – and who not
so long ago had been experimenting with moulded plastic tin-can lids in a disused Belfast factory in the middle
of winter, this was something of a step up. 'I cannot even
imagine the gravity of your responsibility, the greatness of
your assignment or the smallest most mundane task of such
a stewardship. It genuinely overawes me,' Ms Furse Ripley
breathlessly scrawled from her Bleecker Street apartment.

His arrival did not go unannounced. Various newspapers
covered the story, including the regional *Journal d'Extrême-
Orient*: 'Dr Trần Văn Đỗ, Minister of Foreign Affairs, received

yesterday afternoon Mr John Bryan Wood, representing the United Nations Economic Development Programme, who is to replace Mr Thomas Pigot, deceased.' (No mention of how the unfortunate Mr Pigot deceased.) A follow-up art-icle covered his welcome drinks party, with a besuited JBW photographed mingling with government ministers, ambas-sadors and a lone Chinese trade official.

Word of my father's whereabouts eventually made it all the way back to Woking. 'Latest news of JBW is that he has been organizing the refugees in Vietnam for the last eighteen months. He is apparently dodging the bullets, shining up his halo, and being regarded as a saint. Somebody in the office met him on leave in Geneva recently. He said he volunteered to do it as he had no ties and was therefore expendable. I should have thought he had more ties than most.' Since Viet-nam was the first war to be played out nightly on television screens, his presence there gave an unexpectedly glamorous sheen to his otherwise tarnished halo, though not for long. Fathers of small boys in the leafier parts of Woking tended to work in office blocks or business parks – not war zones, and certainly not in Vietnam. As I recall all too clearly, earn-ing myself a punch on the nose at school for my honesty. Or rather, for my 'blether' – from which, as my mother had always cautioned, no good could ever come.

Given that updates on JBW's whereabouts generally only reached us through the 'office' grapevine, I'd always taken it for granted that Shergy had known about his former col-league ending up in Vietnam. Clearly not, given his reaction when I told him. Ironically, he'd been talking me through something of his own history at the time, the cue for which had been the launch of SIS's first ever in-house magazine, which had kicked off with a feature on 'Living Legend Harold

Shergold'. He was happy enough with the 'living', he said, less so with 'legend'.

The CIA had gone one better, inviting him over as an honorary guest for their fiftieth anniversary dinner, where ex-President George Bush Snr was the main speaker. Former Langley colleagues still dropped by from time to time to wish him well or else tap him for background material for Cold War publications such as *Battleground Berlin* (occasionally supplied, on the understanding that he himself wouldn't be credited). With the conversation centring on America, I'd happened to mention in passing about JBW having been in Vietnam.

Clearly the 'somebody in the office' who had met JBW on leave in Geneva all those years ago had failed to pass on the update to Shergy. Somewhat thrown by the news, he made no immediate comment but simply stared into the middle distance with slightly furrowed brow, before eventually concluding, 'Well, there's no way he could have gone out there without the Americans knowing about it.'

As they surely had.

On the face of it, JBW was an unlikely candidate for such a sensitive post: an avowed pacifist at a time when the US military presence in Vietnam was close on 400,000 troops (with more on the way), who only a year before had added his name to Canada's nuclear disarmament movement and who can hardly have endeared himself to his future hosts by publicly talking up Canada's 'handsome' contribution to UN development projects 'at a time when a number of others, including our neighbour, [are] being somewhat unforthcoming'. And yet self-evidently the Americans had raised no objections, may even have put his name forward for the role in the first place. The explanation for which dates back to

JBW's 'factory' visit to the so-called Zenith Technical Enterprises, headed up by Bill Harvey and Edward Lansdale.

Both men's reputations had suffered in the aftermath of Operation Mongoose, with Harvey all but sidelined and Lansdale packed off to the relative backwater of America's 'Food for Peace' programme. But Lansdale still had his supporters within Congress who, unhappy about what had become an almost purely military approach to Vietnam, tasked him with heading up a 'pacification program' – hoping that he might repeat the success of an earlier tour of duty back in the 1950s at the tail end of France's involvement, when Lansdale had been posted as a 'military adviser' to Vietnam, only to end up as President Diem's right-hand man, even moving into the Presidential Palace itself. Convinced that with his knowledge and insights on both the country and its culture, the war could still be won by winning over hearts and minds rather than by force of arms, Lansdale set about assembling a team of like-minded talents, most of whom had worked with him before at one time or another, or else had enjoyed similarly unorthodox career paths, few more so than JBW.

And so to Saigon.

As with Baghdad, it was billed as a temporary posting and came slightly out of the blue. He was still keeping up his CUSO connections during his last year in Iraq – somehow managing to wangle a leave of absence to oversee CUSO's summer seminar in Santiago, Chile – and was still holding out for a possible UNDP slot in Latin America, with his fluent Spanish and his Stanford qualification in Hispanic Studies. Indeed, only a few weeks before arriving in Saigon he was still firing off applications to universities in Canada and further afield, including Delhi, Cairo and Beirut. Thankfully however, on yet another seminar-cum-workshop, this time on behalf of the UNDP in Turin, he was sounded out for a possible last-minute slot in Saigon, once again as a result of the incumbent having (fortuitously) fallen ill.

Given the hazardous nature of the post, most UN officers declined, citing family considerations – which clearly hadn't weighed too heavily on my father. The UN HR department – no doubt relieved that he had accepted – agreed to him taking his usual circuitous route to the new post:

> I would be grateful if you would arrange with Cooks for the issue of the necessary tickets to Saigon via Europe, Montreal, New York and Vancouver. This would enable me to take most of my belongings as accompanied airfreight and clear it through customs at Montreal for onforwarding to Vancouver. Re the European Agencies: Jean Pierre Martin, the newly appointed Director of the UN Social and Economic Office in Beirut, was particularly keen that I should spend a full day with him before leaving the area. I then presume I would need three or four days each in Rome, Geneva and Paris for de-briefing and re-briefing. I would only take in IAEA in Vienna if you thought this desirable, but would like a day at least with ICAO in Montreal en route to NY. If time permits, I would also like to ask four or five days' annual leave in Europe.

After arriving at New York's United Nations Plaza Building to sign on the dotted line and receive his briefing, like many a diplomat heading out to Vietnam, he used the time to read the French-American war correspondent Bernard Fall, whose dispatches from there were regarded as amongst the more insightful, underpinned by Fall's belief that 'military tactics and hardware are all well and good, but they are quite useless if one has lost the confidence of the population among whom one is fighting'. A belief that might not have endeared Fall to the US military but certainly resonated with both Lansdale and JBW.

Leaving Furse Ripley's Bleecker Street apartment in the early hours – and mistakenly, in the darkness, leaving his copy of Fall's latest book on her bedside table – he walked up to St Vincent Hospital to catch a cab for the airport, flying to Geneva first to pick up his UNDP accreditation papers and undergo his medical, before heading to Rome, then Paris for 're-briefing and de-briefing', in between managing to squeeze in a few days' holiday to 'see something of Europe' (more accurately, to call in on his mother), before setting off for South East Asia. His first stop was the UNDP's regional headquarters in Bangkok's Sala Santitham, with vague plans of safely housing Rita and daughters there – wives and partners would, of course, not be allowed into Saigon – only for Rita to opt to stay put in the relative comfort of Limassol, Cyprus, where she and their daughters had moved several months earlier (partly for schooling reasons). Leaving JBW to carry on to the so-called Paris of the Orient *tout seul*. Outcome all too predictable.

A first sighting of the Vietnamese countryside through the clouds prompted him to jot down a few (possibly culled) lines on airline paper to be posted back to Furse Ripley on arrival.

In from the South China Sea the long-held lands look neat and tidy and deceptively peaceful. Palm and thatch and little compact communities hugging the banks of the great brown snaking rivers betray, from a safe height, no vestige

310

of violence. But below the steel birds of prey, the lightning swift hawks and the heavy hovering buzzards sit brooding in their little cages awaiting the command of their electronic masters. Behind the imposed apparatus of war lies the abandoned wardrobe of France, here a Mediterranean roof, a tree-lined avenue and all but the Pernod on the now empty terresses (sic), beyond that gentle south east Asia, prey as ever to conquering armies and militant creeds.

His request for a civilian flight refused, he endured the 'Welcome to Saigon' white-knuckle near-vertical descent into Tan Son Nhat Airport familiar to countless thousands of GIs, before being driven to his official residence in Saigon's Rue Nguyen Dinh Cheiu, little more than a ten-minute walk from the Presidential Palace. Like many a first-time visitor to the city, the sights and sounds and smells clearly left an indelible impression, even on someone who had spent large chunks of his life circling the globe (he subsequently spent as much time talking about Saigon to my brother and me as about all his other various postings put together).

JBW gently eased himself into Saigon life with the occasional game of tennis and early-morning swim at the Circle Sportif Club (rechristened after the war as the 'Labour Culture Palace'). The city still retained a degree of the sophistication of its former occupying power, not least in its cuisine (La Cigale restaurant a favourite), with cinemas showing the latest French films and the language itself widely spoken among the well-to-do. Nevertheless, knowing that he would likely be spending as much time out in the field as in Saigon itself, he started to learn Vietnamese, not the easiest of languages, but then he had tackled harder. 'I try to assure myself that you already have a few special Vietnamese friends & that, being you, now you have enough of the language,' Furse Ripley scribbled. 'I keep trying to move the soldiers aside on the idiot box so I can catch glimpses of the country where you are,' before signing off – possibly more in hope than expectation: 'Just tell me something of how your days are spent . . .'

Welcome drinks and credentials presentations aside, his first few weeks were spent getting to know his team – a diverse staff of all nationalities, many loaned from the World Health Organization (WHO) or the Pasteur Institute, with expertise ranging from electrical engineering to environmental health, TB and leprosy and soil science. Most were housed just off Nguyen Hue, the tree-lined central avenue familiar to anyone who's ever visited the city.

And then it was time to head off to the 'palm and thatch and little compact communities hugging the banks of the great brown snaking rivers' he had glimpsed from above. 'We see young soldiers kill and be killed & every time they burn down the huts of the village I picture you with another 1500 [refugees] to be cared for,' Furse Ripley empathized. 'Given your inner force – your serenity – your detachment & your hope for the future – I should think it would break your heart all the slaughter and destruction every day.'

With rice yields severely affected by the war (the country was now a net importer), the UNDP's efforts in the Mekong Delta were focused on soil fertility and improved irrigation methods for the delta's vast rice paddies. Even this paled in comparison with the refugee problem: up to a million people had fled North Vietnam following the country's partition. Alongside rehousing projects and optimistic attempts to set up safe zones, JBW helped to set up a string of village-based, artisan workshops repairing or rebuilding anything and everything metal or mechanical, from ten-ton trucks down to two-dollar wristwatches, with his own gold Omega, handed down from his father, one of the first to be reconditioned, its long-since-dormant innards completely replaced, body regilded, good for a few years yet.

Not that he spent much time discussing soil fertility, irrigation methods or watches with my brother and me. Instead he spent the best part of that rainy weekend following his mother's funeral taking us through some of the scrapes he'd been in while out and about in the Delta region, where, as his various newspaper cuttings noted, the Viet Cong 'played by its own rules'. Half-remembered highlights: an overhead Huey patrol pointing out to him via loudhailer the inadvisability of attempting to navigate his jeep along a waterlogged track ('A lot more dangerous with you lot above me,' he'd shouted back); being called in to help calm a captured VC commander beside himself with fury after an Australian patrol had silently dug a shallow trench close to where he was sleeping, then simply banged a gong, resulting in the panicked commander falling head over heels as he rushed out to see what was happening; local villagers helpfully pointing out a string of buried IEDs he might want to avoid.

Others, of course, did not escape so lightly.

Ever since arriving in Saigon he'd kept a file of sorts, in which he dumped random cuttings, official invitations and light-hearted ephemera: *Nguyen Charlie* cartoon strips (GI inspecting an aerial poking out from the ground: 'When they put up their TV aerial they are not coming out'); an 'Order of Service to be Used in Government Offices' ('O Lord, grant that this day we come to no decisions, neither run we into any kind of responsibility'); a bright-yellow card with 'PS I LOVE YOU' scrawled on it in large letters.

In amongst these were the not-so-light-hearted, mostly routine Reuters bulletins: 'Thursday April 13th 1967, 56 people killed by VC terrorists last week'; 'Thursday May 4th 1967 – Viet Cong terrorism – officials attacked – sabotage at elections – anti-religious violence'; along with a torn-out article reporting Bernard Fall's death. He'd stepped on a land-mine just a few weeks after JBW took up his post. Whether or not they'd had the chance to meet in person, the loss of a like mind left its mark. 'While still on the aspect of needing word (your physical safety etc.) I wept at the death of Bernard Fall,' Furse Ripley commiserated, 'partly in fury at the snide way the news media here described him & because we need more minds like his & they are so few.'

Honeymoon period over, by May he was gloomily telling his UNDP bosses in New York: 'Now that a compromise political settlement becomes less and less likely, the US desire to have us here may have diminished accordingly [. . .] though our stock has admittedly risen somewhat since the Secretary-General along with Charles de Gaulle was burned in effigy in February.' That same month he flew to Hawaii to attend a UN-sponsored seminar on Vietnam – both Fall and Lansdale had been speakers the year before – and on his return updated the Assistant Secretary-General: 'The situation here seems to favour the hawks increasingly, prospects of any détente seem ever remoter – though maybe it is just the fact of having been away for a few days in a normal country that reinforces that impression.'

Lansdale was coming to much the same conclusion. Though he was still working out of the US Embassy build-ing, within military circles he was viewed as something of a spent force, irreparably damaged by Operation Mongoose and his much-ridiculed plans for dealing with Fidel Castro, 'his villa a Saigon landmark where he poured tea and whiskey for second-generation spooks who adored him, even now that his batteries were dead'.

By contrast, after his years in the wilderness, JBW's career was very much on the rise. Before setting off for Hawaii, New York had telegrammed to confirm that he was being taken on as a permanent staffer and as such was being pencilled in to take over as head of station in Bolivia – the return to Latin America he had long been angling for. With no sign of the war ending any time soon and his Saigon contract coming to a close, he had all but packed his bags, concluding, 'There is little one can do other than rationalizing and tidying up the programme which is now largely in hand.' His Bolivia start date had only to be finalized.

Six months later he was still in Saigon. 'We are still pursuing the plan to assign you as Resident Rep in Bolivia. This idea has, however, caused, I understand, some concern in the United States Embassy in Saigon and in the United States mission in New York; they have a high opinion of your performance in Saigon and would be glad if you agreed to stay there.' Lansdale was still working out of the Embassy building and clearly the hawks were not having it all their way – as further correspondence underlined: 'A strong feeling persists in USA circles that your departure from Saigon at this time would be a mistake [. . .] and that unless there are some very strong reasons for you to wish to leave Saigon, we would rather request you to stay on for some time.'

New York's letter was sent three days before the start of Tet, the Vietnamese Lunar New Year, and arrived three days after, by which time there were possibly very strong reasons for JBW wishing to leave Saigon.

'The Resident Representative will hold Open House (Cocktail) on January 1st, from 6.30pm to 8.00pm to consolidate the New Year,' JBW had cheerily posted in the 'UN Family' newsletter at the start of the Christmas truce period. 'So if you're at a loose end, just pop along – with a friend if so desired.' Having duly 'consolidated' the Western New Year in modest style, everyone was expecting the Lunar New Year (Tet) to be more of the same. 'As many people will want to slope off on Friday for the Tet holidays, the date for the next meeting will be Thursday 25th January 1968. After that we should be back to the usual Friday routine.' But of course they did not return to the usual Friday routine.

Barely had the Tet holiday begun than the Viet Cong broke their ceasefire, launching surprise attacks all across South Vietnam. Saigon – and JBW – were taken completely unawares; some of the Viet Cong fighters even managed to enter the US Embassy compound through a hole they'd blown in the outer wall. And though he might have felt that he had put his former career firmly behind him, it seems Hanoi was unaware of his Damascene conversion, leaving a calling card – to be retrieved at a later date, a cherished souvenir of his Vietnam days. 'On the bookshelf behind the desk – top shelf left, you will find a small pile of stamps held down by a telephone bell as paper-weight. In that pile there should be a small piece of jagged metal – this is in fact a bit of a 122 m/m rocket that came sailing through my bedroom window and if it is still there I would like to keep it as a memento to my closest contact with socialist realism.'

But stay he did, reassuring New York a few weeks later that 'things are more or less back to normal. The curfew is still maintained from 7pm to 7am, a few large (121mm) mortars are lobbed into the city for good measure most nights; statistically the chances of one landing on one's head are no greater than being run down by a drunk driver in the US, but for some reason mortars produce more emotional steam.' As Furse Ripley confirmed: 'I hope your war is still "selective" but from what we hear of Saigon I'm worried. Please say you're intact still.'

Though JBW was still very much intact, in the aftermath of Tet, with the American public back home suddenly aware that they were not winning the war, the hawks took over and by June a disillusioned Lansdale was heading home to pen his memoirs. That same month JBW was promoted to Senior Officer (P5) level – salary $18,400 per annum, along with an 'assignment allowance' and accompanying 'post adjustment' of $4,200 per annum, roughly equivalent to some $210,000 or £160,000 in today's money, tax-free. A slice of which eventually made its way back to Woking in the shape of two crisp $5 bills, along with a (slightly suspect) Omega watch.

He remained in Vietnam until November 1968, though had both JBW and the Americans had their way he would have stayed still longer. *Le Journal d'Extrême-Orient* was on hand to record his departure, a besuited JBW photographed clutching a glass of champagne as a Mr Lê tai Triên of the Mekong Delta Committee bid him a fond farewell: '*J'ai toujours admiré le courage tranquille et la foi dans l'amour de ceux qui, sans fanfare ni trompette, travaillent pour le bonheur de l'humanité au milieu même du vacarme de la guerre, alors que, des deux camps adverses, les gens s'ingénient à se détruire les uns les autres.*' ('I have always admired the quiet courage and the faith in love of those who, without fanfare or trumpet, work for the happiness of humanity in the very midst of the din of war, while, on the two opposing sides, people are doing their best to destroy each other.')

As outgoing Resident Representative, he was invited to the National Day celebrations held every 1 November at the Presidential Palace, the formal italicized invitation card reading: 'The Government of the Republic has decided not to celebrate public rejoicings on the occasion of its National Day this year on account of the recent Tet and the subsequent Communist attacks and its consequences. On the contrary indoor ceremonies will be still maintained.' His allotted slot was 10.50 a.m., at which time JBW and the Apostolic Delegate (a Vatican diplomat – an unlikely pairing) were 'met by the Director of Protocol of the President of the Republic, ushered into the Grand Hall and guided to their respective positions by Protocol Officers'. A speech by President Nguyen Van Thieu was followed by yet more champagne, after which JBW headed back to his apartment to pack, star once again very much in the ascendant. Well, for a few weeks yet at least.

Athens, March 1970.

Newspaper article revealing the UN's man in Malawi as being simultaneously employed by a Canadian university, December 1970.

Mr & Mrs Wood (IV) arrive in Malawi, October 1970.

4.

Bolivia, Athens, Malawi

'His conduct in this affair shows a total lack
of veracity and integrity on his part.'

UNDP report to Secretary-General
U Thant, 27 January 1971

Ever since first arriving in Latin America as Farmer Jøn
Wood, JBW had always been looking to head back there,
even telling my brother and me that should he ever retire
he planned to see out his days in Rio de Janeiro, not least
because his United Nations (dollar) pension would be more
than enough to live on.

To begin with the most likely route back had been with
the Sufi movement, as successor to Shabaz Best, later on via
a teaching post at one of its universities – hence his Hispanic Studies at Stanford – and now via the United Nations
Development Programme. His request had been duly
noted, with Vietnam initially presented as just a short-term,
stop-gap residency – 'Your mission in Viet Nam would be
limited to approximately eleven months' – along with a
promise that 'efforts will be made to offer you an alternative
assignment which you would prefer to be in Latin America'.
True to their word, towards the end of his secondment the
UNDP had confirmed that he was in line for the Bolivia

post – welcome news: 'I am certainly most grateful to you for bearing in mind my Latin-American predilections. As it happens, Bolivia is the only one of the Republics that I have not visited.'

'The assignment is not an easy one but represents at the same time many challenges,' New York's personnel department had cautioned, though it seems unlikely that the challenges would be of the same order as Vietnam. In any case, Bolivia came highly recommended by its previous incumbent: 'What attracts me is the fact that we obviously have a very good programme there and I know that Joan Anstee very much regretted leaving the post.' Just when it had seemed that he might finally be on his way, the Americans had put their foot down and, slightly reluctantly, he had agreed to stay for another year. However, in the meantime the highly rated Anstee was proving a hard act to follow – unsurprising given she would go on to become the first female Under-Secretary-General at the UN – and twelve months later the Bolivia station position was still unfilled.

If a year alone in Saigon at the height of the Vietnam War was a long time, two years alone was a very long time. 'Although you're not a madly verbal type & for all I know don't need to talk about yourself at all, I still ache with a deep grieving anxiety at how lonely it must be for you in Saigon,' a concerned Furse Ripley had written when she learnt that JBW would be spending a second year in Vietnam. She needn't have worried. Like many a first-time Westerner in South East Asia, Lansdale included, JBW had fallen for the charms of a local woman, Liên Nguyen, daughter of a Saigon police chief and a mere twenty-nine years younger than him. As a result of which, had JBW had his way he would have stayed on even longer. But the UNDP could not be seen to be bowing to American pressure a second time: on 1 January 1969 JBW finally – and very reluctantly – left Saigon (5 metres above sea level) for La Paz (3,625 metres above sea level).

'In many ways Bolivia is a very interesting country [. . .] the only problem is the altitude, but unless there is a medical contra-indication, most people I know seem to have adapted themselves to the high altitude much more easily than they expected at first,' the UNDP's HR head, Karol Kraczkiewicz, advised. When Joan Anstee took up the post, she had wisely chosen to arrive by rail and road from Montevideo. Whereas JBW flew directly into La Paz. The standard remedy for first-time visitors to the world's highest capital – which had only recently acquired its first fire engine (lack of oxygen largely prevented conflagrations from spreading), had no bull-fighting arena (the thin air defeated the bull's stamina to charge), nor any wind section in the country's orchestras – was to drink copious amounts of *maté de coca* and hole up in a darkened room for twenty-four hours or so. But not a whole month, not if you're the incoming UNDP head of station, with your arrival heralded in the country's newspapers.

'The Andean gods seem to have taken a violent dislike to yours truly,' he lamented to Joan Anstee's partner Robert Jackson ('Jacko'). 'I thought perhaps with Joan's safe conduct things might be better! I regret to say that the altitude knocked me for a loop. The doctor told me to spend ten days in bed, which of course I can't do – may as well pass out in the office as in the hotel.'

Less than a month into his new post he was already preparing an exit strategy, telegramming his concerns to his UNDP bosses Paul Hoffman and David Owen in New York, along with the head of personnel, John Birt, even roping in one of his former American counterparts from back in Berlin, John W. McDonald, now similarly reinvented as head of the US Economic Mission to the UN in Washington: 'My first couple of weeks in this backwater have hardly been auspicious. The altitude gives me a pounding headache that resists all the local potions. Fortunately there is a pleasant office, but if this is supposed to be the best-kept UNDP mission in the whole of South America, then I hate to think what the others must be like [. . .]. Since I know you have your ear pretty close to the ground in our shop, I would be glad of any views you may have.'

This was of course not the news Messrs Hoffman, Owen or Birt wanted to hear, nor expected to, given JBW's longtime hankering for just such a post. But they were not to know that JBW now had a headache of a different kind, one that no amount of *maté de coca* was likely to alleviate, with Liên marooned back in Saigon. Likely explaining his 'medical contra-indication', which was showing no signs of letting up. 'Wrote to Paul Hoffman last week to ask if he could discreetly extricate me into something where I might be able to do a reasonable job. Oh, for nice peaceful tranquil Saigon!'

Given that his UNDP bosses might reasonably expect him to stick it out until acclimatized, JBW had opened up a second exit gambit, claiming that his 'wife' – Rita, that is – needed to undergo an operation and 'this is hardly the place to take a convalescent mother to with all the problems of packing, uprooting children, etc. All in all I feel I shall have to ask the powers-that-be to release me from this assignment in the hope of there being something less exacting available', signing off with a possible cure for his malaise: 'However I don't want to do anything that might rule out a subsequent and expanded assignment in Viet-Nam.'

The convalescent-wife approach clearly did the trick, and before anyone knew it JBW was flying out on a month's leave of absence. 'Everybody was astounded when they heard you had left,' Maria, the office manager, wrote from La Paz. (Rita would have been astounded too, had she but known.) 'A few letters have arrived for you by ordinary mail. Most of them seem to be bank statements, plus one from somebody in Viet-Nam ['Liên' JBW helpfully clarified in the margin]. Nothing so far from one John McDonald, but will be looking out for it and cabling you if important.'

Having exited Bolivia without so much as a by-your-leave, JBW faced an uncertain future. Fortunately, as ever with the UN, where one door closes soon enough another opens – or rather another Resident Representative drops dead. On this occasion it was no less a figure than Gustavo Duran, one of the founders of UNESCO and head of the UNDP in Greece. Duran was one of the few staffers to have a profile outside of the UN itself, not least as one of the Republican officers portrayed in his friend Ernest Hemingway's *For Whom the Bell Tolls*, grounds enough for him to have been (wrongly) denounced as a communist by Senator McCarthy. 'It is no easy task to step into the shoes of as great and as popular man as was Gustavo Duran,' a grateful JBW wrote to Paul Hoffman. However, with a long-term replacement for Duran already lined up, Athens was only ever going to be an interregnum post, which meant JBW would need to find a new residency – South-East Asia still preferred, ideally Vietnam. 'The Americans were in fact enquiring about just such a possibility before my departure from Saigon . . .'

With this in mind he cabled New York about a possible

opening with his old Mekong Delta Committee partners: 'Reliably informed Umbright definitely not taking Mekong post. Can you please activate request.' Or failing that, Indonesia, for which he was able to pull yet another language from his back pocket: 'As it happens I can also read and speak passable Dutch which I understand is an advantage still in those parts.' Or Singapore perhaps. Or maybe even Ceylon. Only for the UNDP to come back to him with Malawi, hardly ideal geographically with Liên some 5,000 miles away: 'Very pleasant living but uninteresting in almost every other respect I would imagine. Though I must admit I know nothing whatsoever about Africa.'

'We were of course disappointed that the possibility of Malawi did not appeal to you,' New York responded, but with the start date for Gustavo Duran's replacement looming ever larger, Africa suddenly began to look more appealing. 'Will gladly pursue Niger or Togo. Also Gabon, if they have a watching brief on ex-Spanish Guinea, then my Spanish might be put to some constructive use.' Or Yemen, 'having acquired some knowledge of Arabic and Islam in Iraq. I realize, of course, that the living conditions are abysmal.' He eventually settled on Gabon, which by contrast came with 'a delightful home with two bedrooms and a study, well situated with a garden giving on to the beach and a clear view across the Gabon estuary'. Only for Gabon to reject his candidacy on the basis that, for whatever reason, they didn't want a Canadian.

And so at the start of November 1969 JBW, along with Rita and their two daughters, returned to a wintry Canada, resigning himself to once again beginning the search for some sort of academic post.

Only for New York to come back to him a few weeks later asking whether he might reconsider Malawi. Cue some hurried backtracking: 'The only sort of comment I made when the question of Malawi first arose was that I am basically interested in a more challenging post, programme and development-wise, and that I thought you could probably get more mileage out of me in a French-speaking post,' before signing off – because God loves a trier: 'I would also like to reconfirm my interest in a posting to South-East Asia as and when suitable vacancies arise in that area.' And so Malawi it was. On 1 February JBW arrived as the UNDP Resident Representative in what, then as now, was one of Africa's poorer countries.

But not for long.

Even before his first month was up he was putting in a request for a week's leave due to 'unforeseen personal reasons', this time to relocate his (supposedly) ailing mother from England over to Canada. Two months later he was at it again, requesting anything from six months' to a year's leave of absence in order 'to be near to and to take care of my ailing aged mother in Canada'. (His mother, fit as the proverbial fiddle, had not set foot in Canada since 1924.) And on the basis that he would be largely unoccupied while looking after said ailing aged mother, he suggested to the UNDP in New York that he might usefully occupy his time helping out at the Canadian University Service Overseas (CUSO) offices in Ottawa, given that their work inevitably overlapped with that of the United Nations Development Programme. 'I should be able to make a useful contribution towards reorganizing some aspects of the administration and field service, which is apparently what is wanted,' he wrote, before going on to argue that he was not the first person to put in such a request: 'My colleague Joan Anstee had been given a year off before going to her present post in Morocco for the very same reason – i.e. to look after her mother and that she worked on some economic research for the British government during that time. Consequently I [would be] following precedent.'

Unsurprisingly, New York did not quite see it that way.

'I would only hand in my resignation with the greatest of reluctance, but if it has to be, then I guess it has to be,' JBW regretfully conceded, receiving a tersely sympathetic farewell note by return of post: 'Fully understand the nature of your problem. We shall naturally regret your leaving.'

Only for JBW, bags packed ready to head back to Canada, to receive yet another last-minute reprieve, this time courtesy of his new-found friends in Zomba, the then capital of Malawi, where he and the UNDP were based. In spite of his initial reluctance to accept the post, in his usual way he was very taken with both the country and the people, and they with him – certainly if an invitation from the Malawi Minister of Trade to act as interpreter to the national football team for a possible away fixture in (French-speaking) Madagascar was anything to go by.

Rather than go through the palaver of finding a replacement, an exasperated UNDP agreed to a leave of absence, the hoped-for year or minimum six months whittled down to forty-seven and a half days, his return scheduled for the start of October in time for the United Nations Day celebrations, held in the grounds of Government House. A newspaper cutting of the event shows a besuited JBW – in spite of the heat – listening on as the Minister of Agriculture gives a speech in praise of the UNDP's Fisheries Training Project, alongside a second photograph showing 'Mr and Mrs Wood welcoming the Hon. R. J. Sembereka, Minister of Labour and Local Government'.

This was not, of course, the legal Mrs Wood (unbeknown to JBW now re-employed by SIS), nor was it the Mrs Wood who had accompanied him to Baghdad ('Margaret' Rita, left behind in Canada with his daughters), but a very much younger Mrs Wood, from here on in referred to simply as Liên to avoid confusion.

Festivities over, the latest edition of Mr and Mrs Wood headed back to 3 Naisi Spur (tel. Zomba 254), from where JBW once again resumed his relief work and field irrigation projects, driving the length and breadth of the country – 'nice climate and there are lakes and mountains to explore in abundance' – to oversee the establishment of a network of rural health projects, more often than not with Liên taking the wheel, rifle perched on the back seat – strictly for duck-shooting purposes only.

Normal service resumed. Once again, if only for a few months.

As countless observers and the occasional BBC documentary have noted down the years, short of committing a serious crime, it is virtually impossible to get fired from the United Nations. A feat that JBW was about to manage with no great difficulty, chalking up a notable first.

His undoing came about largely by accident. His deputy in Zomba, one Victor Furst, had happened to be leafing through the English-language *Rhodesia Herald* in an airport lounge only to come across an article reporting that CUSO, up until then a largely apolitical organization, had come out in support of African liberation movements, placing it at odds with the UNDP's humanitarian and politically neutral stance. Hardly a surprise, since this was very much in line with most student politics at the time. However, what *did* come as a surprise to Herr Furst was the article's reference to CUSO's 'new Executive Director, John B. Wood'.

After an initial (limp) attempt to explain this away as coincidence, 'John Wood being a common enough name', his line of argument soon changed, with JBW claiming that he'd never made a secret of his association with CUSO. And besides, as the *Rhodesia Herald*'s follow-up article noted, he had voted against the motion, saying that 'as CUSO is embarking on a political course which I consider incompatible with development I would therefore disassociate myself from it'.

Unsurprisingly, once again Hoffman and the UNDP hierarchy did not quite see it that way and summoned him to the UN Plaza headquarters in New York. JBW's defence did not get off to the best of starts when it was discovered that he was currently absent from Malawi – having slipped away yet again to attend to his (supposedly) ailing mother, who now turned out to be not in Canada, as previously stated, but back in England. For which there was a perfectly straightforward explanation: 'As it happened my mother changed her mind at the last moment, but since all the physical arrangements for this had been made in the course of my previous visits to Canada, a postponement would have fouled them all up.'

In the meantime the UNDP had written to CUSO requesting a clarification of JBW's role with them, though a glance at the front cover of the autumn edition of *Cuso '70* would have told them all they needed to know: 'Pictured: CUSO's new Executive Director, John B. Wood, Chief Executive Officer since July following five years with the United Nations Development Programme as its Resident Representative in Iraq, Vietnam, Bolivia, Greece and Malawi.' What *Cuso '70* omitted to mention was that their new Executive Director was being paid a salary of $23,000 per annum (equivalent to over $180,000 today), for which once again there was a perfectly reasonable explanation: an administrative error; he paid it back in full the moment he became aware of it. Or more precisely, the moment the UNDP became aware of it.

Concerned at his continued absence from Malawi, his office manager in Zomba cabled: 'There was quite an article in the *Rhodesia Herald* about CUSO's vote on the Sth African issue and you were registered as voting against participation – your title being "Executive Director". Everyone seems to know that you are in some way associated with CUSO? Speculation about your return/non return is rife.'

In the event he did make it back to Malawi, but too late to save his job. A UNDP report into the whole affair summarized: 'He took up a continuous and outside occupation without the prior approval of the Secretary-General [. . .] His conduct in this affair shows a total lack of veracity and integrity on his part [. . .] After due consultation with and the approval of the Secretary-General [he is to] be dismissed from the service.'

As with Dick White's decision to fire him from SIS fifteen years earlier, few would condemn the UN's decision as unjustified (offspring included). News of his dismissal made it back to England quicker than might normally be expected; his Cambridge bank wrote to inform my mother that he would be discontinuing our £44 monthly funding, which was instead being put towards a lengthy and correspondingly eye-wateringly expensive appeal he was lodging with the UN Joint Appeal Board in New York.

'Let us know all the facts – even those of advantage to the Administration,' his lawyer urged. 'If you hold anything back [. . .] this could, of course, come out at the Appeals Board hearings.' But since most – probably all – the facts were likely to be advantageous to the Administration, his lawyer swiftly changed tack, arguing that JBW's dismissal was unduly harsh, given that – as was well known – no one is ever dismissed from the UN. A claim that the Secretary-General's office happily confirmed a few weeks later: 'There have not been any cases of summary dismissal or dismissal for misconduct of senior staff in the UNDP.'

Even so, his (increasingly concerned) lawyer felt that his client's best hope lay with a forensic examination of whether the UN had observed all the correct legal procedures, which boiled down to the legalese terminology employed and whether JBW had been 'summarily dismissed' or simply 'dismissed'. 'The procedural difference is that the Secretary-General can decide on "summary dismissal" completely on his own, whereas in the case of mere "dismissal" he has to employ the Joint Disciplinary Committee in New York and Geneva. It is perhaps not the most satisfying way to win a case, but the safest and certainly the most congenial one,' his lawyer wrote, before signing off: 'As a gentleman, of course, you will destroy this note after you read it.'

The wording had been nothing more than 'a slip of the pen', the UNDP argued (weakly), and with that the tide began to turn in JBW's favour. 'On the whole, I am rather optimistic,' his lawyer cabled. 'This feeling is not based on any conviction that you are free of guilt – the contrary is the case.' In the end a fudge of sorts was agreed, with Secretary-General U Thant accepting JBW's offer of resignation – submitted three days prior to the date of his dismissal, 29 September 1972, which if nothing else would allow him to save face, a not uncharitable move given that his United Nations career was now finished.

If not for long.

THE TIMES

White flags fly in Phnom Penh as Khmer Rouge enter city

Fugitive officials reported to have flown to Thailand

Phnom Penh. By his own admission a close
shave, managing to clamber aboard the second
to last plane out, April 1975.

Lusaka, 1979. Having always done his best to avoid
all things British, suddenly there was no escaping it.

FOOD AID
THE CHALLENGE AND THE
OPPORTUNITY

HANS SINGER
JOHN WOOD
TONY JENNINGS

Food Aid: a return
to academia.

5.

Phnom Penh, Lusaka, Brighton

'I believe Indonesia is no longer a
possibility – in the meantime my candidacy
was presented to the Khmer Republic.'

JBW, letter to the HR Director, UNESCO,
Paris, 12 September 1974

As was the way with the UN, where one door closes – or
in this instance slams shut – soon enough another opens. A
mere two days after his dismissal from the United Nations
Development Programme, much to their annoyance – not
to say anger – they were approached by its sister organization, the United Nations Educational, Scientific and Cultural
Organization (UNESCO). 'We would wish to be able to
consider Mr Wood for suitable vacancies in our field pro-
grammes. It goes without saying that before doing so we
would take into account, along with other factors, the facts
about Mr Wood's previous employment.' Or not, as the case
may be.

The role was billed as 'roving consultant', neatly bypassing
the need to run his appointment past Messrs Hoffman and
Birt of the UN's HR department in New York, for whom
JBW was by now an all too familiar headache.

UNESCO was based in Paris, where the twenty-one-year-old JBW had spent a post-Cambridge year at the Sorbonne (or, rather, the Sufi school in Suresnes), so it was a return to old haunts. Only now he could afford to rent a flat in the fifteenth arrondissement's Rue Antoine Bourdelle, a twenty-minute walk to his office (Room 123) on the sixth floor of UNESCO's Place de Fontenoy headquarters – with a not unpleasant view across the Champs de Mars to the Eiffel Tower. He spent his first few weeks undergoing the sort of induction period large multinational organizations tend to go in for: a twelve-day 'statistics' course, a UN interagency 'games weekend' in Vienna (no record of what that involved) and the first of many visits to the UN's Food & Agricultural Organization (FAO) in Rome. Where, as he may or may not have been aware (more likely the former), he was following in the footsteps of one John Cairncross, soon to be outed as the so-called Fifth Man of the Cambridge spy ring, whose CV has a faintly familiar ring about it: ex-Cambridge and Sorbonne, ex-SIS, gifted linguist, hauled up for illegal currency dealings (in Cairncross's case earning him a jail sentence). But of course those days were long in the past for JBW.

Unlike his talent for underhandedness.

After losing his job with the UNDP he'd eventually relayed the news back to our mother, saying that as a result he would no longer be able to continue his (slim) monthly alimony payments (which his mother had strong-armed him into). And yet somehow he omitted to mention that he was now on UNESCO's payroll.

'Had a letter from JBW saying that as he had lost his UN job (which I knew already) he has cancelled my monthly allowance,' my mother wrote to a sympathetic Aunt A. 'As I have now no income from him, I have accepted the job

336

at the training camp. PS: Thanks for the £1 (returned herewith). Keep it for your old age to buy a bun.'

And with that JBW settled into his new role. Too old for a permanent contract in any case – he was now fifty-six – he was nevertheless too worldly-wise and too experienced an aid worker for an organization such as UNESCO not to try and put his (more commendable) talents to good use, as his annual performance reports make clear. 'It is highly desirable that the Organization retains the services of Mr Wood for as long as possible so that Member States can continue to benefit from his achievement capabilities, all the more remarkable as they are underpinned by a clear vision of the requirements of international action and the sense of responsibility that results from it.'

Life as a 'roving consultant' was not without its perks, be it heading up a conference in Barbados for the World Food Programme evaluating its school meals projects, a seminar at Klagenfurt University, another in Athens, but following a short-term project management slot in Yaoundé, the Cameroon capital, he was finally granted his wish to return to South East Asia, with a posting to the recently created Khmer Republic (aka Cambodia). Only for the Director-General of UNESCO to overrule the appointment, informing JBW that he would instead be going to Indonesia. Only for the Deputy Director-General to then overrule the Director-General, telling JBW to ignore Indonesia and revert to the original plan and head out 'to the Khmer Republic as a matter of urgency'. Or, in UNESCO-speak, 'to DC/KMR/72/011/EP/001 as a matter of urgency'.

The Khmer Republic had been in existence for little more than four years, after a coup d'état saw off the previous regime, which the military viewed as having been too accommodating towards Cambodia's North Vietnam neighbour – with some justification, given that communist forces controlled most of the eastern half of the country. Just to add to their problems, they also faced the Chinese-backed Khmer Rouge.

As with JBW's appointment to Vietnam, and as Shergy had observed, the Americans would all too likely have had a hand in his appointment – given that they were propping up the new regime with vast amounts of weaponry and money. By the time he took up his post – towards the end of September 1974 – Phnom Penh and its vital Mekong River lifeline (bringing in food and supplies from South Vietnam) were just about the only areas of the country still in government hands. With some three million refugees out of a total population of seven million crowding into the capital, his role with the United Nations Educational, Scientific and Cultural Organization was always destined to be more humanitarian than it was educational, scientific or cultural.

The upshot was that he ended up staying rather longer than was wise, and though he may have accepted the post on the basis that (Liên aside) he 'had no ties and was therefore expendable', by his own admission he cut it fine, later telling my brother and me that he had barely managed to scramble aboard the second-to-last plane out of Phnom Penh, the advancing Khmer Rouge close enough for him to be able to pick out individual soldiers heading towards the airport perimeter. And yet just an hour later he was dusting himself down in the safe haven – and comparative paradise – of Thailand.

A few days later, on 17 April 1975, Phnom Penh itself fell, and two weeks after that Saigon went the same way, news-reels capturing the moment a North Vietnamese Army tank crashed through the entrance gates of the same Presidential Palace where not so long ago JBW (accompanied by the Apostolic Delegate) had been sipping champagne with President Nguyen Van Thieu.

With Saigon's fall, Liên was to all intents and purposes stateless, marooned back in Paris with a now worthless passport. She had been with him for close on a decade and had been listed in the UNDP's own handbook as Mrs Wood when she had first arrived in Malawi – all that was lacking was the supporting paperwork.

To which end, in early December 1975 John Bryan Wood (fifty-eight) married Thi-Liên Nguyen (twenty-nine), daughter of (Police Chief) Dinh Tan Nguyen, in the unlikely setting of Brighton Registry Office – the choice of country down to the need for her to obtain a European (rather than Canadian) passport, the choice of venue down to JBW having accepted a 'visiting lecturer' role at Sussex University. This had come at the invitation of Hans Singer, a former UNDP colleague and feted economist, best known for his work with developing countries, who had set up the highly regarded Institute of Development Studies (IDS) department at Sussex. Singer saw JBW as, in his own words, 'my man in the field', able to provide a rare firsthand insight into the challenges such countries faced. And given his close shave exiting Phnom Penh, academic life likely had a renewed appeal for JBW.

Our mother had long since cleared the way for him to remarry, an amicable enough arrangement whereby she had walked away with our old Woking house, in return for which he was freed from any financial obligations for his two sons (hardly a loss, she noted, given that 'he gave up the business of financing the boys many years ago'). Not that we were his sons, of course, at least not as Liên understood it, having been led to believe by JBW 'that his ex-wife was called Margaret and had two sons from her lover', just as our Canadian half-sisters, Sophie and Louise, 'were the daughters of his half-brother who disappeared while on business in South America'.

Newly married (again), he returned to Paris to await his next posting – filling the time with the usual merry-go-round of conferences, consultancies and committees, an occasional lecture at Sussex, even a week-long visit to his daughters ('nieces', as Liên understood it) back in Canada (as ever, arriving without warning – to the understandable irritation of their mother, Rita), followed by a visit to the FAO's Rome headquarters, where he was a familiar-enough face to be sounded out for a post in Zambia with the World Food Programme. On the basis that this was likely to be slightly less hazardous than his previous posting, and an area of Africa where he had unfinished business after his (truncated) stay in neighbouring Malawi, he and Liên were soon packing their bags again, arriving in a country whose endemic problems – falling copper prices, rising maize prices, malnutrition, child poverty – he understood only too well. The situation was further exacerbated by the war in neighbouring Rhodesia (Zimbabwe), which regularly spilt across into Zambia itself, with Patriotic Front guerillas said to control areas of the country; this too was a familiar-enough scenario after Phnom Penh. Not that this stopped him travelling the length and breadth of Zambia, more often than not with Liên at the wheel, posting updates and reports to Rome – cc'd to Hans Singer back at Sussex University (JBW's contribution necessarily anonymous, given his troubles with the UNDP and CUSO).

Having done his best to avoid all things British for the

majority of his sixty-three years, all of a sudden there was no escaping it. In July 1979 Queen Elizabeth arrived in Lusaka on an official state visit, followed a few days later by Margaret Thatcher, who was attending the Commonwealth Heads of State Conference, hoping to thrash out a solution to the Rhodesia problem. Whether or not JBW attended the conference itself, he was certainly not afraid to voice his (prescient) concerns about the country's future leader, Robert Mugabe.

In November he returned for his mother's funeral – only to learn that she had cut him out of her will – and enjoyed a pleasant enough reunion with his ex-wife – only to find that she was back with SIS – before spending a rainy few days running my brother and me through (heavily edited highlights of) his career to date, escape from Phnom Penh included. As he was getting in his car to leave, our mother had one last (unsuccessful) go at wheedling out of him where he was heading off to, following which he got out a camera, took a last photo of my brother and me, and then – because old habits die hard – drove off before our mother had time to fetch her own camera.

Quite what he told Liên about where he'd been, let alone about his mother's will or meeting his ex-wife and two sons for the first time in twenty years, only he would know. Then again, he'd had plenty of practice down the years.

And with that JBW went back to, well, he never did say, while our mother in her semi-retirement went back to her bridge classes and her whist drives, occasionally reprised her role as Lady d'Arcy and, of course, took up writing – or rather Maggie Ferguson and Felicity Gray took up writing – more than a few of her short stories featuring a thinly disguised JBW. She would have continued on for a

341

few years more but for that ailing SIS officer happening to tune in to one of her hospital radio plays.

She did, however, write one last piece. But this had little of Maggie Ferguson's or Felicity Gray's romantic sheen, nor was it set in Berlin. She'd found a lump in her breast and over the coming months unflinchingly recorded the path it took. The doctors did their best, but it was a long, drawn-out exit, time enough 'to properly tidy everything away', leaving just a few faded photographs of her old Berlin gang gathered round the pool of Grunewald's Blau-Weiss Club, skiing in Garmisch-Partenkirchen, riding a donkey across the floor of the Golden Horseshoe nightclub, which she couldn't quite bring herself to throw out.

She'd 'hung around' (her words, not mine) to see a first grandchild, the medics carrying her upstairs for one last visit home – touch and go, a grizzly story of having to drain her lungs with the aid of a knitting needle – before lowering her back down. Back in hospital she spent the best part of a morning, as she did every morning, working her way through a chequerboard of pills of all colours, shapes and sizes that the doctors had prescribed – and some say a rather larger pill that the doctors certainly hadn't prescribed – before signing off, aged just sixty-one, with one last *tsk-tsk* for John II for allowing her glass of water to drip over the bedspread.

It was a big funeral, perhaps the only thing to be said for going before one's time, amongst the mourners several of the original Berlin tunnel team, including Lunn, Wyke, Shoebottom and, of course, Shergy. 'The office' had laid on one of the camp's blue Ford Transit vans from London, George at the wheel as ever, into which half a dozen or more managed to squeeze. But then they were probably used to operating in confined spaces. Aunt A made her own way down. She'd stayed at the training camp on a couple of occasions, though only after much persuasion – 'There are no Broadway Beagles about here at weekends (it is deserted then) so you won't be exposed to Communist influence' – but chose instead to take the train, on the basis that having never been stationed in Berlin, she barely knew Shergy or the rest of the tunnel team. Or perhaps she was simply wary of being exposed to 'fellow travellers' of any kind.

Shergy gave the eulogy. For someone said to be 'utterly dedicated to the idea that SIS should sustain the secrecy of its people and its operations beyond the grave', he gave a surprisingly candid speech, recalling – outing, to most of those attending – the tall, red-haired, twenty-one-year-old innocent from Whitley Bay who early one July morning in 1949 had stepped off the train a hundred miles behind the Iron Curtain and into the Wild West of espionage that was West Berlin. Before the service began he'd taken my brother and me to one side, warning that he might be making some less than complimentary observations about our father and hoped we wouldn't mind. I didn't. But others did, not least SIS, reputedly earning Shergy a first-ever ticking off from on high.

After the service we regrouped at a nearby hotel, my mother's old Berlin friends making their way through the throng to give me a hug and a last ruffle of my hair. There was much discussion of the wording of Shergy's eulogy, though no one could quite agree on what exactly he had said about JBW, only that he probably shouldn't have but they were somehow glad he did. By way of small talk, I'd asked some of them if they'd read Ian McEwan's fictionalized account of the tunnel operation, *The Innocent*, coincidentally published a few days before. But none had, nor did they show any interest – and probably thought less of me for thinking that they might. Afterwards the London contingent squeezed back into the blue Ford Transit, Aunt A once again preferring to make her own way back to her bedsit, her travel books and her diaries. But the diaries make no mention of the funeral, and from that day onwards she never wrote another entry. But then, to be alone was not a fate she would have wished on anyone, as an earlier diary entry, for Sunday, 1 September 1963, had noted: 'Guy Burgess died of heart trouble in a Moscow Hospital on Friday, in his sleep from heart disease. There was an Englishman with him at the end, probably Kim. Poor Kim, now he will be all alone in Moscow with nothing to do but drink. I don't think he was friendly with Maclean. No one to talk to can be too awful.'

Every now and then I'd call in on her, but as the stacks of newspapers and travel books grew ever taller, we'd instead meet up for tea and a sticky bun on Putney High Street. And then one morning I was called to Roehampton Hospital, where she was laid up after a bad fall – one of the floor-to-ceiling stacks she'd been hoarding had toppled over as she negotiated a path through. She'd lain there for more than a day before her moans were heard, pinned under an avalanche of Freya Starks, Wilfred Thesigers and Lawrence Durrells – the way she would have wanted to go, given the choice. She made a partial recovery, following which the hospital called me in to face a semicircle of well-meaning assessors. Did I know anything about her past? What happened in Warsaw? What did she do for a living before the BBC? Apparently it's not unheard of for elderly patients to hint at having led a shadowy prior existence, but this was the first time anyone had confirmed that there might be some substance to it all.

But she never did get to go back to her bedsit. And so I was left to sort through all her travel books, her stacks of old newspapers and, hidden away, her diaries and several bundles of my mother's letters.

Towards the end, my mother had fretted that JBW might reappear after she'd gone, but for the most part he kept his distance, responding to news of her death with a mumbled silence, if such a thing is possible. From time to time we'd get word of his current whereabouts; the occasional card; a note to say that he'd written a book (which, likely to the relief of his former employers, turned out to be nothing more contentious than a worthy tome on Food Aid co-authored with Hans Singer); even, on one occasion, an overnight stay at my brother's house (out of the blue, with no warning). He was, he explained, on his way down to Brighton where, unbeknown to Hans Singer (and us), he had owned a house for the past twenty years. When I eventually got to meet Singer, this came as something of a surprise to him, just as he knew nothing about JBW's SIS past, his Sufism or that he had children. (Not altogether surprising, Singer's PA explained as I was leaving; Singer had worked with John Maynard Keynes for many years and never realized he was gay.)

But it was largely one-way traffic, inevitably so, given that we had no idea where in the world JBW was most of the time – the best I could manage being to pass on my regards via an aid worker friend, who at least knew *of* him. Too complicated to go into details, I'd simply said that I was a distant relative and had only met him properly once, which was true enough. Duly reciprocated by JBW, I heard back, albeit a couple of years later.

In the meantime, my father's odyssey showed no signs of any let-up, the nomadic existence of his childhood turning full circle: well into his seventh decade he was still camped out (literally) in some of the less-hospitable corners of the globe, a final buffing up of the halo that would take in the likes of Somalia, the Yemen, Baghdad (again) and, in his late seventies, Sudan. His daily routine had not much changed in thirty years of work with the various United Nations agencies, more often than not with Liên by his side or behind the wheel. Sixty years after his conversion to Sufism, he was still managing to keep up with his fellow Sufis, Erica Hathaway and Vera Corda included, the Sudanese postal service permitting. 'There is not much food, almost no social life and no alcohol of any kind or bacon, ham etc. – but we are able to catch fish from the Red Sea where the coral and marine fauna are fantastically beautiful. Fortunately, there are no tourists as they cannot get visas so the beaches and fishing and diving are unspoiled. There is also plenty of sunshine, heat and sand but one survives.'

Survive he did, and but for the need to return to Paris with a troubling eye infection might have continued indefinitely with one or other of the various UN-affiliated aid agencies. Thoughts of retiring to Latin America had long since given way to a small pensione he'd bought in Bormes-les-Mimosas on the French Riviera, an area he knew well from his youth and surely as good a place as anywhere to recuperate after an eye operation. But no cure for ever-itchy feet.

And so, finally, to Bosnia.

JBW, back to camera, Mostar, 1996.

'Dr John Wood u Starom Grabovcu kraj Novske'
('. . . in Stari Grabovac near Novska'), 1996.

6.

Bosnia. And beyond . . .

'I met Jøn on the other side – "Erica!" he said.
"Fancy meeting you here!"'

Erica Hathaway, letter to the author

At the age of seventy-eight, J B W, now Dr Wood – still time
for one last reinvention – exchanged the pastel colours of
Bormes-les-Mimosas for the rather less obvious charms
of war-torn Bosnia. He'd volunteered his services to Diakonie, a German charity operating under the umbrella of
the United Nations High Commission for Refugees. He was,
of course, no stranger to the region, which along with his
passable (if by now slightly rusty) German had likely over-
ridden any concerns about his age, though how exactly he
had acquired his German or how he came to know the Balkans was another matter, best skated over. To begin with he
was based in Zagreb, moving down to Bosnia in November
1994 after Diakonie opened a second office in Medjugorje,
fifteen miles south of Mostar.

Mostar was as divided a town as anywhere in the entire
conflict, its Muslim eastern half cut off from the Bosnian
Croats' western half, a chasm all too visible following the
destruction of its famous bridge twelve months earlier.
With UN forces constructing a temporary replacement

structure, Diakonie weighed in with a rebuilding programme of seventy-five houses and a new school, along with a skills workshop teaching everything from carpentry to beekeeping (something of a specialist subject for JBW). This was one of several Diakonie-funded initiatives across Bosnia, which inevitably meant that much of his time was spent on the road. Negotiating the endless checkpoints made for a stop-start progress of sorts, while the scarcity of overnight accommodation often meant having to fall back on the kindness of strangers, though given the country's sizeable Muslim population, his Sufism and knowledge of Islam would have done him no harm. Lifelong polyglot as he was – he once told my brother that he was 'comfortable' in seventeen languages – he had finally called time on the endless hours spent with headphones clamped to ear – one of his few concessions to old age being the luxury of an interpreter, Iva, who was based alongside him in the Medjugorje office and who would often accompany him on such road trips. His other concession, of course, being the services of a full-time driver: Liên.

Liên and he had by this time been together for over twenty-five years, by some distance the most enduring of his various liaisons. They'd met back in 1966 in Saigon – a time when he had, as my mother observed, 'more ties than most' – but eventually Furse Ripley's scrawled notes via Grand Central Station had tapered off, Rita and his daughters were safely explained away, my brother and I hidden away. Not that JBW had entirely mended his ways: a few months before heading off to Bosnia he'd written to Vera Corda in California suggesting she might want to up sticks and see out her days with him in Bormes-les-Mimosas – just as half a century back he'd urged her to leave her husband and join him in Bermuda. Duly ignored, thankfully.

As with the vast majority of frontline aid-agency efforts, Diakonie's work in the Balkans would go largely unheralded and, but for its own in-house magazine, largely unreported. Under the heading 'A Journey Through Bosnia', one of its directors recorded a typical day in the life of their man in Medjugorje – and his driver – in the process giving a rare window into the life that my father had by then been living for several decades.

The sky is grey and overcast when we leave Zagreb for Bosnia. We, that is John Wood from our office in Medjugorje, his wife Liên (she is our driver), Horst Voigtmann, radio journalist, and myself [. . .] continue our drive to Tuzla [. . .] A lot of windows cannot be shut any more (mine among them), in some other [building]s the window panes are missing, the heating makes rumbling noises but functions, the carpets are worn down, there are no teaspoons [. . .]

We drive to Vive Zene [. . .] An old man approaches us with shaking hands asking for 'one marka' (1dm) which Horst Voigtmann gives him gladly. I am curious and ask him where he comes from. He is a Muslim and was evicted from his village near Srebrenica in the middle of last year. Has he got a family? Yes, his wife is with him, but she is sick. The man is at the end of his forces, he is hungry and close to tears: his two sons were killed, and he does not know what to do, where to go, how to survive [. . .]

We pass the ruins of former villages and drive through the mountains. The rain turns into snow. The road is slippery and the slush covering the tarmac also hides the potholes. Liên apologizes each time she hits one of the potholes. Just around the bend is the IFOR checkpoint. This time we have to get out of the car (despite the snow) [. . .] A female soldier – she comes from sunny California – checks Liên and I. Over the radio they inform the next checkpoint about our registration plates and confirm that we are 'OK'. After a three-hour drive the snow turns to rain and Sarajevo is in sight. A huge graveyard with a lot of new graves extends over the hill and continues – as in a nightmare, under the grey sky – across the road towards the city centre [. . .]

We set out for our journey 'back home' to Mcdjugorje. Once more the road winds its way through the mountains. The sky is still grey and overcast, it is cold but it doesn't rain any more. Once more we pass through shelled villages, we see houses without roofs, doors or windows, burnt down. At sunset we reach Mostar; the devastation of this city, especially of the Muslim section, causes me again to be dumbfounded.

A rebuild project a few miles south of Brčko somehow found its way onto YouTube, though with his back to camera you'd do well to spot Dr Wood amongst the huddle of refugees and UN soldiers. But I recognized the unkempt hair and the hands-behind-back walk easily enough – even if he was a little unsteadier than I remembered.

And by way of a last word, a lengthy article about his work in Bosnia in which, guard finally lowered, he touched on something of his past.

For a quarter of a century he has been travelling by car, train and boat, to Sudanese villages on the edge of Nubian and Libyan desert, the length and breadth of both the Blue and White Niles, or along the small villages near Somali's rivers Shabel or Juba, or to settlements around Malawi's

Lake Nyasa, hurrying on the roads in Vietnam and Cambodia, or by sampan along the Mekong. Two and a half years ago, he arrived from Sudan to Zagreb. In that short time, Dr Wood has got to know Croatia's problems along with Bosnia's troubles, its exiles and refugees.

The article then takes the reader through renovating a primary school in Mošćenica, helping refugees escape from Posavina across the Sava River and, finally, to Sarajevo itself. 'I found the situation in Sarajevo very depressing. It reminded me of the time when the Russians occupied Berlin (1945–50). One could not cross from one sector to another due to all the shooting.'

'Books, or perhaps a documentary movie in episodes, could be written about the humanitarian Dr Wood,' the article concludes (unknowingly echoing Dorothy Maclean's summary: 'Books could be written about his intrigues and deceptions – but no one would believe them').

A few weeks later, on their way back from Diakonie's Zagreb office, Liên behind the wheel as usual, their Land Rover burst a tyre and overturned, killing my father instantly and leaving Liên badly injured. Given his colourful past, inevitably some read more into the circumstances of his death than the facts probably support, with talk of a largeish amount of cash he was couriering back to the Medjugorje office nowhere to be seen and all his papers being hurriedly incinerated within a few days of his death, but the truth was likely more mundane: simply an icy February road.

His funeral was held in Medjugorje's St James's Church, where just a few weeks before he had made an improbable last-minute conversion to Catholicism, to the subsequent dismay of his Sufi friends. It was standing room only, the numbers swelled by a large contingent of Muslim Bosniaks specially bussed in for the service. Liên, badly injured, just about made it to the front of the church, where she was joined by his daughters, Sophie and Louise – or as Liên had always been led to believe (and would continue to believe), the daughters of his (entirely fictional) half-brother.

A few months before, Sophie had ventured out to Bosnia. Her unexpected appearance would, of course, have posed problems for JBW. And so before she knew it, she found herself being whisked off on an impromptu road trip round Bosnia, an unintended consequence being that she had him all to herself. And didn't waste the opportunity to ask the occasional awkward question, most of which he skilfully fended off (years of practice), if sheepishly confirming the rumour that, yes, he also had two sons. And if she had reason to suspect that there was more to her father than esteemed frontline aid worker and university lecturer, which she certainly did, then she didn't have to wait long for confirmation. Pulled up at a checkpoint for being out and about after curfew, poker player to the very last, he'd calmly spread out a flush of five different-coloured passports, selected the appropriate one and was waved through. Given his age – he was by now in his eighties – at Sophie's prompting he'd called in for a check-up at one of the UN field hospitals, leaving her contact details just in case. Not that she and her sister need worry, he'd promised – they'd be well looked after should anything happen to him. Needless to say . . .

Before saying her goodbyes, she teasingly asked in a where-did-it-all-go-wrong way how someone with all his intellectual and linguistic gifts had ended up living the life he did, sleeping on a camp bed with little more than a rug for warmth, ankle deep in mud as he toured yet another war zone – and, had she but known it, having left both SIS and the UN under a cloud. But instead of the great political cause that I and others might have expected (suspected), there had been no tap on the shoulder from any NKVD Cambridge recruiter or laying-on of hands from Comrade Trotsky. He simply blamed it all on having had a rather over-bearing mother.

In the event Sophie and Louise were possibly not the first to receive news of their father's death, with both Vera Corda and Erica back in California claiming to have intuitively 'felt' his passing. A few weeks before, he'd written to both, out of the blue – as was his way to the very last – and even managed to track down a number for Cil (his Norwegian, she was surprised to hear, still as word-perfect as it was the last time they had spoken, over half a century earlier). He'd also telephoned Dorothy Maclean ('John? John who?'), the first time she'd heard from him since they had gone their separate ways in Oberammergau, back in 1950. For a while she'd survived by pawning her husband's family jewellery and doing a little secretarial work, supplemented by (very) occasional cheques from his Bene't Street account, through it all some-how managing to retain her trademark smile. Then, in 1962, she'd hitchhiked up to the small coastal village of Findhorn in northern Scotland, living in a shared caravan and growing her own food – an alternative way of life that had its follow-ers: Findhorn would grow to become the largest and most successful alternative community in Britain, and that same caravan now listed, as is her childhood home in Guelph. And yet, despite everything, to the very last – she lived to be a centenarian – Dorothy never uttered a bad word about JBW.

'I took it for granted that you knew I thought he was special, in spite of himself.'

For my own part, I can't claim to have had any such intuitions, other than a sudden thought one evening that I really should give him a call, if for no better reason than at eighty-one he wasn't getting any younger. Added to which, I'd always been slightly troubled by that slightly blurred photograph in which I can just about make out my brother and me standing in front of the garage of our old Woking home, in amongst all those pastel-coloured files (mistakenly) handed over to us in the Happy Eater car park. Which, I couldn't help but conclude, he must have fired off from across the road – explaining the slight blurring – only to then drive away for fear of being spotted. Somehow or other I even had a number for his office in Bosnia, but when I reached for the phone, just as on that drive back to our home after his mother's funeral when I couldn't quite bring myself to raise my arm in response as he'd waved at me from his car, I couldn't quite bring myself to tap out the numbers. (Where to begin? What to say?) And so the moment passed, the arm slumped back down, opportunity gone.

News of his death took several months to reach my brother and me, and even then largely by chance, following which I belatedly contacted the person who dealt with such matters to register his death. I'd never met Ms Kerr, but we'd spoken a few times down the years, given that most of my family had at one time or another been with SIS. There were the usual forms to fill in so that they could update records, stop pensions, perhaps pen a line or two of obituary for the staff newsletter. I'd managed to track down a death certificate, signed by a Dr Josip Skavic of the Institute of Forensic Medicine in Karlovac. Cause of death:

'*Contusio diffuse gravis cerebri*' – 'massive head injuries'. He was eighty-one years old. 'In Bosnia? At the age of eighty-one?' Ms Kerr had queried, before running me through her list – dependents, religion, nationality – but she wouldn't accept guesses, even educated ones, so we ended up with little more than his place of birth and date of death.

A few days later Harold Shergold had asked to see me. This was, of course, not altogether unexpected.

And so I arrived at his Richmond home to be greeted by Westley and Larry, tails wagging, before heading across the road to the Star & Garter Home to see Bevis's various medals and certificates, then back for lunch and the usual conversation: his health, dogs past and present, what John II was up to, where I was working, etc. But even as he shuffled me through to the familiar fraying armchairs, I was aware that my visit would be different this time, and that discussion of my father's death was unlikely be held back until I had my coat on ready to leave – even without Shergy's sudden, unexpected seizure.

Shergy, needless to say, was curious to know how his former colleague had come to end his days, not in quiet anonymity or on the golf course – nor, like one or two, in Moscow (not that Shergy, perhaps surprisingly, had ever met Kim Philby, let alone Burgess or Maclean). But in war-torn Bosnia? Aged eighty-one? I explained that he'd been working there for Diakonie, carrying out 'good deeds'. Cue Shergy's familiar wry smile.

I talked him through what I knew about my father's death, which Shergy sat through without comment, other than to ask how I could be sure it was really him under all that marble. I explained that, rather helpfully, undertakers in that part of Bosnia were in the habit of inserting a small window

357

into the lids of coffins, so I had it on good authority (my half-sisters, Sophie and Louise) that yes, it was definitely him, if a little green around the gills.

Above all, Shergy was curious to know what my father had been doing in the forty-something years since his dismissal from SIS. And, more especially still, for whom. Perhaps I might want to look into it?

And so I began. Unsuccessfully at first, with a visit to Eardisland and JBW's birthplace, before heading out to California, home to JBW's fellow Sufis Vera Corda and Erica Hathaway, then on from there to what would be the first of several meetings with Dorothy Maclean.

Vera was still leading much the same life as she had back in Kaaba Allah, with a ground-floor room in a Potter Valley timber-frame house, which, *Seven Brothers for Seven Sisters*-style, was being constructed around her by her fellow commune members as we chatted. She and JBW had, she claimed, been together in previous lives, both in India and China – and but for Hathaway Snr's intervention might have been in this one. In preparation for my visit she'd dug out some of my father's letters, the last of them asking her to join him in Bormes-les-Mimosas, somehow making no mention of Liên. Given that up until the day I turned up Vera had still had no idea that Sophie and Louise were JBW's daughters – despite their having lived with her while he was at Stanford – I hadn't the heart to tell her about pretty much everything else. Only that he had turned out all right in the end.

Erica, by contrast, was rather more wise to JBW. After all, they went all the way back to pre-war Munich, back when he was Bryan, not Jøn, not Norwegian. And understood as well as anyone his talent for duplicity. Even so, news of his last-minute conversion to Catholicism came as a shock, a betrayal even (not the first he'd been accused of). Gripping the arms of her chair, in spite of her age – she was by now in her nineties – Erica slowly raised herself up almost on tiptoes, pointing an outstretched finger up to the heavens: 'Spiritually there was no one higher. No one. Not even Samuel Lewis, not even Murshida Martin. Everything came from him.' Only to then bend over double, pointing so low to the ground I could hear the creaking of bones. 'Morally? No, morally there was no one lower. Oh no, not anybody, nobody!'

For Erica, death was not quite the barrier it is to most: my father, she insisted, had simply stepped across to 'the other side'. 'Erica, fancy meeting you here!' he'd said when she'd happened to run into him there. Granted, I was not the most receptive of audiences, not being entirely wedded to the existence of an afterlife. (Dorothy Maclean would find my inability to see the 'devas' or angels equally baffling: 'You're just not trying . . .') Even so, once or twice a year I'd head up to Erica's Santa Barbara home, where in the shade of her jacaranda tree, to the sound of more wind chimes than was strictly necessary and under the watchful gaze of the obligatory stone Buddha, she would talk me through her various meetings with JBW, during which she would update him on what his fellow Sufis and my brother and I were up to on terra firma. In truth I can't claim to have heard much news in return – as Erica conceded, mostly he would simply nod and smile without ever giving much away. Then again, he never did. Nevertheless, I'd come away from Santa Barbara having arguably had more contact with my father than I ever did when he was alive.

A more evenly balanced – and more sympathetic – account of his life might have devoted as many pages to his last thirty years as to the previous thirty. For which, mea culpa. After all, even the gold Omega he'd sent me from Vietnam all those years ago, supposedly handed down from his own father, had turned out to be not quite the fake I'd always written it off as. It had indeed been his father's, given a new lease of life in one of the small artisan workshops he had helped set up in the Mekong Delta, where obsolete watches would be stripped down and given new movements, sometimes whole new faces, just one of the hundreds of such projects he'd initiated, unknowingly kick-starting a whole industry.

And so, with this in mind, to Medjugorje.

These days the town is easy enough to reach, just over an hour's drive up from the Adriatic coast, a popular day trip from the tourist hotspot of Dubrovnik, twenty minutes from Mostar and its famous bridge, now fully restored. Most visitors will be heading for the shrine of the Blessed Virgin Mary, where shortly before the start of the Bosnian conflict a group of local children claimed to have seen Mary appear in person. Further visitations have been reported, along with the occasional miraculous healing, unexplained spinning lights and illuminated crosses, but after three decades of peace the only miracle today's visitors are likely to witness is economic: there are barista bars, trattorias, crêperies and spa hotels everywhere, with TripAdvisor lauding infinity pools, water jets, even an imported beach.

Rising above all this glitz are the immaculate, lemon-white twin bell towers of Medjugorje's Catholic church, now very much a worldwide centre of pilgrimage, attracting some three million visitors a year from all four corners of the globe, with a vast outdoor area for open-air masses, its own visitor centre and, in one of the gardens, a bronze statue of the Risen Christ, said to shed real tears.

Tucked out of sight a few hundred yards behind all this, set against a backdrop of the Dinaric Alps in the quiet of the church's surprisingly small cemetery, is where you'll find him. In place of the simple marker stone I'd always half-expected, there's an impressive polished red-granite affair, in a 'prime spot' as it were, with his name and dates of birth and death all neatly chiselled. So I hadn't the heart to point out to the priest that, needless to say, they aren't entirely accurate. 'Did I know him?' the priest had asked when I first visited. Back then I gave the honest answer – no, I can't say I really knew him at all.

One of the quirks of being born into an entire family of SIS employees is that one gets to know one's relatives better in death than one ever did in life.

Acknowledgements

Anyone hoping to navigate the proverbial wilderness of mirrors that is the espionage world needs all the help they can get.

Granted, my early years within the SIS training camp gave me something of a head start, so too my off-the-record briefing by the former head of anti-Soviet intelligence, not to mention my unexpected 'windfall' of several boxes of my father's papers (much to his annoyance).

Even so, all this barely got me to the start line. So I am indebted to those who, over many years and in many countries, helped let a little light into this most travelled and secretive of subjects: former colleagues of both my mother and father, anonymous and otherwise; the Sufi communities in California, Norway, Holland and France; various far-flung relatives, not least Sophie and Louise in Canada; and, ahem, all my former employers who unknowingly helped finance such research trips.

I shall always be grateful to John Synnott (John II), who, surprisingly perhaps, first encouraged me to make a record of his predecessor's adventures and misadventures. I am only sorry that he is not around to see the results – no one would have enjoyed them more. To Aunt A for secreting away her diaries and all my mother's letters in a place only I would know; my brother J for sharing whatever came his way, most usefully our father's early passports; Sophie for all her help re Bosnia; and, dare I say it, my mother, who against her better judgement let me keep hold of JBW's papers rather than hand them over to her employers (as Lady d'Arcy would surely have insisted). That said, had she and others, myself included, had their way this book would have remained for private consumption – and but for a passing remark to Mary Sayers, might well have done. The fact that it has seen the light of day is in no small part thanks to Mary's endless encouragement and enthusiasm; she it was who eventually steered a reluctant author towards his literary agent, Charlie Viney. I am especially grateful to Charlie for taking on and championing a first-time author – and for occasionally letting me beat him at tennis.

I am of course indebted to Rowland White at Michael Joseph for his leap of faith, and to his team for taking the time and trouble: Alan Samson for helping bring order to chaos, Emma Horton for fine-combing and fine-tuning, and to all those at Penguin Random House who steered me towards the finish line – Nick Lowndes, Ruth Atkins, Gaby Young, Mubarak Elmubarak, Katya Browne and a host of others.

Finally, I am grateful to Cozzie, Poppy and Oliver for their tweaks, IT know-how and their curiosity – and oh so grateful to Charlotte for putting up with all this blether down the years. And me. And for all the wonderful food.

Picture credits

PART TWO

Chapter 1
John Atkinson Wood & Gladys Eleanor Wood (Greenhough)

Chapter 2
1. Bergen friends: Photographer unknown
2. Hudson 8 car: Cecilie (Cil) Egeberg

Chapter 4
1. Rio de Janeiro: JBW postcard
2. T. Ifor Rees: Llyfrgell Genedlaethol Cymru | The National Library of Wales, Zenobia-Juan Ramón Jiménez House Museum

Chapter 5
1. Samuel L. Lewis: Unknown (JBW's own)
2. Vera Corda: Sufi Ruhaniat International
3. Erica Hathaway & JBW: Bill Hathaway

Chapter 6
1. JBW in Panama: Unknown (JBW's own)
2. 'Jardin El Rancho': Unknown (JBW's own)

Chapter 10
Uruguayan Railways & SS Rippingham Grange: Library footage

Chapter 11
JBW at Kaaba Allah: Erica Hathaway

PART THREE

Chapter 1
JBW with VW: Unknown

Chapter 2
All from Margaret Miller (Wood) photo albums

Chapter 3
Allan Batham & JBW on boat: Margaret Miller (Wood)
Russian zone recce photos: Margaret Miller (Wood)

Chapter 4
Mother with SIS 'minder': Unknown
Cakor Pass: J. B. Wood

Chapter 5
Vespa: J. B. Wood

PART FOUR

Chapter 1
All Margaret Miller (Wood)

Chapter 4
Athens: Unknown

Chapter 5
Mostar photograph by kind permission of Sophie Wood
'*Dr John Wood u Starom Grabovcu kraj Novske*', D. M., Moj Bliznji'
    (translation Anita Mušić Maksimović)